Planet of the Apes as American Myth

Planet of the Apes as American Myth

RACE AND POLITICS IN THE FILMS AND TELEVISION SERIES

by ERIC GREENE

McFarland & Company, Inc., Publishers
Jefferson, North Carolina, and London

The present work is a reprint of the library bound edition of
Planet of the Apes as American Myth: Race and Politics
in the Films and Television Series, *first published in 1996*
by McFarland.

LIBRARY OF CONGRESS CATALOGUING-IN-PUBLICATION DATA

Greene, Eric, 1968–
    Planet of the apes as American myth : race and politics in the
films and television series / by Eric Greene.
       p.   cm.
    Includes bibliographical references and index.

    ISBN-13: 978-0-7864-2663-8
    softcover : 50# alkaline paper ∞

    1. Planet of the apes films.   2. Planet of the apes (Television
program).   3. Race relations in motion pictures.   4. United
States—Race relations.   5. Motion pictures—Political aspects—
United States.   I. Title.
PN1995.9.P495G74   2006
791.43'75'0973—dc20   95-44163

British Library cataloguing data are available

On the cover: (background) Gorilla ©2006 Image Source; *(foreground)*
Statue of Liberty and beach ©2006 PhotoSpin

Manufactured in the United States of America

McFarland & Company, Inc., Publishers
  Box 611, Jefferson, North Carolina 28640
   www.mcfarlandpub.com

To Gloria Greene, my mother,
to Jeffrey Greene, my brother,
and in memory of Charles Powell
for his selfless help,
this book is thankfully dedicated

Contents

Each of us has within him an "Under-Man," that primitive animality which is the heritage of our human and even our prehuman past. This Under-Man may be buried deep in the recesses of our being; but he is there.... This primitive animality, potentially present even in the noblest natures, continuously dominates the lower social strata ... civilization's "inner barbarians." Now when society's dregs boil to the top, a similar process takes place in individuals, to whatever social level they belong. In virtually every member of the community there is a distinct resurgence of the brute and the savage.

Dr. Theodore Lothrop Stoddard
The Revolt Against Civilization, 1922

Man was born of the ape and there's still an ape curled up inside of every man. The beast that must be whipped into submission. The savage that must be shackled in chains. You are that beast, Caesar. You *taint* us. You poison our guts. When we hate you, we're hating the dark side of ourselves.

Governor Jason Breck in *Conquest of the Planet of the Apes*, 1972

The necessity, then, of "those lesser breeds..." — those wogs, barbarians, niggers — is this: one must not become more free, nor become more base than they: must not be used as they are used, nor yet use them as their abandonment allows one to use them: therefore they must be civilized. But, when they *are* civilized, they may simply "spuriously imitate [the civilizer] back again," leaving the civilizer with "no satisfaction on which to rest."

James Baldwin
The Devil Finds Work, 1976

Preface

Recently, a friend asked me why I wrote this book. A reasonable query, and I'd like to begin by answering it. I began researching this book in the autumn of 1990 while working on a Ford Foundation Academic Associates Fellowship in the English Department at Wesleyan University. Asked to write about some aspect of U.S. myth and popular culture, I decided to write about the ways in which the five *Planet of the Apes* films allegorized racial conflict during the late sixties and early seventies.

One of my earliest memories of movies is being five years old and going with my older brother Jeff on opening day to see *Battle for the Planet of the Apes*. Because the previous showing had not yet finished, when we walked into the theater the first thing I saw was an explosion from the film's final battle scene. Right then I knew that the planet of the apes had something to do with war.

Later, I became fascinated by the other *Apes* films as I saw them on television and in revival theaters. I did not know what drew me to the *Apes* movies, but I suspect that as someone of mixed racial background I was particularly interested in the way the films dealt with the conflict between different groups. I knew the filmmakers were trying very hard to say something about fear, hatred, violence, war, cruelty, revenge, compassion, reconciliation and peace. What I did not realize was that these same concerns were at the heart of the political issues troubling the nation when the *Apes* series was produced, and that these films I rushed home from school to see on the three-thirty movie confronted those political conflicts.

Except for the overtly political "message movie," we tend to think of politics as one thing and movies as another. This book looks, however, at some of the ways in which politics and movies are in fact connected and how both are influenced by issues of race.

The writing of this book coincided with a time of extraordinary interest in race, politics, and popular culture. Events of the past few years have sadly demonstrated what needed no demonstrating: that race is still very much an issue in the United States. Reactionary attacks on affirmative action, multicultural education, immigrants, and minority voting rights have all demonstrated that racial difference still makes a difference.

But the most vivid reminders, for those who were happy to forget, came in 1991 when a videotape exposed white Los Angeles police officers crossing the thin blue line and brutally beating an African-American man named Rodney King, in 1992 when an almost entirely white jury declared the officers innocent of any wrongdoing and Los Angeles exploded in fury, and in 1995 when the trial and acquittal of O.J. Simpson on double murder charges became a spectacle which dramatically exposed how race and class impact our views of truth and justice.

Recent years have also seen an extraordinarily high interest in the relation between popular culture and society. This interest was spurred on, in large measure, not by artists or by critics or by audiences, but by a politician. In May 1992, Vice President Dan Quayle, seeking to shore up conservative support for the upcoming presidential election, made a speech full of condescending assumptions about the poor and people of color. But the white press did not focus on that part of the speech. They instead focused on the disparaging comments Quayle made about someone like themselves: a white news professional. And what crime did this person commit that so disturbed the vice president of the United States that he felt compelled to publicly denounce her? She had a baby.

The catch was that this woman was not in fact real. She was the title character in the popular television comedy series "Murphy Brown," which Quayle criticized for mocking the value of fathers by having the single Brown give birth to a child out of wedlock. White House spokesman Marlin Fitzwater, not wanting to alienate any of the show's 38 million viewers, later backtracked by stating that because the Brown character did not terminate the pregnancy, the show demonstrated "strong family values."[1] The confusion made a public issue of what President George Bush actually thought about the show, but also raised the deeper questions of whether and why all this mattered and how it came to pass that the nation's chief executives had become television critics. After the inevitable jokes about Quayle's seeming inability to distinguish real life from television subsided, a considerable amount of public discussion about popular culture's influence on the nation's values ensued. Quayle, it seemed, had struck a nerve.

Bush himself contributed to the sense of virtual reality by declaring that "we need a nation closer to 'The Waltons' than to 'The Simpsons.'"[2] Apparently having "family values" was all just a matter of emulating the right television show. As expected, the television shows retaliated: on "Murphy Brown," the Brown character watched Quayle's speech and "responded" that she had agonized over her decision, and the offended Simpsons shot back at Bush by "answering" that like the Waltons they too spent a lot of time praying for the depression to end. The surrealistic attack-counterattack between the country's politicians and the country's television characters led one observer to decry "American history deteriorated to *Roger Rabbit*, to interactive slapstick, to 'toons."[3]

The debate did not end with the election. A torrent of talk about popular culture and society ensued: front pages, nightly news broadcasts, and politicians addressed issues of "cultural elites," "obscene art," music's influence on the young, and the mores of movies and television.

And so the debate goes on. Yet these types of debates tend to be sporadic and rarely ask what it is about the relationship between popular culture and other parts of our national life that gives a television show or movie enough significance to be considered "controversial." These discussions also tend to be one-sided: they concentrate, and not always very thoughtfully, on popular culture's influence on society. Yet it is also the case that popular culture is *influenced* by society and that is what this book examines.

Most of us probably recognize as "political" those movies that explicitly deal with governments or with issues of public concern. Thus *JFK* is seen as political, *The Untouchables* is not. I think we need a broader definition of political film that includes any movie that explicitly or implicitly deals with the use of, struggles over, and control of power and privilege or that suggests ways of responding to societal conflicts. This definition includes *The Lion King* no less than *Judgment at Nuremberg*.

Even on the surface level, the *Planet of the Apes* movies raise questions about power: who gets it, how they get it, what they do with it, and what the ramifications are for those involved. The *Apes* movies, therefore, can be usefully understood as political films.

As political texts, movies from *Star Wars* to *Forrest Gump* have their own sets of ideological assumptions. If we view movies as being apolitical and having no ideological axe to grind, however, we will not see or understand their implicit political values and assumptions. It is easy to miss what we do not expect to find. Unnoticed and unquestioned assumptions are powerful, in part, *precisely* because they remain unnoticed and unquestioned, beyond the realm of critical examination. But what we regard — or, more accurately, disregard — as trivial often contains the core values we accept as given.

The goal of this book is simple yet difficult: to contribute to a more thoughtful questioning and a greater understanding of the possible meanings and implications of the political formulations and representations produced, sold, and consumed as "entertainment." I want to suggest ways that race, politics, and movies interact, always remembering two points. First, that if we want to understand how movies may contribute to our interpretations of our ongoing national drama of race, it will be helpful to see how films have done so in the past. And second, that in addition to providing entertainment, "film is the site of a contest of representations over what social reality will be perceived as being and indeed will be."[4]

My intention is not to embark on an elaborate excursion into cultural theory in an attempt to explain definitively the complicated nexus of relationships between race, politics, and popular culture. Rather, this book is a more modest attempt to understand those relationships by examining a specific set of films produced during an exceptionally volatile time, films that addressed a particular set of issues. Specifically, through close analysis of the creation of the *Apes* films as political parables and cultural myth, I am seeking to explore ways in which films are affected by, enter into, and engage in political debates.

The introduction lays out the theoretical framework within which I view the *Apes* series by discussing some of the relationships between ideologies of race and discourses about apes. The introduction also discusses the relationships between politics and popular culture that enable films to address political issues. Chapter One examines how with the first *Apes* movie, *Planet of the Apes*, the filmmakers started to fashion a story about conflict among apes and between apes and humans that allegorized racial conflict and the Vietnam War. Chapter Two addresses the intensifying of the Vietnam War concerns in the second film, *Beneath the Planet of the Apes*, and the shift of attention to domestic racial conflict in the third picture, *Escape from the Planet of the Apes*. Chapter Three, which focuses on the fourth film, *Conquest of the Planet of the Apes*, traces the series' increasing emphasis on violent domestic racial conflict and examines the cultural impact that the race riots in the sixties and the "Black Power" movement began to have on the series. Chapter Four notes the continuing influence of the tensions between white liberals and African-American nationalists and the effect of white backlash on the series and considers the ways that the fifth film, *Battle for the Planet of the Apes*, challenged some of the ideological assumptions of the earlier films. The conclusion briefly looks at the *Apes* television shows, discusses the continuing presence of the *Apes* phenomenon in the nineties, both in popular and political culture, and notes how the *Apes* framework is again being used to tell stories about racial conflict that are both consistent with and distinct from the sixties and seventies *Apes* films.

I am grateful to many more people than I can practically list who lent their time, energy, and ideas to help me write this book, and my thanks go out to all of them. In particular, thanks go to the following:

For the opportunity to begin the research, the selection committee for the Ford Foundation Academic Associates Program at Wesleyan — Richard Boyd, Peter Frenzel, and Carol Lynch.

For first showing me a different way to look at movies, Bill Blakemore.

For their gracious participation in interviews, Mort Abrahams, Frank Capra, Jr., Joyce Hooper Corrington, Charlton Heston, Charles Marshall, Tom Mason, Hari Rhodes, J. Lee Thompson, and Doug Wildey.

For helpful suggestions and good advice, Jeanine Basinger, Bill Goodwin, Donna Haraway, Indra Karamechetti, Joe Reed, Steven Jay Rubin, Jane Seiter, Susie Shannon, Tom Tullio, Jerry Watts, Heather Weibel, Warren Weitzenhoffer, Rob Westbrook, Jr., Armond White, Patricia Williams, Elizabeth Young-Bruehl, and Jeremy Zwelling.

For providing detailed critiques of various drafts, Mark Cooper, David Greenberg, Saul Kotzubei, Michael McCaughan, Mel Powell, and Christopher Swain. I am sure that for every mistake they found, I later made another.

For assistance with computers and materials, Martin Bischoff, Terry Hoknes of the International *Planet of the Apes* Fan Club, Jeff Krueger, Myra Ming, John Money, Kevin Reed, Alan Sanborn, and the staff of the Margaret Herrick Library of the Academy of Motion Pictures Arts and Sciences.

For permission to publish photos and illustrations, Sebia Hawkins of Greenpeace; Shepard Kurnit, Richard Goldstein, Scott Carlton, Steve Bronston, F. P. Tartaro, and Fred Greller of Kurnit Communications; Dina Waxman; and Rex Perry.

For support, love, and friendship way above and beyond the call, my mother Gloria Greene and my friends Christopher Corey Smith and Aria Smith.

And for skipping the last day of school to take me to my first *Apes* movie, Jeff Greene.

Special thanks also go out to James H. Stone, II, for his constant support and challenging encouragement over the years. The effects of his caring are surely immeasurable and invaluable; I do not know where I would be without them.

And for his engaging, eye-opening, and inspiring guidance, I thank my mentor Richard Slotkin — a model "of" and a model "for" indeed — without whose tremendous help and exceptional talents this book would not have been possible.

Finally, I would like to express my hope that the reader finds this book a positive step toward making the unnoticed noticed and calling attention to the language of images and ideas with which we write our popular fictions and our political realities.

Introduction

"Can a planet long endure half human and half ape?" In 1970, advertisements for the film *Beneath the Planet of the Apes* asked North Americans this question. In fact, the ads dramatically declared this the "ultimate question" and pronounced the answer "terrifying." Filled with historical resonance, the question echoed Abraham Lincoln's prediction made over a century earlier that "this government cannot endure permanently half-slave and half-free." Lincoln saw one ideology as destined to overwhelm the other in time. The issues of racial conflict and racial oppression at the heart of the crisis which Lincoln addressed are also the central issues of the five films that comprise the *Planet of the Apes* film series. Like Lincoln, the filmmakers lived amidst severe racial conflict and racial violence. And like Lincoln, the filmmakers envisioned racial politics as a power struggle allowing only one victor.

In the fall of 1971, following the release of the third *Apes* film, *Escape from the Planet of the Apes*, reviewer Frederick S. Clarke wrote that the *Apes* films should be viewed not as separate entities but as one great work, a rich mosaic which had "the promise of being the first epic of filmed science fiction."[1] While race relations may be more or less foregrounded in a given film, when seen as one epic work, the *Apes* saga emerges as a liberal allegory of racial conflict.

As the series progressed, the racial conflict theme increasingly took center stage. While racial conflict is embedded in the first two *Apes* films — *Planet of the Apes* and *Beneath the Planet of the Apes* — the films' political implications are not always highlighted. In the later three films, however, the racial concerns were foregrounded. The third film, *Escape from the Planet of the Apes*, details the fate of racial strangers in a strange land. The fourth film, *Conquest of the Planet of the Apes*, is modeled after the Watts "riots." And the fifth film, *Battle for the Planet of the Apes*, keys off White phobias of Black Power. What had been a fairly general commentary on United States racial relations in the first two films, had become by the last three a more urgent address to the crisis of racial power dynamics. The last

1

two films also constitute a pointed debate on the nature of the black liberation movement, and specifically on the use of violence as a means to achieve
racial justice.

Since the release of *Planet*, the *Apes* series has been recognized by
audiences, critics, and the filmmakers as an allegory of racism, and the saga
has even entered into the national discourse on U.S. racial conflict. While
at times this thematic concern was the result of deliberate choices made
by the filmmakers, at other times the concerns and issues of the era may
have been subconsciously incorporated into the films.

I can think of no better illustration of the above point than the following story related to me by Mort Abrahams, the associate producer of *Planet*
and *Beneath*: After the opening of *Planet of the Apes* in early 1968, Abrahams
and producer Arthur P. Jacobs (whose APJAC productions was responsible
for all five films) bumped into entertainer Sammy Davis, Jr. Davis
embraced Jacobs and proclaimed that *Planet* was the best film about black-
white relations he had ever seen. Neither Abrahams nor Jacobs knew what
Davis was talking about. What Davis was talking about — the ways *Planet
of the Apes* and its sequels functioned as allegories about racial conflict and
addressed this "ultimate question" — is the focus of this book.

The *Planet of the Apes* saga began with *La Planète des Singes* (*Monkey
Planet*), a 1963 novel by French author Pierre Boulle that combined speculative fiction adventure with Swiftian social satire. In 1964, publicist-turned-
producer Arthur P. Jacobs read the book and with the help of associate producer Mort Abrahams began working to bring it to the screen. The process
was long and difficult. After Jacobs joined with Blake Edwards, who was
to direct the film for Warner Brothers, the studio estimated the budget
would surpass $10 million. No one in Hollywood or in Europe was willing
to risk that much money on a concept as unbelievable as a planet of talking
apes. In time, Edwards departed for other projects and the on-again, off-
again *Apes* film was shopped around and rejected by the studios for years.

Eventually the tenacious Jacobs secured the involvement of writer
Rod Serling, actor Charlton Heston, and, on Heston's recommendation,
director Franklin J. Schaffner. Jacobs' APJAC productions brought the
budget estimate down to $5.8 million and produced a screen test starring
Heston as Astronaut Thomas and Edward G. Robinson as the orangutan
Doctor Zaius. The test utilized paintings to depict major scenes which led
up to the filmed confrontation between Heston and Robinson, which was
written by Serling and directed by Schaffner. The minifilm proved to the
executives at Twentieth Century–Fox that a talking ape would not evoke
unwanted laughs and Fox gave *Planet of the Apes* the green light and
$5 million.

The investment paid off. *Planet* was a commercial and critical success — so much so that the studio requested a sequel. And another. And

another. And another. In all, five films were released: *Planet of the Apes* (1968), *Beneath the Planet of the Apes* (1970), *Escape from the Planet of the Apes* (1971), *Conquest of the Planet of the Apes* (1972), and *Battle for the Planet of the Apes* (1973). Seen from the United States to Japan, from Britain to Israel, the *Apes* films were well received both by audiences and by critics, one of whom lauded the series as "perhaps the most successful ever to blend intelligent and thought-provoking story matter with broad entertainment values."[2] Following Jacobs' death in 1973, Fox followed the movies with the *Planet of the Apes* television show in 1974 and with the *Return to the Planet of the Apes* animated television series in 1975. In addition, there was a myriad of *Apes* merchandise ranging from books and magazines to records and soap to action figures and Halloween masks. The *Apes* saga had gone from a small science fiction novel to a major international popular culture phenomenon.

There was more to this than art and commerce. As Davis seems to have perceived, *Planet of the Apes*, and later its sequels, was also about difference, fear, guilt, survival, violence, and reconciliation. And race. The Davis anecdote, an exchange between an African-American viewer presumably cognizant of issues of race and two white producers apparently less aware, raises a number of important questions whose answers will help in understanding how the *Apes* films addressed racial conflict. First, how is it possible for accounts of ape behavior to serve as a device for exploring human racial relations? Second, how can popular fictions and entertainments engage social and political conflicts? And finally, how can there be such a vast discrepancy of interpretation between producer and viewer? In this introduction I will address these questions in order to set the context for considering the *Planet of the Apes* films as political movies.

How is it possible for stories about apes to serve as a device for exploring human racial conflict? Three explanations readily emerge. One explanation lies in our popular views towards biological evolution. The belief that humans are descended from apes, who are our closest relatives in the "animal kingdom," carves out for apes a singular relationship to humans and shapes our views of both "nature" and "civilization."

As Donna Haraway notes in her analysis of Western primatology, *Primate Visions: Gender, Race, and Nature in the World of Modern Science*, "monkeys and apes have a privileged relation to nature and culture for western people: simians occupy the border zones between those potent mythic poles."[3] In Western science and in Western fiction, apes are figured as liminal creatures, simultaneously like and unlike human beings; they are located between the worlds of "nature" and "civilization" and between the worlds of "origin" and "destination." Both scientific studies of, and popular fictions about, apes explore questions about the distinctions between, and the meanings of, those worlds. Studies and fictions about apes also help

construct the conceptual boundaries between those worlds and debate the
permeability of those boundaries.

Apes' liminal position allows us to see or imagine ourselves both in
their image and apart from their image. The similarities between apes and
humans are regarded as an indication of our origin, while the differences
help shape our ideas of ourselves as both being distinct from our animal
"ancestors" and possessing a "unique" destiny. Constructing and exploring
human self-identity has been an important part of our fascination with apes.
As Haraway observes: "Origins are in principle inaccessible to direct testimony; any voice from the time of origins is structurally the voice of the
other who generates the self. . . . Western primatology has been about the
construction of the self from the raw material of the other."[4]

This process of counter-identification, of constructing the self "from
the raw material of the other," is often integral to self-identification. Thus
images of "blackness" are central to images of "whiteness," constructions
of "savagery" are used to construct "civilization," and "heathens" are used
to shore up the identity of the "faithful." In this way the "other" forms the
border of the "self."[5] Likewise, primatology's constructions of apes are
integrally linked to our constructions of human beings.

The production, release, and initial popularity of the *Apes* films (roughly
1967 to 1973) coincided with a remarkable increase in the number of scientific studies of nonhuman primates. Haraway records the Science Information Exchange statistic that between 1965 and 1971 the number of science
projects using primates grew from 666 projects to 1183, an increase of over
77 percent. Similarly, "total primate references listed by the . . . Washington Primate Research Center grew from 5,000 in 1960 to 35,000 in 1971,"
a jump of 600 percent. Haraway also notes that between 1962 and 1965 "the
number of 'man-months,' devoted to field studies of *ecology* and *behavior*
of non-human primates more than exceeded the total of all previous
research" (emphasis added).[6]

These research statistics are particularly noteworthy in that this period
was a time when the scientific community, rather than focusing solely on
medical data, was increasingly concerned with the *social* aspects of primate
life. Apparently, producers of science during this time were particularly
hopeful that observations of, constructions of, and interpretations of ape
and monkey behavior could improve understanding of human beings.
Their hopes were shared by the producers of culture.

As different segments of our national life are intertwined and mutually influencing, we might expect that increased interest in apes would
simultaneously register in both the science and entertainment industries.
And it is possible that a rising national interest in apes and monkeys,
exemplified by the increased amount of time and money given to primate
studies, preceded and contributed to Twentieth Century–Fox's willingness

to finance a film that the studios had previously been unwilling to produce.

The makers of the *Apes* films also told stories about simians in order to talk about people. Co-writer Michael Wilson said the "key point" of *Planet* was that "it was more about the human predicament than it was about apes."[7] Thus the *Apes* series can be seen as consciously fictive primatology, a deliberate use of particular constructions of apes to advance particular constructions of humans.

As Haraway points out, in the sixties, primatologists' stories about apes were seen and prescribed as potential sources of redefinition of human experience. And as the above research figures indicate, the hopes that producing narratives about apes would yield better understanding of human beings were quite high. Even the similar language used to promote the products of scientific primatology and the products of popular culture primatology spoke to those hopes. A 1965 film about primatologist Jane Goodall, *Miss Goodall and the Wild Chimpanzees*, predicted that her ape study would "lead to a redefinition of the word *man*."[8] Along the same lines, three years later the theatrical trailer for *Planet* echoed Goodall's promise and proclaimed that the film would "challenge every idea you've ever had about civilization." Thus from the beginning, publicity for Fox's simian saga alerted audiences that the "key point" was that "it was more about the human predicament than it was about apes."

The *Planet of the Apes* series could also function as a discourse about race in the United States because historically discourses about apes and monkeys and discourses about race and "people of color" have been continually intertwined. Haraway points out that "traditionally associated with lewd meanings, sexual lust, and the unrestrained body, monkeys and apes mirror humans in a complex play of distortions over centuries of western commentary on these troubling doubles."[9]

It is not only apes and monkeys who have been burdened by these associations. Such stereotypes of morally polluted hyper-carnality have been integral components of the prejudices directed against a variety of racial, ethnic, and cultural "out-groups." Africans, Asians,[10] Jews, Latinos, women, homosexuals, and bisexuals, all of whom are constructed or have been constructed in the Western imagination as primarily and overly *bodily* and *sexual*, have all had these same associations and stereotypes forced upon them.[11] And in the case of people of African descent in particular, "ape" and "monkey" are still commonly encountered racial slurs.

Because apes and monkeys resemble humans but are still animals, "ape," "gorilla," "monkey" and related terms became favorite epithets to degrade those whose otherness and inferiority were believed to be manifested by and *inscribed* upon their bodies, people who, while they appeared human, were seen as less than human. For example, Edward Topsell's indignation in 1607 over apes' "indecent likeness and imitation of men" suggests that, used as a slur, "ape" indicates a subhuman masquerading as human.[12]

In the racist imagination, the "lower" orders masquerading as the "higher" threatens to compromise racial or even species purity. The human being called an ape is condemned as a racial imposter. Such was the case in a "liberal" eighteenth century Bavarian writer's assertion that "excluding the Indian fakirs, there is no category of *supposed* human beings which comes closer to the orangutan than does a Polish Jew" (emphasis added).[13] As Winthrop Jordon has pointed out, "to liken . . . human beings . . . to beasts [is] to stress the animal within the man."[14] The use of "ape" and related terms as slurs is a means of asserting nonrelation to those who appear similar but are still regarded as inferior. This would explain the use of the terms "ape" and "monkey" by Europeans to downgrade Africans, who must have seemed a startling and profoundly unsettling combination of difference and similarity. This assertion of difference staves off relatedness to the inferior "other" and maintains a sense of superiority by both accounting for and discounting likeness.[15]

Comparing apes and monkeys to "inferior" people confers upon the disfavored human beings the connotations of these simians' assumed carnality and lust. For instance, in 1945, as Europe reeled from Nazi attempts to destroy those with "inferior" genes, a book released in the United States advocated sterilization laws for all biologically and socially "inferior" types. The threat from these misfits supposedly arose in part from their "reckless breeding," which threatened to turn the United States into a "monkey house."[16]

Africans were seen as "reckless breeders" hundreds of years earlier. Jordan writes that in the time of initial contact between the English and Africans, "common and persistent was the notion that there sometimes occurred 'a beastly copulation or conjuncture' between apes and Negroes." He also notes that "a few commentators went so far as to suggest that Negroes had sprung from the generation of ape-kind or that apes were themselves the offspring of Negroes and some unknown African beast."[17]

As we have already seen, apes are laden with more meanings in the Western imagination than those of racial difference. Likewise, the *Apes* films were not focused on racial conflict as an isolated issue. Rather, race was a key component in a constellation of problems plaguing U.S. society which the films addressed. And like race, the related social and political themes the series addressed have historically been important parts of the study of apes. As Haraway points out:

> Questions about the nature of war, technology, power, and community echo through the primate literature. Given meanings through readings of

the bodies and lives of our primate kin . . . reinvented origins have been figures for reinvented possible futures. Primatology is a First World survival literature in the conditions of twentieth-century global history.[18]

The *Apes* series could function as a consideration of the social realities of humanity because the *Apes* movies were within the precedent of primate studies (and the precedent of science fiction and social satire) functioning in this capacity. Given the *Apes* films' apocalyptic images of cataclysmic race wars, nuclear destruction, struggles for dominance, ecological and biological devastation, enmity, suspicion, and corrupted innocence, the themes and problems of primatology resonate throughout the *Apes* saga. In the films, apes are not just our evolutionary predecessors; they are our evolutionary successors. Thus, as in the science of primatology, the focus of the *Apes* films on "reinvented origins" is in fact a look to "reinvented possible futures." And with their preoccupation with the future of humanity and its possible demise, the *Apes* films are indeed meditations on the survival potential of humanity, or at least Western humanity.

While stories about ape civilization might be entertaining and interesting, for most of us they would be less pertinent and powerful than stories about our own civilization. This brings us to the second question raised by the Sammy Davis, Jr., anecdote. How can popular fictions and entertainments engage social and political conflicts? When considering the political agenda of popular culture, some may be inclined to object that movies should not be taken so seriously, that they are just fiction with little or no social pertinence, simply entertainments for an afternoon or evening that should be enjoyed with popcorn and forgotten. This view is too uncritical and dismissive. Since their producers and their consumers do not exist in cultural vacuums, any cultural product — and by this I mean everything from books to films to political speeches to food packaging — can and should be seen as a text that is suggestive of the cultural context out of which it emerges.[19]

In the United States, we put an enormous amount of time, energy, and resources into the production and "consumption" of movies. There must be reasons, aside from the technical skills of the makers and the formal qualities of a given project, why audiences are especially responsive to particular films. There must be reasons why some films are exceptionally popular and have a stronger staying power; why some films are invested with extraordinary amounts of cultural capital, remaining in the public consciousness and even entering political discourse; why some films are recycled more often through sequels, imitations, or films that echo their themes, structures, or images.

Any film, in order to be effective, must connect in some way with audiences — with their memories and misfortunes, experiences and expectations, fantasies and fears. Many movies, including the *Apes* films, succeed because they connect with the individual or collective experiences of large numbers of the consuming public. We create culture and look to it to help us make sense out of the world around us. This function is likely to become particularly crucial in times of tremendous change, conflict, and instability. The late sixties and early seventies were just such a time for the United States, and the cultural production of the time dramatically registered that fact.[20]

For the United States, the sixties and early seventies were marked by a number of wars — the cold war, the Vietnam War, civil rights battles, "the war on poverty" — that were tumultuous public contestations of the character and meaning of United States society. These events provoked a stinging sense of despair that pervades the *Apes* series. *Planet of the Apes* was released on February 8, 1968, one month after the country had experienced the shock of the Tet offensive and just prior to the horror of the Martin Luther King, Jr., and Robert Kennedy assassinations. It was at the close of a decade that had seen Americans release attack dogs on other Americans demanding basic human rights. The Vietnam War was losing its public support and would produce the horrifying images of the My Lai massacre, but on March 10, 1968, roughly a month after the film was released, General William Westmoreland asked for 206,000 additional men for the prosecution of that war. The political and cultural crisis in the United States had led Dr. King to observe that "we are not marching forward; we are groping and stumbling: we are divided and confused. Our moral values and our spiritual confidence sink, even as our material wealth ascends."[21]

The *Apes* sequels came out in the midst of continued cultural shocks — Kent State and Watergate among them — that challenged U.S. citizens' estimations of their own society. The Vietnam War also took its toll on the U.S. self-image, a toll that weighed heavily upon the popular culture: on records the ever-apocalyptic Bob Dylan sang of the "Tombstone Blues." On "Star Trek" the USS *Enterprise*'s weekly television adventures on the "final frontier" often recalled the adventures of the United States in Vietnam — our latest frontier. And in the movies, John Ford's cavalry was transformed into Sam Peckinpah's *Wild Bunch*, "who came too late and stayed too long" in somebody else's war and who, like the United States in Vietnam, were "unchanged men in a changing land. Out of step, out of place and desperately out of time."[22] In 1973, critic Pauline Kael noted the Vietnam War's influence on popular film:

> The Vietnam War has barely been mentioned on the screen, but it has been overwhelmingly present in the movies of the past decade. . . . In action pictures, there was no longer a right side to identify with and nobody you really felt good about cheering for. The lack of principles was the same on both sides; only their styles were different, and it was a matter of preferring the less gross and despicable characters to the total monsters.[23]

The entire *Apes* saga unfolded at a time when the culture's moral coordinates were askew, a time when on- and off-screen, to use the American mythic language of racial heroism and racial villainy, the cowboys were becoming Indians and the Indians were becoming cowboys.

This dismay is reflected in the continuing perspective shift throughout the five films. While chimpanzees are always the good apes, the audience's point of identification changes from film to film. Sometimes the audience is supposed to identify with the humans against the apes, at other times with the apes against the humans, at times with some humans and against other humans and at other times with some apes and against other apes. From the closing moments of one film to the opening moments of the next (and indeed in the case of *Conquest* and *Battle*, at various moments within the film), we are not always entirely certain for whom we should be rooting. The filmmakers continually moved the lines separating the heroes from villains. Watching the *Apes* films on movie screens year after year was likely to provoke the same sense of moral confusion as watching the news on television screens year after year.

The *Apes* series depicted, commented upon, and engaged in, the painful convulsions of the changing times. It was for this reason that the studio could claim in *Planet*'s advertisements not only that the film was "unusual" but also "important." Although fiction, the *Apes* films were potent and successful, in part, because they related to the social and political realities, pressures, and crises of the time.

In *Mechanic Accents: Dime Novels and Working Class Culture in America*, Michael Denning discusses the manifestations of social struggles in popular fictions:

> Social cleavages ... do not present themselves immediately.... If historical struggles ... take place in borrowed costumes and assumed accents, if social and economic divisions appear in disguise, then the source for these and the manifestations of these roles lie in the conventional characters of a society, played out in its popular narratives.[24]

The *Apes* series was in fact a fictive disguise for political struggles and public anxieties that had produced profound national cleavages. The makers of the *Apes* films created fictional spaces whose social tensions resembled those then dominating the United States. They inserted characters into those spaces whose ideologies, passions, and fears duplicated the ideologies, passions, and fears of generations of Americans. And they placed those characters in conflicts that replicated crucial conflicts from the United States' past and present. The films were attempts to explore the meanings of those cleavages and understand what they said about the character of the society and its people both as U.S. citizens and as human beings.

Movies are an integral part of our society's culture. As such, they are always bound up with the meanings we assign to our experience.[25] Therefore, when those meanings are in debate, when the character of the country is facing a crisis of self-definition, we should expect films not only to reflect, but to participate in, that struggle. In fact, during these times, responding to, regulating, and arguing for particular interpretations of political and social events may be one of the most important, if unacknowledged, functions of the culture industries.

Some have claimed that movies are the most telling art form for understanding a society's cultural values and responses to its experiences. In a commencement address at Smith College in 1973, Pauline Kael argued that "of all the arts, movies now come closest to expressing the changes in our attitudes and the tensions in our lives."[26]

Some have made that point even more emphatically. Joseph Reed asserts that "how we see ourselves, what we think of us, what we think our world is like, how we think it works all come from the movies (and now from television as well)."[27] This is too strong a statement because other institutions such as schools and religion obviously play a significant role in shaping our worldview. But Reed's point should not be easily dismissed. For most of us, filmed depictions of major life experiences ranging from sex to work to war are likely to precede (or in the case of combat even *substitute* for) our actual encounters with them. As Reed points out, much of what we think we know of life comes not from direct experience but from simulated experiene delivered through the vicarious and highly mediated format of films and television (both entertainment and news programming). I would add music to the list.

Popular culture media such as these may give us the only "knowledge" we have of races we have never encountered personally, places we have never been, and experiences we have never had. Therefore the way we see, understand, and misunderstand experiences of the past, present, and future is largely shaped by popular culture. Thus movies, especially those which are very popular with audiences, demand critical assessment and careful interrogation if we are to understand what they say about the concerns and the values of the people and times that produced them. Such is the case with the *Apes* films.

Franklin J. Schaffner, the director of *Planet of the Apes*, once compared the film to a mirror of human society. In fact, this is only partially true. *Planet*, like the rest of the *Apes* series, was not just a mirror of the time but a response to it. Films are not simply indiscriminate reflections of society, nor are they disinterested. Films are specific representations and stories constructed in particular ways. As with any representation, with movies conscious choices are made about what will be included and what will be excluded, what will be explored and what will be ignored, what information the audience will be given and what will be withheld. The *Apes* films are particular shots of particular aspects of "reality" that privileged particular viewpoints.

The images we get from movies and other popular culture media, especially the images that are repeated often or are especially popular or powerful, will likely influence how we view the world, which in turn must influence how we act in it.[28]

Thus movies, in the United States at least, become more than stories or pastimes. They function as myths that are an integral part of the process through which we remember history, interpret experience, and prescribe a course for future action. As a result, the *Planet of the Apes* series can be understood as more than escapism, fantasy, or science fiction adventure. The *Apes* movies were also *political* films which, to use Haraway's description of the stories told by scientific primatologists, were "science fiction, where possible worlds [were] constantly reinvented in the contest for very real, present worlds."[29]

In *Bond and Beyond: The Political Career of a Popular Hero*, a study of the James Bond phenomenon and its relationship to the sociopolitical dynamics of Great Britain, Tony Bennett and Janet Wollacott make some thought-provoking arguments about popular fiction's role in cultural debates: "Popular fictional genres tend to rise to a position of pre-eminence in terms of both production and reading because they re-work current ideological tensions to effect, in their specific narrative forms, either a repetition of existing subject identities or a shift of such subject identities." They point out that it is not accidental that during the seventies, when "the dominant articulating principle of hegemony was a discourse of 'law and order,'" the most popular television dramas were police shows in which both "reservations about and identification with the law could be put into play."[30]

Similarly, during the late eighties and early nineties, in a time of public expressions of despair over the divorce rate and the demise of the nuclear family, there was a rash of situation comedies on television that had the nuclear family as their focus. These range from "The Cosby Show" and "Growing Pains," both popular exaltations of the nuclear family, to "The Simpsons" and "Married with Children," both popular critiques of the nuclear family, or at least critiques of traditional television images of the family. These shows emerge as explorations of and debates within the perceived crisis of the family.

Social cleavages and public crises open up spaces for artistic debate over the character of society and the meanings of its experience. When the status quo is challenged, popular culture may come to its defense, join the attack, or even do both.

Bennett and Wollacott make a tentative suggestion along these lines when they offer this speculation:

> Periods of generic change and innovation in popular fiction often coincide
> with those in which the ideological articulations through which hege-
> mony was previously secured are no longer working to produce popular
> consent. . . . The emergence of popular heroes, such as Bond and Sher-
> lock Holmes, often born in moments of crisis, may . . . play a particularly
> significant role in acting as a sounding board in relation to which generic
> readjustments in the fictional field may be articulated. . . . Figures like
> Bond and Holmes . . . may thus serve a crucial role in reorganizing the
> configuration of the ideological field.[31]

Ronald Reagan's presidential career offers some of the clearest recent examples of using popular heroes to produce popular consent. Reagan's referring to film characters like Rambo in attempting to gain support for his
administration's foreign policy and his quoting Dirty Harry's line "make my
day" when challenging Congress were deliberate uses of popular culture
figures to shape ideological debate by appealing to popular characters
and the cultural capital which audiences—voters—grant them. Arnold
Schwarzenegger, who came to public prominence during Reagan's presidency, learned the same tricks. While stumping for George Bush's presidential campaign, he warned that when it came to the economy, Michael
Dukakis would "be the *real* terminator." Similarly, the common application
of the term *Star Wars* to Reagan's space-based missile defense program
gave the veneer of the clean, efficient military technology of space fantasy
to Reagan's highly controversial proposal.

We can also view the *Apes* films as part of a cultural debate about the
direction and character of U.S. society. At the time that the *Apes* series was
produced and released, the racial power dynamics of the United States
were under sustained, often furious, attack. This "crisis" of threatened
racial hegemony—and we must ask for *whom* was it a crisis—had been
represented both by peaceful civil rights protests and violent encounters
involving African-Americans against police and military units. The sense of
instability engendered by these events was heightened by national shocks
such as the escalating war in Vietnam, the assassinations of U.S. political
leaders, and the growing civil unrest on college campuses. Such shocks
necessitated a response from various quarters of the society and opened up
a space that presented great ideological maneuverability. The *Apes* films
were attempts to respond to those events and provide credible meanings
for crises that seemed to defy understanding. The *Apes* series confronted
what was nothing less than a national crisis of identity, and, as James
Baldwin has observed:

> The question of identity is a question involving the most profound
> panic—a terror as primary as the nightmare of the mortal fall. . . . An iden-
> tity is questioned only when it is menaced, as when the mighty begin to
> fall, or when the wretched begin to rise, or when the stranger enters the

> gates, never, thereafter to be a stranger: the stranger's presence making *you*
> the stranger, less to the stranger than to yourself [emphasis in original].[32]

The sixties identity crisis was as ominous as the warnings of the *Apes* series about how the crisis might end.

As ominous as the warnings given by the Apes series are, the difficult question of intentionality often arises. Indeed, the most frequently asked question I have encountered when describing this book to others is whether the filmmakers *intended* the *Apes* movies to be political allegories of racial conflict. Undoubtedly, as I hope to demonstrate, much of it was intentional and the political moves of the series grew even more self-conscious in the last two films.

It is possible, however, that some of the political content of the films was unintended. Indeed, it is likely that, at times, the nature and dynamics of the United States' political struggles affected the artists' formulation of conflict and were thereby unconsciously worked into the films.

The persistence of certain ways of conceptualizing, representing, dramatizing, and resolving conflicts — in politics, art, leisure, and other fields of culture — express and speak to deeply held notions about the nature of conflict and how to respond to it. Artists, like the rest of society, derive their ideology, conceptual vocabulary, and means of expression in large measure from the culture around them, often, if not always, with little or no self-reflexive attention to where these cultural conventions came from, how they were formed, or what they might mean.

Even if artists do not consciously attempt to make "political statements," artists exist in a world of political and social relations. If political and social events are significant, they will, consciously or unconsciously, make an impression on artists and evoke a response. We can reasonably expect therefore that, consciously or not, political realities, events, and themes will register in an artist's work. In fact we should be shocked if a country's political conflicts and social biases do *not* find their way into its cultural production.

Stuart Hall has correctly pointed out that "an ideological discourse does *not* depend on the conscious intentions of those who formulate statements within it" (emphasis in original). [33] Furthermore, as Denning argues, "to be content . . . with the culture's self-understanding, is to abdicate the historian's task, which is to understand the way *a culture's social and political unconscious overdetermines its self-consciousness*" (emphasis added).[34] Thus the question of what an artist intended to put on the screen (or in a book or an advertisement, etc.) is in certain respects not as pertinent as the issue of what actually appeared on the screen, the relationship between the film and the political and cultural context of which it is a part, and what meanings and impact the film might have had for its audiences.

Thus, intentionality is not the only, nor the best, way of assessing a cultural product's meanings. The question of intentions is in some regards an irrelevant question, for it assumes that all effects are intended. As most of us are probably aware from our daily experiences, what we say and do may be the source of numerous unintended meanings and consequences. These meanings and consequences, even misunderstandings, exist and are no less real for having been unintended, however. Take for instance the argument that movies often support racism. I suspect that filmmakers rarely set out with harmful intentions, but effects do not always respect intentions. The issue is not one of assigning artists guilt for malicious motives but of artists accepting responsibility for the results of their actions. Raising the question of an artist's responsibility for her or his work shifts the emphasis away from the rhetoric of blame—a rhetoric that tends to raise defenses and lower understanding—and towards confronting consequences.

Lorraine Hansberry persuasively made this point in a debate with director Otto Preminger about the stereotyping of blacks in his film *Porgy and Bess*. Hansberry argued against stereotyping on artistic grounds, pointing out that stereotypes "constitute bad art" because the "artist hasn't tried hard to understand his characters." When Preminger asked if she suspected the motives of those who made *Porgy and Bess*, Hansberry correctly recast the issue from the comparatively trivial question of artists' intentions to the more important question of the art's material effects:

> We cannot afford the luxuries of mistakes of other people. So it is not a matter of being hostile to you, but on the other hand it's also a matter of never ceasing to try to get you to understand that your mistakes can be painful, even those which come from excellent intentions. We've had great wounds from excellent intentions.[35]

As Hansberry's comment suggests, the intentionality question may be a distraction from substantive issues.

One of the important ways that film affects our social and political culture is to influence our ideas of what "race" is and how different races are. As Hall puts it, "amongst other kinds of ideological labour the media construct for us a definition of what *race* is, what meaning the imagery of race carries and what the 'problem of race' is understood to be" (emphasis in original).[36] While filmmakers may not feel comfortable acknowledging that they can have this degree of influence and may not actively seek it, the fact remains that our fantasies impact our realities.

To return to the stereotyping issue as an example, it is not necessary for filmmakers who traffic in bigoted stereotypes to *intend* to malign anyone. But artists—whatever their background—share with the rest of society a cultural language steeped in racist, sexist, anti–Semitic, classist, and other biased assumptions. It takes a tremendous amount of work to unpack and discard those assumptions. To unselfconsciously speak that language is natural and requires no malicious forethought, or any forethought at all for that matter. Nonetheless, lack of bad intentions is an inadequate excuse when it comes to recycling or promoting bigotry and rationalizing oppression.

We now turn to the third question raised earlier: How can there be such a vast discrepancy in interpretation between producer and viewer? To understand this, we must understand that, as with any text, the meanings of the *Apes* films cannot be located solely in the minds of their creators or even in the images on the screen, but are found also in the interpretations and experiences of their audiences. Although filmmakers can attempt to influence the audience's reading of a film, they cannot control it. There is thus an interplay between artist, text, and audience out of which meaning is formed. Ultimately, the meanings lie in the interpretive activities of the audience and are determined, in part, by the extratextual conditions, pressures, and experiences that influenced both the filmmakers and the audience.

The *Apes* movies address U.S. racial politics by referencing events and images in the audience's cultural memory. All cultural products rely on and play upon cultural memory. By cultural memory, I mean public memory— the memory of a population's shared experiences, stories, and images and the meanings ascribed to them. Cultural memories may be deep, recalling experiences from the distant or even mythic past, as in the story of the expulsion from the Garden of Eden, or they may be more recent or current, recalling such events as the civil rights struggle or the attack on Rodney King. Cultural products access these memories through symbolic representations, whether through language, visual images, or some other form. When we read of a damsel in distress or watch a presidential inauguration, we understand their meanings in part through internal references and comparisons to other damsels in distress about whom we have read or inaugurations about which we know. Works of culture are largely built upon pieces of earlier works of culture. We know whether a story, a ritual, or a genre film has successfully conformed to our expectations because we have internalized the formula. What we experience in the present is integrally bound up with what we have experienced in the past. Pieces of cultural memory are the building blocks the filmmakers used to construct the political allegory of the *Apes* series.

When metaphoric comparisons are made, like the ones in the *Apes* films or, indeed, like the ones made in this book, the things being compared comment upon each other and their interaction is intended to guide or shift our understanding of them. Anthropologist Victor Turner notes philosopher Max Black's conviction that a metaphorical statement is made up of a principal subject that is being compared to a subsidiary subject, the basis of the comparison. For example, screenwriter Paul Dehn's statement that the ape uprising in *Conquest of the Planet of the Apes* is "like the Watts riots"[37] is a metaphoric comparison in which the film's climax is the principal subject and the Watts riots is the subsidiary subject. Turner points out that rather than single things, both subjects in this type of comparison are in fact "multivocal symbols, whole semantic systems, which bring into relation a number of ideas, images, sentiments, values and stereotypes. Components of one system enter into dynamic relations with components of the other." He goes on to explain that "The metaphor selects, emphasizes, suppresses, and organizes features of the principal subject by implying statements about it that normally apply to the subsidiary subject."[38] What Turner describes is the same process through which metaphorical referencing helps produce meaning in the *Apes* films. When the films depict fictional events that are modeled on actual incidents, as *Conquest* did with the ape revolt based on sixties urban racial violence or as *Beneath* did with a chimpanzee antiwar movement that resembled the student anti–Vietnam War movement, the meanings of the actual occurrences may be supplied as the meanings of the movie's imitation. Thus the resemblance between the chimpanzee opposition to the gorilla army and the student opposition to the Vietnam War may provide the viewer with the moral coordinates to interpret the film the same way she or he interprets the public drama regarding the Vietnam War.

Metaphoric comparisons also work both ways. The actual event may be reread through the film's images and ideological charge. A film may problematize commonly accepted ideas by offering different interpretations to counter traditional views of historical occurrences or by presenting an honored icon in a new light. This may shift the viewer's interpretation of historical or current events.[39] *Conquest*, for instance, may be more than rote repetition of the images of the Watts riots. It may in fact provide a key for rereading the Watts riots as a justifiable violent reaction to intolerable violent oppression, rather than just an outbreak of lawless abandon. A film can also raise questions of value and interpretation or juxtapose different interpretations of the same historical or fictional event without seeking to endorse one particular view.[40]

This is all complicated by the fact that symbols are multivalent — they may carry a variety of sometimes conflicting meanings for different individuals or groups. Therefore interpretations are varied and negotiable. This is one of the difficulties filmmakers face in creating their work and one of the main reasons that producers like Jacobs and viewers like Sammy Davis, Jr., can vary vastly in their interpretations — artists cannot control what associations the audience will bring with them and what interpretations they might create.

A symbol's historic associations and the artistic and political context in which the symbol is used render some interpretations more likely and plausible than others, however. The *Apes* films do employ strategies to place interpretive weight on certain readings, and we will see some of the ways used both to hold out the possibility of multiple readings and to try to guide the viewers toward particular ones. In the absence of detailed studies of audience response when the films were released, however, it is difficult, perhaps impossible, to assess how effective those attempts were.[41]

We must also remember that symbols are fluid and elastic; they may expand or contract over time to admit more or fewer referents. And memory is fleeting. A symbol or image produced in 1968 might have had a multitude of references to easily recognizable events and concerns of the time which might go unnoticed or unremembered by today's viewers. Conversely, in the intervening years, that same symbol or image may have taken on new associations unimaginable at the time of its production.

The meanings of a symbol or image may also change due to the location of the audience. A symbol in an *Apes* film might have particular possible meanings in the United States and very different ones in, for instance, Mexico or Egypt.[42] For example, a British publication noted that the *Apes* series "was laced with racial overtones, easily linked to the civil rights movement in America, Vietnam and Northern Ireland."[43] While U.S. audiences and critics noted the connections to Vietnam and to U.S. race relations, the comparison to Northern Ireland would have been unlikely from someone who was not from the United Kingdom or who was not for some other reason particularly knowledgeable about Ireland.

Given the fluid and varied meanings of symbols and the fact that the *Apes* films were produced, promoted, and seen as multilayered texts which served as, among other things, social commentary, speculative fiction, action-adventure, and fantasy, we can conclude that different viewers would derive different pleasures and meanings from them. A child who might enjoy the films' elements of adventure might not see the connection between the action in the *Apes* films and anxiety over "Black Power," while an adult who did see this connection might not notice the similarity between the racial nationalism of the gorilla generals and that of Theodore Roosevelt. Thus to the extent possible, in addition to my own interpretations, I am trying to discuss the meanings that would have been available to adult U.S. audiences in the late sixties and early seventies.[44]

While it is difficult to know the precise interpretations drawn by the audiences of the *Apes* films, it is certain that a segment of the audience was aware of, and, judging by the series' popularity, responded positively to, the ways the movies functioned as social commentary. Although the political content of the films was handled subtly enough that they could still function as entertainment for several age groups, even on the surface the *Apes* films are too charged with the ideological and social conflicts of the time to have functioned as total escapism for most adult viewers. In 1972, just prior to the release of *Conquest of the Planet of the Apes*, *Time* magazine declared that the film would "find a huge ready made audience of ape addicts, including many intellectuals who enjoy the series' broad, cartoon-like satire of human faults."[45] The following year, in a review of *Battle for the Planet of the Apes*, a critic praised the series as

> both wonderful entertainment and a politically sophisticated fable, a chance for children to learn about the forces that move the world in a way that's accessible and imaginative. Where else can a family audience see greed and ambition so nakedly revealed while simultaneously cheering for idealism in its struggle against evil?[46]

The producers, directors, writers, actors, critics, audiences and those who became fans as the series achieved cult status all understood that social commentary was an essential part of the *Apes* phenomenon.

This remains the case. Mark Phillips of Johnson City, Tennessee, wrote a letter printed in a spring 1991 issue of the new *Planet of the Apes* comic book to respond to an earlier reader's letter criticizing the comic's social overtones. Phillips argued that

> the original *Planet of the Apes* book is a social satire designed to point out [human flaws]. The creators of this comic are advancing along these same lines. . . . The weaknesses of mankind are all played up so that we can possibly learn something about ourselves with our entertainment. Without these elements we might as well have a funny animal comic.[47]

This letter, and other evidence of audience reaction, including the writings of critics and the letters to the mid-seventies *Planet of the Apes* magazine, suggest that the sociopolitical themes and meanings of the *Apes* materials were considered seriously by at least some of the *Apes* audience and were for them part of what made the series worthwhile and about more than funny animals.

One of the characteristics of fiction is the ability to extract controversial problems from their social circumstances and reinscribe them onto fictional, even outlandish, contexts. The acceptability of introducing new worlds and even new forms of life in science fiction and fantasy may make these genres especially flexible in this regard. Difficult issues can be located safely distant, even light years away, from the real ground of conflict and thereby rendered less obvious and less psychologically or politically threatening.[48] Science fiction's distance provides deniability for both the filmmakers and the audience.

The displacement of issues like race relations and Vietnam into the science fiction genre is a mark of the difficulty filmmakers had with openly confronting these problems at the time the *Apes* series was produced. It should come as no surprise therefore that the third *Apes* film, *Escape from the Planet of the Apes*, which is set closest to the audience's time, is also the least violent and the one where the director chose not to "hammer the sociological overtones."[49]

Stan Hough, the producer of the *Planet of the Apes* television program, commented on this aspect of doing the show in a 1974 interview:

> We have so much latitude in what we can say, dressed up in monkey suits. We are enjoying the freedom, the fun, of creating a whole culture and society from the ground up. We can reveal truths and show things we could never otherwise get away with. Make social statements. About the violent side of human nature. About the horrors of the police state. About the blindness of prejudice.[50]

Hough's comments are important both for what they tell us about cultural products and for what they tell us about the understanding of these particular cultural producers. Anthropologist Clifford Geertz notes that cultural patterns are both models *of* reality and models *for* reality. They have a descriptive and a prescriptive component. Hough's explanation of his work on the *Apes* television show touches upon both the descriptive and the prescriptive components of cultural symbols. The ability to use the *Apes* series to "reveal truths," to dramatize what life is, is a function of the descriptive aspect, a function of the way cultural symbols act as representations *of* reality, or of perceptions of reality. At the same time, the ability to use the *Apes* series to "make social statements," to put forth a vision of the way reality should be, is a function of the prescriptive aspect, a function of the way that cultural symbols act as arguments *for* a particular configuration or reconfiguration of reality.

The descriptive and prescriptive components of cultural symbols are integrally related and mutually reinforcing—they borrow authority from and give authority to each other. Thus Geertz notes that "culture patterns have an intrinsic double aspect: they give meaning, that is, objective conceptual form, to social and psychological reality both by shaping themselves to it and by shaping it to themselves."[51] Therefore to understand the development and place of the *Apes* series, we must understand that the series did not just act as a mirror. The movies did not merely record and play back the society's ongoing discourses of racial difference and racial conflict; they entered into and are a part of those discourses. The *Apes* films did not just represent, they presented. They did not just repeat, they spoke. And as we shall see, the films privilege speaking as a most powerful act.

Hough's comments are telling in a further regard. Although his remark that in the *Apes* television show the filmmakers could "show things we could never otherwise get away with" suggests that he still felt the need for deniability, his remark that through the *Apes* television show the producers could "make social statements . . . [a]bout the blindness of prejudice" is evidence that between Arthur Jacobs' 1968 encounter with Sammy Davis, Jr., and Stan Hough's 1974 interview with *TV Guide*, those in charge of developing and exploring the *Apes* property and producing it for mass consumption became explicitly aware of and publicly acknowledged the *Apes* saga as a discourse on race.

ONE

Planet of the Apes

In the Apes series, racial conflict is removed from the audience's present, projected into both the near and distant future, and reinscribed as species conflict.[1] Whether characterized explicitly as race or species difference, however, the salient fact is that *in the Apes series, as in U.S. history, physical difference remains the point of departure for titanic conflict.*

A brief overview of the films may be helpful for those unfamiliar with the series. In *Planet of the Apes* (1968, screenplay by Rod Serling and Michael Wilson, additional material by John T. Kelly [uncredited], based on the novel *Monkey Planet* by Pierre Boulle, directed by Franklin J. Schaffner), white astronaut Colonel George Taylor and his crew crash-land on an unknown planet. Crew member Stewart, a white woman, has died in her sleep during the voyage due to damage to her life-support system. Taylor and the other two survivors, Dodge, an African-American man, and Landon, a white man, set out to explore the planet and search for food. The astronauts encounter a group of mute human beings living in the jungle. Immediately thereafter the astronauts and the other humans are attacked by gorillas on horseback. During the hunt, Landon is captured, later to be lobotomized, and Dodge is shot and killed, later to be stuffed and exhibited in a museum. Taylor is shot in the throat, temporarily loses his ability to speak, and is captured along with the tribe of humans.

Amazed by Taylor's intelligence and his ability to talk once his throat heals, Zira, a chimpanzee animal psychologist, and her fiancé Cornelius, a chimpanzee archeologist, befriend him. They help Taylor escape the ape city, thereby thwarting the will of the orangutan administrator Dr. Zaius, who sees intelligent humans as a threat to the survival of ape civilization and wants to geld Taylor. Accompanied by a white woman named Nova, a mute human also captured in the hunt and later selected to mate with Taylor, Taylor ventures into the "Forbidden Zone"—a mysterious desert area declared taboo by the apes' "Sacred Scrolls." There he discovers that he has returned to Earth 2000 years in the future, the half-buried Statue of Liberty serving as evidence that human civilization has been destroyed, presumably by itself.

The first sequel was *Beneath the Planet of the Apes* (1970, story by Mort Abrahams and Paul Dehn, screenplay by Paul Dehn, directed by Ted Post). In this film white astronaut John Brent is sent to find Taylor. His ship also crashes, and he finds Nova wandering alone in the desert. After being captured in the ape city, Brent and Nova escape into the Forbidden Zone and stumble upon the bombed-out subterranean remains of Manhattan. There they find Taylor held captive by telepathic radiation-scarred mutant humans who worship an atomic bomb powerful enough to destroy the world as the divine instrument of their god. When the expansionist gorilla general Ursus leads an invasion of the city and shoots Taylor, Taylor's dying act is to detonate the bomb and destroy the Earth.

Escape from the Planet of the Apes (1971, screenplay by Paul Dehn, directed by Don Taylor) follows Zira and Cornelius, along with chimpanzee Dr. Milo, who had salvaged and relaunched Taylor's ship just prior to Earth's destruction, as they are catapulted back in time and land on 1973 Earth. Befriended by two white animal psychologists, the apes are initially welcomed as charming celebrities. Once he learns that Zira is pregnant, however, Dr. Otto Hasslein, the white science adviser to the president, becomes convinced that the progeny of the apes will one day dominate the human race and destroy the world. Zira and Cornelius are hunted down and murdered. But their child survives, Zira having switched her newborn baby with a chimpanzee from a circus owned by the sympathetic Latino Armando.

Conquest of the Planet of the Apes (1972, screenplay by Paul Dehn, directed by J. Lee Thompson) picks up eighteen years later when Zira and Cornelius' son Caesar accompanies Armando to an unnamed state's capital city in 1991 and discovers that the humans have turned the apes into a slave labor force. Following a run-in with the police, Armando is held in custody and interrogated. The white Governor Breck, suspecting the true identity of Armando's circus ape, orders a search for the talking chimpanzee. Meanwhile, Caesar infiltrates the slave population and is purchased by Breck. After Armando dies while in custody of the white security inspector Kolp, Caesar, aided by Breck's African-American assistant MacDonald, escapes execution and leads a successful revolt to free his fellow apes from their enslavement.

The film cycle is concluded in *Battle for the Planet of the Apes* (1973, story by Paul Dehn, screenplay by John William and Joyce Hopper Corrington, directed by J. Lee Thompson). In this last chapter, the apes having liberated themselves and acquired the power of speech in the unspecified number of years since *Conquest*, Caesar attempts to create a peaceful community of apes and humans in an Eden-like village. That peace is threatened, however, by tension within the village between the resentful gorillas and the human beings, whom the apes have reduced to second-class citizens. Peace is threatened as well by the hostility of the human survivors of humankind's last war, a nuclear confrontation that left Kolp and his people scarred by radiation and living in the remains of the capital city (these are the predecessors of the mutants in *Beneath*).

Caesar, his orangutan adviser Virgil, and MacDonald's brother venture into the city to view recordings of Zira and Cornelius' disclosures about the fate of the Earth. Assuming the visit to be hostile, Kolp orders his troops to kill them. After Caesar and company escape Kolp's soldiers, Kolp decides to attack the ape village. While the apes are preparing their defenses, the gorilla general Aldo devises a plan to exterminate all the humans in the city, kill Caesar, and seize power. Caesar's son overhears the plan and is killed by Aldo. The apes repel Kolp's attack, and Caesar kills Aldo once the murder of his son and the coup attempt are disclosed. Finally, Caesar begins the task of rebuilding the community and setting the foundations for equality between apes and humans.

The *Apes* series portrays a continual power struggle between human and ape. Structurally, each film is built around the conflict between a racially dominant oppressive group and a racially subordinate oppressed group seeking survival, harmony, or reversal of domination. The plot trajectory of the series arises out of the conflict between these two groups. Each film also presents mediating figures who intervene in the conflict and act as advocates of racial harmony. (See accompanying chart.) These mediators are marginalized members of the dominant group who have suffered or continue to suffer racial discrimination and are at odds with the oppressing group. The oppressed and mediating characters, both of whom the audience is meant to identify with, are, or become, outsiders who run afoul of the power system. The subordinate and mediating characters' conflict with the system is a device which allows the filmmakers to describe and critique that system.

In each film the power structure mirrors the very society out of which the films arose: racial oppression is built into the structure of society and the oppressed and mediating figures appeal to those in control in the name of racial or species harmony. Significantly, the advocates of racial peace never fully prevail. Their appeals fail, and racial hostility invariably results in cataclysmic violence. (While *Battle* has some structural differences, the central conflict remains unchanged.)

The *Apes* films are dystopian and apocalyptic. They are dystopian in that rather than offering a symbolic resolution of cultural tensions and fears, they magnify and extend those tensions to a fearsome conclusion. The *Apes* films arose during a time of perceived crisis, or perhaps more precisely a time of perceived heightened crisis, and such conditions are

RACIAL CONFLICT STRUCTURE

Planet   Dominant: Orangutans
           Mediator: Chimpanzees
           Dominated: White humans

Beneath Dominant: Gorillas and Orangutans
           Mediator: Chimpanzees
           Dominated: White humans

Escape   Dominant: White humans
           Mediator: Latino, liberal white woman,
                     liberal white man
           Dominated: Apes

Conquest Dominant: White humans
           Mediator: Latino, African-American
           Dominated: Apes

Battle   Dominant: Apes
           Mediator: African-American
           Dominated: White humans

Each film is built around the conflict between a racially dominant group and a racially dominated group. The mediating figures are from a group previously discriminated against which is still marginalized and at odds with the dominant group.

---

fertile ground for apocalyptic responses. They are apocalyptic films in that they imagine a dramatic, definitive break with past and present social configurations and depict a radical reorganization of power dynamics — the last shall be first and the first shall be last.

The films are constructed around such inversions, depicting the apocalyptic transformation of racial power relations. This is the main motif, some might even call it an obsession, of the *Planet of the Apes* series. Each film is concerned with and situated in significant relation to that apocalypse: either it has happened or it is imminent. The films' narratives in general concern understanding, preventing, precipitating, or reversing that apocalypse. In this sense, while the series does not symbolically resolve the tensions with which it is concerned, it does project their apocalyptic culmination and eventual termination. The two mutually reinforcing issues with which the series appears most concerned are humanity's potential for destruction and, the primary concern in this book, racial oppression.

White fear of racial apocalypse in the Americas can be traced back as far as the colonial period when the colonists felt themselves encircled by the dark, "savage Indians." Later, Native Americans were joined in white Americans' apocalyptic dread by the other great repository of racial dread, Africans. The threat of slave uprising and fear of racial apocalypse led Thomas Jefferson to

> tremble for my country when I reflect that God is just: that his justice cannot sleep forever: that considering numbers, nature and natural means only, a revolution of the wheel of fortune, an exchange of situation, is among possible events: that it may become probable by supernatural interference! The almighty has no attribute which can take side with us in such a contest.[2]

Still later, when the fear spread that the huddled masses would become a rising tide of color, the forces of racial reaction acted to keep out the wretched refuse through draconian, racially biased immigration restriction.[3] Hence, there is a long-standing fear among whites in the United States of an "exchange of situation," a loss of racial dominance. Those fears were aggravated during the sixties by the war in Vietnam and by the black liberation struggle at home. The sense that the racial violence abroad and at home was beyond control had shaken the security of white racial hegemony and led to a self examination by whites of which the *Apes* films were a part.

Rod Serling wrote the first drafts of the *Planet of the Apes* screenplay for Arthur Jacobs. In the fifties Serling was one of a group of authors, including Paddy Chayefsky, Robert Alan Arthur, and Horton Foote, who were referred to as "the angry young men." Serling had established himself as one of the most talented authors of live television plays with works such as *Patterns* and *Requiem for a Heavyweight*.[4] In many ways Serling's background and prior work made him a perfect choice for the film. A gifted author, Serling was also the creator-producer-writer of "The Twilight Zone" a science fiction television series during the late fifties and early sixties with the exact combination of engaging drama, other-worldly imagination, and daring, thought-provoking scripts that would prove so important to the *Apes* films' success. Serling's exclusion from a fraternity because he was Jewish fed into a long-time interest in writing about prejudice. Asked in 1961 what he would most want to write about, he responded, "I'd like to do a definitive study of segregation—say from the Negro's point of view. A definitive study of what the Negro feels about it."[5]

Serling, who considered himself a conservative liberal, had dealt with race relations on "The Twilight Zone" and had previously written *In the Presence of Mine Enemies* about the Polish Jewish ghetto in Warsaw. Serling was frustrated, however, by the resistance from TV networks and sponsors who were frightened of controversy and who refused to deal directly and honestly with contemporary racial problems in the United States. He complained:

Planet of the Apes offered a primal vision of racial apocalypse depicting the victory of nonhuman over human, East over West, non-white over white.

If you're doing a controversial script, you perform the strange ritual of track-covering. If you want to do a piece ("A Town Has Turned to Dust") about prejudice against Negroes, you go instead with Mexicans and set it in 1890 instead of 1959. . . . If you want to do a play about a man's Communist background as a youth, you have to make him instead a member of a wild teen-age group.[6]

An example of this "track covering" is the final result of Serling's *Noon on Doomsday* for "U.S. Steel Hour." Serling had originally based *Doomsday* on the murder of Emmett Till in Mississippi. But by the time the Southern White Citizens Councils had completed their hate mail campaigns, they had successfully intimidated the network and sponsor into interfering with the project. The "victim was changed from a Negro to a Jew, then to an unnamed foreigner. The locale was changed from the South to an unnamed place to New England."[7] Serling commented, "I think we would have moved it farther north than that if the sponsor hadn't been worried about running into the minority problem of the Eskimo." Firmly believing that television could be used to comment on society's troubles and serve as a forum for "self-examination of the moral climate of the American people," Serling later would criticize television's failure to confront the Vietnam War.[8]

Carrying his concern over racism through the sixties, Serling wrote movingly about the hypocrisy of the white embrace of Martin Luther King, Jr., coming only after King had died: "In death, we offer the acknowledgement of the man and his dream that we denied him in life. In his grave, we praise him for his decency—but when he walked among us we acted with no decency of our own."[9] And in June of 1967, as *Planet* was being filmed, Serling told a newspaper that "the singular evil of our time is prejudice. It is from this evil that all other evils grow and multiply. In almost everything I have written, there is a thread of this: man's seemingly palpable need to dislike someone other than himself."[10]

Given all of this, it is rather surprising that Serling's *Planet* screenplay did not particularly address the racial aspects of the *Apes* material. When he was finally freed from television's timidity, it would have seemed quite natural for Serling to use the *Apes* material as a forum for exploring the issues of racial hate that had so long concerned him. Serling apparently felt obligated, however, to stay close to Boulle's original book, in which racial discrimination was not a major part of ape society. Instead Serling played up the cruelty to animals angle, and his script addressed humanity's poor treatment of other animals more than the poor treatment of some groups of human beings by other groups of human beings. Serling also retained Boulle's thematic focus on humanity's ability to physically, intellectually, and spiritually regenerate itself in the face of a backwards turn in evolution.

Although he received co-writer credit, Serling's screenplay bore little resemblance in story and dialogue to the final film. But Serling's thematic contributions were nonetheless significant. It was Serling who, over Boulle's objection, introduced the theme of nuclear destruction. Further, a line he wrote for an ape reacting to the United States use of nuclear weapons against Japan— "you are scientifically advanced but there remains a question as to *how* civilized" (emphasis in original)—suggests that it was Serling who made the human propensity for war a focus of the film.[11] (Both these themes were consistent with Serling's work on "The Twilight Zone.") Finally, Serling retained the gruesome ape experiments on the humans mentioned in the book, experiments which might have touched upon fears of Communist torture and mind control. Serling added to this a description of the apes' planned economy, which resembled U.S. images of Communist states. This suggests that it was Serling who early in the film's preproduction stage infused the *Apes* project with the cold war themes that remained, though in radically altered form, important in the series.

To finish the work of writing a viable script, Jacobs hired Michael Wilson. Wilson was no stranger to Boulle's work; he had written the 1957 film adaptation of his *Bridge Over the River Kwai*. However, because Wilson had been an unfriendly witness before the House Committee on Un-American Activities, he was blacklisted and received no credit for his Oscar-winning screenplay, which was instead credited to Boulle himself.[12] Wilson also had experience with racial epics, having worked on the screenplay for *Lawrence of Arabia* (1962), for which he also did not initially receive credit. Wilson had established himself as an impressive writer of intelligent adventure-dramas. Throughout his career, Wilson also was drawn to politically "left" films. He shared a best-screenplay Oscar with Harry Brown for *A Place in the Sun* (1952), which dealt with the pitfalls of ambition, and he addressed labor strikes in *Salt of the Earth* (1953). The director and producer of the latter were also blacklisted at the time, and a Screen Writers Guild official had denounced the film as a "Communist propaganda weapon." Wilson wrote about Che Guevara in the 1969 *Che!* (which he later disavowed after he concluded that the changes made by others to the screenplay made Guevara look foolish).[13]

Wilson also had an interest in racial conflict which surfaced in *The Old Man*, a screenplay written for director Robert Wise that concerned John Brown's Harpers Ferry raid, and *Outer Darkness*, a comedy about CIA infiltration of the black liberation movement. Apparently too controversial for Hollywood, which was still reeling from the anti-leftist campaigns of the fifties, the scripts were never produced. It is in Wilson's hands that the screenplay for *Planet of the Apes* began to take shape as an allegorical address of racial conflict and of the Vietnam War.

The filmmakers juxtaposed ape society with human society, most notably that of the United States, and thereby critiqued the latter. Not only was this intentional, for *Planet* director Franklin Schaffner it was a priority. In an interview in *Cinéfantastique* magazine, Schaffner stated: "The approach was to engage an audience in a simian society. I had never thought of this picture in terms of being science fiction. More or less, it was a political film, with a certain amount of Swiftian satire, and perhaps science fiction last."[14]

The film's first few moments establish some of its major political themes. *Planet* opens with a shot of blue-tinged red and white "stars" passing through space. The next shot is of the interior of a spaceship, and the dominant colors are again red, white, and blue. We then see the main character George Taylor (Charlton Heston), who has a United States flag insignia prominently displayed on his sleeve. When a few minutes later we see the ship from the outside, we see that it has red and blue stripes on its white hull. Thus the film repeats the red, white, and blue color motif four times within the film's first few minutes, signaling that something about the United States is at stake here.

In the film's opening scene, astronaut Taylor, who is sending a report back to Earth, sits in the ship and expounds upon humanity's talents for war and cruelty, expressing hope that the humans of the future will be a different "breed." This soliloquy introduces two of the film's major concerns: what humanity is and what it will become. At the conclusion of the scene, Taylor places himself in a suspended animation chamber and drifts off to sleep. His image slowly blurs until it becomes no longer distinguishable and is replaced by the title *Planet of the Apes*, as if to foreshadow that humans as we know them will be replaced by apes.

The plot device of the hero falling asleep and awakening in a different time and place has been used repeatedly in science fiction and fantasy stories and places Taylor in a line of succession with characters like Burroughs' John Carter, Twain's Connecticut Yankee, and Buck Rogers. Typically in these stories, the character awakens in a radically altered world, often a world white men no longer dominate, and the device has become a signal to pay attention to the social and *racial* structure in which the white hero rises.[15]

Although the film did not explain the genesis of the ape society, in story conferences the filmmakers developed the history of the apes' social and racial structure. Abrahams recalls that the gorillas, being physically the strongest, were conceived as having been originally in charge of a military dictatorship. This is very close to the political history described by Pierre Boulle in his original 1963 novel, but Boulle's conception and that of Abrahams, Jacobs, and Wilson began to part.

In the book, Zira explains the racial structure of ape society to the equivalent of Taylor's character, Ulysee Merou, aptly named after another adventurer:

> There are three distinct families, as you have noted, each of which has its own characteristics: chimpanzees, gorillas, and orangutans. The racial barriers that used to exist have been abolished and the disputes arising from them have been settled, thanks mainly to the campaigns launched by the chimpanzees. Today, in principle, there is no difference between us.[16]

But in the minds of the filmmakers, according to Abrahams, as ape society advanced, the gorillas needed the services of the more intellectual apes, presumably opening the way for orangutans and chimpanzees to play important roles.[17] We can assume that the orangutans, portrayed as quite manipulative and shrewd, were able to outdistance the chimpanzees and also reduce the gorillas to a subservient manual labor and military class. The film seems to be set sometime after, or perhaps during, that transition period.

While in the book the ape races are somewhat disdainful of each other, the film goes even further by picturing a society built on rigid racial stratification. At the bottom of this hierarchy in Wilson's early draft were the baboons. The lowly work in ape society is reserved for them. In describing the medical facility, for instance, Wilson wrote that "all menials in the lab, such as guards and janitors are baboons."[18] Right above the baboons are the chimpanzees. The script specifies that the ape legislators be "gorillas, orangutans and chimpanzees, but no baboons." Additionally, there are no chimpanzee legislators seated on the ape assembly dias, presumably the place of highest prestige and power.[19] No such rigid stratification is suggested in the book. Further, Wilson made the allegory more pointed by having the baboons challenge the ape racial hierarchy, just as African-Americans were challenging the racial status quo of the United States. As the main human character, Thomas (an early name for the "Taylor" character), attempts to escape, he passes a baboon protest outside of the ape assembly. The baboons carry signs that read "Baboons Unite," "Down with Discrimination," and "Freedom Now." And as in U.S. society, the demonstration turns into a violent clash with the police. Wilson even has a gorilla assembly member echoing the temporizing rhetoric of whites opposed to equality and justice for African-Americans and other peoples of color:

> We have a government of laws, not of apes. And material gains for minorities can come only within the framework of the law. These agitators don't want orderly change! Theirs is not a peaceful demonstration. They don't even represent our law abiding baboons ... no! They've come to the very portals of the assembly to start a lawless riot.[20]

The proximity in the screenplay of Thomas' escape and the baboons' resistance links the apes persecution of the baboons to their persecution of humans.

Notwithstanding Wilson and Schaffner's political conception however, Abrahams recalls that *Planet* was developed using the "NP" or "no polemic" rule. Political statements were not to be "platformed." The political commentary was never to overwhelm the plot or entertainment value of the picture.[21] Indeed the careful balance of political commentary and entertainment was key to the film's eventual success as social satire. Therefore, whenever the political statements seemed to be coming on too strong during the preproduction process, someone would say "NP" as a signal to tone things down and keep the commentary subtle.

Hence, perhaps in an attempt to keep the commentary more restrained, the baboons and their protest were taken out and the gorillas, who in the early draft had served as clergy and legislators as well as hunters, took their place as the lowest racial class. The film has no lectures or debates on the evils of racial discrimination. Instead, racial antipathy and discrimination are built into the film's conflicts. The audience is shown, rather than told about, the apes hostility for the humans and sees that one ape "race," the orangutans, dominates the chimpanzees and gorillas.[22]

The first scene in the ape city establishes the apes' racial pecking order. Having been captured and shot in the throat, which temporarily renders him unable to speak, Taylor is being treated by a male chimpanzee surgeon and a female chimpanzee nurse. The attendants in the prison infirmary are gorillas. Taylor hears the male chimpanzee, Dr. Galen (Wright King), complaining to Dr. Zira (Kim Hunter) about his work conditions:

> DR. ZIRA: You don't sound happy in your work.
> DR. GALEN: I'm little more than a vet in this laboratory. You promised to talk to Dr. Zaius about me.
> DR. ZIRA: I did. You know how he looks down his nose at chimpanzees.
> DR. GALEN: But the quota system's been abolished! You made it, why can't I?
> DR. ZIRA: What do you mean made it? I'm an animal psychologist, that's all. We have no authority.

This first glimpse into the ape racial power structure is telling. The baboons of the early draft have been removed and replaced by gorillas, who are limited to military service and low-skilled manual labor. Their opportunities have been constrained in much the same ways as those of African-Americans. And like African-Americans, they have been maneuvered into low-status service jobs. The debate between Dr. Galen and Dr. Zira also makes it clear that class cleavages *within* races are a source of friction.

The scene also indicates that chimpanzees had once been denied opportunities for jobs, status, and power by deliberate quotas. Although the quotas have been officially eliminated, the chimpanzees, depicted as pacifists, intellectuals, scientists, and political radicals, still face discrimination in their quests for better positions and are denied true authority. In the split between the apes and the humans, they are part of the dominant group physically, yet they are marginalized and still discriminated against within it. This characterization constructs and positions *Planet's* chimpanzees in ways that make them analogous to Jewish people in the United States at the time. The reference to quotas in particular recalls the restrictive immigration, education, and employment quotas directed against Jews that limited their entry into the United States and their advancement here. Thus situated as analogues to Jews, on the periphery of the power system and not fully sharing all of its privileges, the chimpanzees are structurally positioned to challenge the power system's racial hierarchy and to serve as Taylor's advocate.[23] As a female, the only important ape female visible in the film, Zira has a dual qualification to serve in this capacity.

This racial caste system is a departure from the ape society conceived by Boulle. In the novel, Merou observes:

> In principle [the orangutans, chimpanzees, and gorillas] all have equal rights and are allowed to occupy any position. Yet, with certain exceptions, each species confines itself to its own specialty. . . . From far back in the past, when they used to reign by force, the gorillas have preserved a taste for authority and still form the most powerful class. . . . It is they who administer at a very high level most of the great enterprises. . . . The gorillas who do not occupy positions of authority are usually engaged on lesser jobs requiring physical strength.
>
> [The orangutans are] pompous, solemn, pedantic, devoid of originality and critical sense. . . . They form the substratum of every academy. Endowed with a good memory, they learn an enormous amount by heart and from books. . . . Almost every orangutan has behind him a gorilla or a council of gorillas who support him and maintain him in an honorable post, seeing to it that he is granted the titles and decorations that are dear to his heart—until the day he ceases to give satisfaction. Then he is dismissed without mercy and replaced by another ape from the same species.[24]

The power arrangements described above differ considerably from those that are depicted in the film and these changes are significant—they are differences that *make* a difference. Originally, Boulle attributed to the dark-skinned gorillas a dignified bearing with "the manner of aristocrats"[25] as well as some political skills (albeit coldly manipulative skills). They were not defined solely as belligerent and stupid. Some gorillas had chimpanzee servants, and the gorillas were not strictly confined to the lowest stratum of society. Furthermore, in Boulle's novel the ape races confined *themselves* to specialties. Likewise in Rod Serling's original 1964 screenplay, the occupations of the apes were not as strictly tied to their race. Serling's script, for example, had gorilla doctors and gorilla members of the scientific assembly. It is thus evident that as preproduction progressed the filmmakers made a deliberate choice to veer away from the direction of Boulle and Serling's original conceptions and to construct an ape society based on racial hierarchy in which the darkest apes were at the bottom. This choice probably brought a certain "social relevance" to a film that had been rejected for years and was in a genre—science fiction—that was still struggling to be taken seriously. The choice was probably also a response to the questions of racial inequality stressed by the black liberation movement, issues which demanded response in the field of cultural production.

Boulle's novel and Serling's screenplay were more concerned with the potential of humanity to destroy itself or to degenerate into an animal state and with the ability of humanity to regenerate itself in the event of such a fall. Both Boulle and Serling envisioned the main character's mission to be the reeducation of his fellow humans and their elevation back to their state of intelligence, speech, and dominance. (Boulle would further develop this concept in his proposed *Planet* film sequel, *Planet of the Men*.) Serling's December 23, 1964, draft even attributes to the main character, Thomas, a kind of telepathic ability to communicate with the less advanced humans. (Paul Dehn would endow the ape liberator Caesar in *Conquest of the Planet of the Apes* with similar capability.) Like *Tarzan of the Apes*, Boulle's and Serling's *Apes* texts ask what it is that separates human beings (in the case of *Tarzan*, explicitly white human beings) from animals and elevates humans above animals. Furthermore, Boulle and Serling asked how that difference may be asserted and maintained.

This remains a question in *Planet*, but it is both asked and answered differently. Human beings are not constructed here as superior to the apes, and the film presents social domination (of human over ape, of orangutan over chimpanzee and gorilla, or, by extension, of white over black, or of gentile over Jew) as primarily a function of political or violent subjugation rather than biological superiority. Furthermore, humanity's potential for biological regeneration was not at issue in *Planet*.

The most telling evidence for this latter point is the omission from the film of the plot point that spoke most to the question of human regeneration: Nova's pregnancy. Her pregnancy introduced the implication that Nova and Taylor could begin the human species again with a reinvigorated intelligence. (Taylor mentions this possibility in *Beneath*, more as a self-mocking daydream than an actual plan for a new human race.) In *Planet*, Nova seems to serve little purpose other than being a vessel for the planting of Taylor's ("civilized" humanity's) seed. All references to her condition were excised. Wilson had been told that the deletion had been "at the insistence of a high-echelon Fox executive who found it distasteful. Why? I suppose that, if one defines the mute Nova as merely 'humanoid' and not actually human, it would mean that Taylor had committed sodomy."[26]

If regeneration of the species had been a central concern of the film, the scenes dealing with Nova's pregnancy could not have been deleted. Out of the issues introduced in Boulle's novel, however, it is not the potential for regeneration, but rather humanity's potential for self-destruction which the filmmakers stressed. As the *Apes* series progressed, the issues of racial conflict and domination, both powerful examples of our impulses for self-destruction, were given heightened importance.

It is difficult to ascertain the filmmakers' exact reasons for creating an ape society more rigidly differentiated along racial lines than the one in Boulle's book. Crucial members of *Planet*'s creative team, Arthur Jacobs, Rod Serling, Michael Wilson, and Franklin Schaffner, have all passed away. Abrahams believes, however, that the changes arose out of discussions regarding whether the romantic couple Zira and Cornelius should be of the same or different ape races, which then lead to discussions about the role each race would play in the fictive society. From these discussions it was decided both that Cornelius and Zira should be of the same race and that the role of each ape in the ape society would be determined by race, unlike in the novel, in which all three groups "had equal rights and [were] allowed to occupy any position."[27]

That a decision in favor of racial differentiation and separation arose out of a discussion of possible ape miscegenation is in itself not surprising given the historic American preoccupation with "'race mixing'." The decision speaks to the degree to which a culture's traditional biases, in this case attitudes regarding interracial romance, are unknowingly reinforced. Although Abrahams and his colleagues were not necessarily opposed to "race-mixing," their decisions regarding Zira and Cornelius and racially determined societal position were consonant with long-standing social and political prejudices. For example, in the Dred Scott case, the U.S. Supreme Court reasserted the belief of the colonists that

> a perpetual and impassable [legal] barrier was intended to be erected between the white race and the one they had reduced to slavery . . . which they then looked upon as so far below them in the scale of created beings that intermarriages between white persons and negroes and mulattoes were regarded as unnatural and immoral, and punished as crimes.[28]

The assumption of the colonial legislators and of the Supreme Court—an assumption, as James Baldwin has pointed out, born out of white peoples' delusion that they are, in fact, white—was replicated by the makers of *Planet*.[29] This assumption, fiercely held and desperately clung to, is the belief that racial boundaries are after all—and above all—sexual boundaries that must not be crossed.

Although the novel presented an ape society in which "the racial barriers that used to exist have been abolished and the disputes arising from them have been settled," the film presented an ape society rife with racial inequality and discord. While the specific motivation for the alterations in the apes' racial organization from book to film may be hard to ascertain, the effects of the changes may be assessed. The primary effect was the most crucial thematic shift from the novel to the film: the changes brought racial injustice to ape society, making it a replica of U.S. society and allowing racial conflict eventually to become the series' central issue.

Roughly half of *Planet* is set in an ape city. There is a certain spatial dislocation that pervades the film, so we are not certain where the city is or what relation it has to the ape world. It could be the only city, or it could be the capital of a larger ape country. The presence of important ape administrators and institutions lets us know at least that it is an important city. Despite this lack of definition, we get a considerable glimpse of the apes' social organization.

Ape society is made up of three distinct racial groups: orangutans, chimpanzees, and gorillas, with skin color and body type apparently serving as the primary biological markers of racial difference. Importantly, the apes see each other as distinct races, and there exists a considerable amount of prejudice among them. Zira laments that Doctor Zaius (Maurice Evans), the orangutan minister of science, "looks down his nose at chimpanzees." Zira returns the antipathy: in *Escape*, she dismisses the orangutans as "a bunch of blinkered, pseudo-scientific geese" and the gorillas as "a bunch of militaristic nincompoops." In *Beneath* she also laments that the gorillas are "all bone and no brain." The apes also exhibit a certain racial pride. Zira, for instance, maintains that since they are intellectuals and pacifists, the milk of chimpanzees is "the milk of kindness."

One fascinating feature of the film's production is that the race consciousness of the apes even continued off camera. An article in *Starlog* magazine reports that actress Kim Hunter's "most powerful memories of her days on the set concern the segregation of the characters, wherein during filming breaks, the chimps sat with the chimps, gorillas with gorillas, and so on."[30]

And, of course, there is also considerable hostility directed against the inferior humans. In fact the apes' dislike of humans is expressed in terms modeled after well-known human racist ideologies: "man has no understanding, he can be taught a few simple tricks, nothing more," Zaius insists. Ape religion, developed and ministered by orangutans, maintains that "the Almighty created the ape in his own image. . . . He gave him a soul and a mind. . . . He set him apart from the beasts of the jungle and made him lord of the planet." An orangutan official points out that human beings are soulless, while the simian brain carries a "divine spark." Similarly, we are told that "all men look alike to most apes," and a gorilla labels humans "natural born thieves." The above comments, of course, recall condemnations of non-whites often made by white Westerners.

These racist phrases are embedded in what I am referring to as "cultural memory." They are recognizable formulations that have been an important part of U.S. history and culture. These phrases, along with others like "human see, human do" and "I never met an ape I didn't like," in addition to adding humor to the film, are points of correspondence with human culture that signal the audience that it is in fact human culture that is being spoofed and critiqued. As Schaffner noted: "It must occur to you as you are watching an ape society, you are looking into a mirror. That's the purpose of that picture. That the human mores are no different than that of the ape society and they were fairly ridiculous, and a lot of our mores, habits, customs, attitudes, etc., are pretty ridiculous."[31]

Taylor returns the apes' animosity in kind, with lines like "Get your stinking paws off me, you damn dirty ape!" and assertions of human superiority such as "[Man] was here before you, and he was better than you are!"

The film also presents visual correspondences to the racial conflicts of the times. In one scene, Taylor is subdued by his gorilla captors with a water hose. The sight of a water hose used as a tool to enforce racial supremacy and quell resistance was a familiar one in the sixties, when civil rights demonstrators were repeatedly attacked with the same weapon.

The mirror aspect that director Schaffner discussed was observed by others involved in the film, as well as by the critics and the general public. Numerous critics noted the film's commentary on U.S. racial relations. Frederick S. Clarke, for instance, recognized that the chimpanzees were a "disenfranchised minority."[32] And Kim Hunter recalled the reaction of a six-year-old boy to *Planet*:

> It's quite extraordinary when a film can reach a six-year-old child saying: "You know I think I understand now why people are afraid of other people. It's because they're different and they're strange." This child got the reverse thing, that apes were afraid of humans because they were odd, they were different. Whereas this is half our problem in the world today.... We're antagonistic and we're aggressive, and we're all of these terrible things that human beings can be because we don't understand [those who] are different.[33]

Similarly, *Life* magazine critic Richard Schickel said the film taught his young daughter that when people are "scared of the unfamiliar" they can be "foolish and prejudiced."[34]

Planet thus identifies fear of the "other's" difference as a central cause of racism and racial violence. *Conquest* and *Battle* later provided the further insight, present just below the surface in *Planet*, that racism stems not only from a fear of the "other's" difference, but also from the fear that the "other" may in fact—and in very significant ways—be the same.

We have already noted another crucial point of correspondence between the apes and humans: while the official rhetoric holds that "all apes are created equal," the reality, as Taylor points out, is that "some apes . . . are more equal than others." What we are shown of the ape social structure and work force is rigid racial hierarchy. The apes, whose character and temperament are depicted as a function of their race, fulfill roles determined and circumscribed by race. The orangutans are at the top of society as the religious, bureaucratic, and political power elite. Chimpanzees are in the middle as pacifistic intellectuals who serve as academicians, scientists, and doctors. There is even Lucius, a young anti-establishment chimpanzee radical, complaining about "money-mad," authoritarian "grown-up[s]"; he serves as a link to the young liberals of the sixties and suggests a simian "generation gap." At the bottom of the social ladder are the gorillas, serving as the army, police force, and menial labor.

Taylor's interrogation by the ad hoc tribunal of the apes' National Academy of Science brought Taylor into conflict with the ape power elite and was a useful plot device for revealing the power structure's dynamics. In the tribunal scene, what we see of the apes' political apparatus is controlled by male orangutans. The state prosecutor, the president of the academy, the commissioner for animal affairs, and the minister of science are all orangutan males. Thus there is also a gender hierarchy at work here, although the series does not significantly confront the issue of gender inequality.

It is somewhat surprising perhaps, given the frequent connection between race and gender, that gender is not more of an explicit concern of the series. Neither, however, is it irrelevant. In *Planet* there are three women: Zira, a desexualized, highly intelligent ape whose stolen kisses with her fiancé Cornelius are more humorous than passionate; Nova, a hyper-sexualized mute human, played by former Miss Maryland, Linda Harrison, who spends the entire film clad in an animal-skin bikini; and Stewart, a woman astronaut with a male name in traditionally male space who is dead before the events of the narrative begin.

After Taylor delivers his opening soliloquy on the faults of "man," the film shows Stewart asleep, encased like the other astronauts in her suspended animation chamber. During the flight, her life-support device malfunctions and when the ship crash-lands, the other astronauts find her dead, withered body in the chamber. From the opening scene of the film, Stewart is thus physically enclosed and sealed off from the film's action and is dead before it really starts. The segregation and elimination of her presence seems a strategy to communicate that gender is not an issue on the planet of the apes. In the context of this study, however, the film's curious treatment of Stewart has precisely the opposite effect: it raises the issue of gender.[35]

The fact that *Planet*'s producers put a woman into space fifteen years before the U.S. space program did, only to kill her off within the first fifteen minutes of the film, suggests that the presence of women in outer space, or at least in the fictional space of *Planet*, posed a problem for the producers. Of the three woman characters in *Planet*, Stewart has violated male space in both name and body and, having spoken not a word, dies almost immediately, thus neutralizing her as a source of competition for power

with the male astronauts. Zira, who is perhaps stronger and more committed to "scientific truth" and interspecies understanding than anyone in
the film, stands alone as the only female character in the film who can talk
and who does compete with males. She competes with male apes as a
career "woman," in her work position over the male chimpanzee surgeon
and over the male gorilla attendant Julius, in her successful goading of the
otherwise timid Cornelius (Roddy McDowall) to be stronger and more
assertive, and in her bold challenging of the all-male orangutan political
elite.[36] There seems to be some kind of "logic" at work that states that
because she is intelligent, articulate, and assertive, she must therefore also
be "ugly" by traditional standards.[37] By contrast, Nova is beautiful, but
literally and figuratively dumb. In *Planet* a woman may be physically attrac-
tive (Nova) or smart (Zira), but she cannot be both (Stewart). Therefore
Stewart is eliminated before the story begins, and the images of women are
split between what are presumed to be the mutually exclusive poles of
beauty and brains.

With the exception of Zira, a character of great courage and conviction, the women in *Planet* and the supportive, nurturing, and by-and-large
deferential women characters in the other *Apes* films seem to represent
certain fantasy types and images of limited female possibility. In fact, the
series seems so intent on preserving these types that immediately after
Nova finally speaks in *Beneath* (and her only word is "Taylor"), she is shot
and killed by a gorilla. Message? Beautiful women should just be beautiful —
and keep their mouths shut.

The tribunal, ostensibly called to allow Zira and Cornelius to present
their case on Taylor's behalf, is shown quickly as an attempt to frame Zira
and Cornelius, who are denounced as "perverted scientists who advance
an insidious theory called evolution." The orangutans prevent Taylor from
explaining himself and concoct a story charging Zira with "tampering with
his brain and throat tissues to produce a speaking monster." When Zira and
Cornelius try to assert their theories, suggesting that apes evolved from
humans and that Taylor is "a missing link in an evolutionary chain," they
are silenced and indicted for contempt, malicious mischief, and scientific
heresy.

The sequence touches upon many contemporary issues: tensions
between religion and science, embodied both in the conflict in the scene
and in Zaius' dual appointment as chief defender of the faith and minister
of science; suppression of free thought and speech; government conspiracy
to withhold the truth from the masses; and reactionary suppression of dissent. For co-writer Michael Wilson, a victim of black-listing during the
McCarthy-era "Red Scare," these themes may have had particular relevance.[38] The tribunal scene is also crucial because it is here that Zira and
Cornelius' appeals for racial understanding fall upon deaf ears.

Because of the references to the debate over evolution, the tribunal scene has most often been compared to the infamous "Scopes monkey trial." However, the ape state's insistence that because Taylor is a man "he has no rights under ape law" replicates the rationale of the United States Supreme Court in its infamous *Dred Scott* decision. In the Dred Scott case, the Supreme Court held that because his ancestors were slaves and were not meant to be part of the nation when the constitution was framed — and when they were effectively framed by it — Dred Scott was not protected by the constitution and had no rights that the nation was obliged to recognize. Wretchedness, after all, is often, perhaps always, mistaken as a justification, or a demand, for its continuance.

The audience is meant to view all of this from the perspective of Colonel George Taylor. Taylor was typical of the heroes in Franklin J. Schaffner's films. Schaffner explained that "I've been doing stories about people out of their time and place. A thread of loneliness seems to have coursed through the films I've done — the loneliness of a man on the level of command and simply on a personal level."[39] Erwin Kim, in his 1985 Schaffner biography, points out that the prototype for Schaffner's displaced hero was Chrysagon in *The War Lord* (1965), another character played, fittingly, by Charlton Heston, the same actor who played Taylor. Kim writes that in *The War Lord* "the core ingredients of a Schaffner film and hero are made manifest: Chrysagon is a gifted but obsessive man who is trapped in the wrong time; his obsession reveals flaws that have been otherwise concealed by his talent and skills. . . . Schaffner's heroes can escape neither their flaws nor their times."[40] Taylor has many of the same qualities. "You thought life on Earth was meaningless," Landon accuses. "You despised people. So what did you do? You ran out." But as Taylor has become the symbol of humanity, he cannot so easily escape its flaws and its time.

Taylor, a misanthropic high-ranking officer who despises war and the value system of a world in which there is "lots of love-making but no love," had left the Earth convinced that "somewhere in the universe there has to be something better than man." His position as expedition commander suggests that he is a relatively elite member of his society, yet he feels himself alienated from it. His alienation made him a figure with whom many U.S. audience members could particularly identify and align themselves. Much like Taylor, many viewers would have felt themselves alienated from and disgusted with U.S. society. Even those who reacted negatively to Taylor's unpleasant character might have sympathized with his outsider stance.

The critical choice of casting Charlton Heston in this part was extraordinarily astute and was an effective means of conveying some of *Planet*'s most important themes. Abrahams remembers that Heston had the qualities of "good physicality" and "intelligence" that the part required.[41] Indeed these are among the first features that one might think of if one were

looking for an representative for, or the last member of, a species or a race.
The casting produced a visual element that reinforced certain of the film's
narrative and thematic elements: because of Heston's height, Taylor towers
above everyone else in the film. Even half-naked, wounded, mute, and
caged as an animal, Taylor's stature, perhaps inside as well as outside we
may ponder, overpowers that of his captors. His cage is on a platform that
makes him even taller and results in the visual irony that while Dr. Zaius
expounds on the inferiority of "man," he is forced to look up at the object
of his derision.

In the past, Heston had chosen parts that were in his assessment
"alienated, iconoclastic, even misanthropic,"[42] and like so many of our
heroes, the characters were men in the middle, men who were on the edge
of one or more societies, or segments of society, yet did not truly fit into
any of them. Kim discusses the ending of Schaffner's *The War Lord* and
notes the relation of Chrysagon to Heston's other roles:

> In the end, the War Lord is as he was in the beginning—alone. He no
> longer has family ties; he has relinquished love and freedom.... The sight
> of the weary War Lord favoring his wound as he rides off into the horizon
> ... [is where] Heston's contribution is most keenly felt. Still looking
> physically invincible, he plays a middle-aged man who has been a loner
> in life, and who, despite his rigorous attention to his duty, feels he has
> missed something meaningful in his life and is desperately trying to find
> it. This personal theme has influenced Heston's choice of material: it was
> explored in other films the actor made ... most notably *Will Penny*
> (1968), in which he played an aging cowboy, and *Number One* (1969), in
> which he played an aging quarterback.[43]

Playing Taylor allowed Heston to expand this persona, and the character
seems to have had a particular fascination for him. "Of all the roles I've
played," Heston told Kim, "this is the closest to my own personality."[44] In
Planet, Heston is again out of place, trapped between worlds. Taylor is
physically separated and psychically alienated from his own time and society. Lost in the future, he is simultaneously "superior" to the humans that
inhabit the planet, yet nonetheless looked down upon as at worst a "monster" and at best "a mutant" by the ape population. And again, the Heston
hero is lonely and looks in vain for some meaning for his life.

Kim notes that "Taylor is another obsessive Schaffner character, literally out of his depth and time"[45] and offers some useful insights into the
effectiveness of using Heston as Taylor:

> Heston ... is effective both for those who like him and those who do not.
> Physically he looks exactly right as astronaut or captive. Hardly a sym-
> pathetic character, Taylor, in his capacity as an astronaut, literally starts
> at the top of the world, quite happy to be leaving earth. Taylor is arrogant,
> overbearing, just begging for a fall; it comes immediately.... With such

> a drastic reversal, the audience becomes sympathetic if not to Heston
> then to Taylor's plight: if it can happen to Charlton Heston, it can happen
> to anyone.[46]

This last assertion is particularly striking in that it suggests that Heston brought something more than his considerable physical presence or a tradition of playing lonely characters. "If it can happen to Charlton Heston, it can happen to anyone." Why so? What was the connection between Heston and the moviegoing public that would lead Kim to conclude that, more than with any other actor, "a drastic reversal" of Charlton Heston's fortunes could provoke a sense of vulnerability in the audience? And precisely who is the "anyone" for whom Heston acts as surrogate?

The answer to these questions lies in the fact that the Heston hero was characterized by more than an internal crisis: functioning as symbol, the Heston hero's personal identity crisis was doubled and enlarged as a political identity crisis of the "West." Heston had developed his star persona, in part, by playing the central figure in a number of "epic" films concerning the struggle between Western interests and non–Western natives. Through these films, Heston became a film icon of white heroic strength and Western indominability.

In *Gunfighter Nation: The Myth of the Frontier in Twentieth Century America*, cultural historian Richard Slotkin discusses the typical Heston epic of the era, in which Heston portrayed "a 'hard' and self-willed White male hero . . . who stands for the highest values of civilization and progress but who is typically besieged from without by enemies (often non–Whites and/or savages) who greatly outnumber him and beset from within by the decadence, corruption, and 'softness' of his own society."[47]

In the sixties Heston seemed to be perpetually fighting a "last stand" battle to defend a fort or outpost of Western "civilization" against the onslaught of hordes of non–Western, dark-skinned "barbarians."[48] This persona goes back at least to *The Naked Jungle* (1954), in which Heston is a plantation owner who is convinced he is bringing "civilization" to South American natives and fights off a massive horde of killer ants. In *El Cid* (1961), Heston is the white man against hordes of North African Muslims; in *55 Days at Peking* (1963), Heston becomes a white man against hordes of Chinese; in *Khartoum* (1964), the white man has to defeat hordes of Arabs;[49] and in *Planet* (1968), the white actor as Taylor defends civilization against the apes and fights off the darkest of the apes, the gorillas.[50]

Thus, I refer to Jacobs' casting of Heston as Taylor as astute because by the time *Planet* was filmed in 1967, Heston's repeated appearance as the central hero in films where racialized struggles between white and non-white peoples were coded as struggles between "civilization" and "savagery" had deeply encoded Heston's screen persona with the very issues of Western dominance and racial conflict at the heart of the film.[51]

Slotkin discusses Heston's epic films and other "epic treatments of 'western' history, recreations of best-selling novels, lavish musicals, 'Bible' and 'Roman' epics and grandiose treatments of the Victorian Empire after the manner of *The Charge of the Light Brigade*" in the context of the "New Frontier" policies of the John Kennedy and Lyndon Johnson presidential administrations:

> The grandiose scale of these epics and the worldwide scope of their production techniques and historical references corresponded to the administration's vision of an incomparably wealthy and powerful America confronting global issues in "a time of greatness." Moreover the recurrent themes of the epics promulgated the worldview that closely corresponded to Kennedy's sense of America's place in the world as a nation noble and strong but sorely beleaguered in a "darkened" and hostile political environment.[52]

As Slotkin points out, in the early sixties the United States felt threatened by "the sense that communism was expanding throughout the third world at the expense of the United States and Europe. [These films] represent a fictive working out of the premises of the policy of counter insurgency, through which the Kennedy administration hoped to defeat wars of national liberation and create a new frontier of American power."[53] Heston's race war epics and their repeated thematic refrains gained currency in the midst of a crisis of confidence in Western dominance in the face of Communist and anticolonial movements and victories across the globe that threatened Western world supremacy.

These films were efforts at a reassurance of Western supremacy and stability. The films attempted a mythic reconstruction of the image of the invincible West by depicting the ultimate success of Western interests in struggles that represented the opposition of polarized and *racialized* abstractions: civilization versus savagery, trustworthiness versus treacherousness, reason versus fanaticism, and whiteness versus darkness.

Planet shares important aspects of Heston's other race-war epics and his role in them. As Taylor, Heston is again at odds with a corrupt and decadent society—he laments human beings' propensity for war and their willingness to keep their "neighbor's children starving," and he bemoans a world in which there is "lots of love-making, but no love."

The purpose of Taylor's mission is not stated, but it is conceivable that it is part of a program of colonial expansion, indeed he does express imperialist ambitions to rule the planet. Taylor is captured as a brute animal, having lost his power of speech, his tools, and his clothes—all the physical vestiges of his civilization—yet he ironically finds himself the lone embodiment and representative of the civilization he had despised and abandoned in search of "something better." Apparently, the values and character of "true" civilization are so deeply ingrained in the Heston hero's core that even when he is stripped of the trappings of civilization, he remains civilization's embodiment and symbol.

Since apes, gorillas especially, are considered non–Western animals, *Planet* again has Heston defending that civilization, both philosophically and physically, from the onslaught of yet another dark-skinned non–Western horde. Thus Taylor was in many ways an extension of personas that audiences had already seen Heston develop. And in a celebrity culture that encourages the conjunction of current and past personas, Heston brought to Taylor an important ideological charge. So much so that, for some, throwing Heston as Taylor into jeopardy meant throwing the United States, indeed all of white Western humanity, into jeopardy, a move that could provoke a profound sense of insecurity and the fear that "If it can happen to Charlton Heston, it can happen to anyone."

Kim's assertion might suggest that some saw Heston as more than just a Western hero. Indeed, one commentator made precisely this claim when he wrote that "Charlton Heston, in both his personality and his role, is the embodiment of self assured 20th century man, and a perfect choice to be thrust into a reversed world."[54] Thus the Western hero is here universalized into the symbol of humanity in the twentieth century.

It is crucial to note that although some might have seen the particular dilemma of the Heston hero as universal, Heston was not a suitable identification figure for all Americans. Cultural critic Blanca Vasquez recalls pointedly that she did not feel sympathy for Heston because he represented the America of John Wayne and Richard Nixon.[55]

Vasquez's negative reaction to Heston as a symbol of conservatism and the fact that he could evoke those associations are, however, themselves evidence of the effectiveness of casting Heston as Taylor. Regardless of whether Heston's past roles or political affiliations made audiences more or less inclined to *like* Taylor, the cultural and political conservatism represented by Wayne and Nixon were precisely what *Planet* is rebuking.

The fact that *Planet* fits well within the framework of other Heston racial epics does not mean that it shared the same ideological project. The makers of *Planet* were not interested in providing a therapeutic balm for the psychic wounds of a beleaguered empire. That *Planet* contained so many aspects of Heston's myth enabled the film to perform one of its critical tasks: to call that myth into question.

Schaffner had in fact begun puncturing Heston's myth three years earlier in *The War Lord*. In this 1965 film, Heston plays Chrysagon, a Christian Norman knight sent on an assignment nobody else wanted: to impose the Duke of Normandy's will on his vassals and protect an outlying druid village from Frisian raiders. Chrysagon is attracted to a peasant woman from the village who will soon be married. Chrysagon is persuaded to invoke the archaic "droit du seigneur," a rarely observed druid fertility ritual in which the lord of the community may have sex with a woman on her wedding night. When the night is over, Chrysagon refuses to end the affair. This antagonizes the villagers, and the enraged groom forms an alliance with the Frisians and attacks Chrysagon's castle. Eventually, Chrysagon's brother Draco brings reinforcements and saves the day, but Chrysagon kills him when he attempts to wrest control and restore order in the duke's name.

Rather than focusing on racial dilemmas, *The War Lord* stresses religious conflict. Here Heston is the representative of Christianity fighting off hordes of savage pagans—at one point Heston fights them off with a giant cross. (The pagan wedding ceremony even resembles the debauchery of the wayward Hebrews in the desert from Heston's *The Ten Command-ments*.) Although there is a shift in emphasis from race to religion, in this film Heston's mission is once again protecting "civilization."

In contrast to the situation in most of his epics, in *The War Lord* Heston completely fails to fulfill that mission. In a story that anticipates criticism of the involvement of the United States in Vietnam, Chrysagon, though ordered by the duke to "keep their good will" (read: win their hearts and minds?), antagonizes the natives, stumbles into a war that he cannot win, and puts himself in a situation from which he cannot get out: the land is no longer his and he cannot continue to kill all the representatives the duke sends nor kill the duke himself.[56] In a significant departure, instead of the invincible Western hero, Heston here is a petty failure whose own arrogance and greed eclipse his virtues and bring everything he touches to ruin. Having begun the process with *The War Lord*, Schaffner would continue to deflate the Heston myth in *Planet*.

Planet was in fact a countermyth to many of Heston's other films and to the other "new frontier" epics. Heston's performances as the representative of a variety of Western nations was important to the ideological project of the films. That project was to express a sense of Western, not just United States, beleaguerment. These epics were wishful fantasies that depicted the West's successful management and containment of revolution, to use the political terminology of the time. They typically ended with the stabilization, or promise of stabilization, of the threatened empire. *Planet* does precisely the reverse.

Casting Heston, who had played the symbolic representative of a number of Western powers—the United States in *55 Days at Peking*, Britain in *Khartoum*, Spain in *El Cid*—rather than using an actor identified exclusively or primarily with U.S. heroism (John Wayne for example) enlarged the scope of the critique from the United States in particular to the West in general. *Planet* shows not only the failure of the favored Western hero to symbolically manage the crises of the time but also the failure of Western civilization to survive.

Heston's success as one of Hollywood's biggest stars and his roles in some of Hollywood's most prestigious epics made audiences well acquainted with this Heston hero. Much like current stars such as Arnold Schwarzenegger, Heston brought with him a number of expectations regarding what kinds of struggles he would be in and how they were likely to end. Audiences would be prone to expect that Heston would successfully defeat the non-white threat to white dominance or that if he failed, his failure would eventually have a redeeming symbolic value.

As Slotkin notes, in the heroic style of the Heston films, the hero "always achieves his final victory . . . by suffering a last stand and risking or actually undergoing a personal martyrdom."[57] This was not the case in *Planet*, however. *Planet* invoked those expectations and then subverted them. *Planet* uses the last-stand device in order to expose its bankruptcy by denying the Western hero both victory and the mythological gesture of martyrdom.

In U.S. fictional and mythological tradition the American hero is often separated from society and sees himself (and it usually is *him*self) as above it. Nonetheless, his efforts and suffering usually bring some benefit to society. But this is not the case with Taylor, for there is no society left for him to help. Near the film's end, Heston fights off gorilla soldiers who are attacking the cave in which he is holed up. The cave is an archeological dig in which Cornelius has found ruins of an ancient human civilization.

Thus *Planet* gives us a last stand in which the protected space of white power is utterly devoid of force or meaning other than that of an archeological curiosity. In what seems a pointed political critique of American mythology and foreign policy, the Western hero is no longer protecting an outpost of imperial power but only remnants of the past. His compatriots are now fossils. There is no one left to remember the Alamo, and Little Big Horn is no longer the site of Custer's redemptive last stand — it has become a mere graveyard, a monument to the rule that whatever rises will fall. The image of "civilization's" last stand against "savagery," at Little Big Horn, at the Alamo, in the Philippines, or, more to the point, in Vietnam, has here been emptied of its traditional mythic power.

Heston's previous race-war films, and other films that malign non-white and non–Christian peoples, participate in the construction of the necessary ideological support of racism and imperialism by constructing whiteness and Christianity as civility, order, rationality, and imperial privilege, while defining the non-white and the non–Christian as hostile, chaotic, untrustworthy, irrational, and deserving of domination. Without this ideological underpinning, undertakings like the Vietnam War would have been far more difficult to initiate and sustain.

Yet *Planet* reverses these poles of racial character and imputes to white humans, through the use of one of Hollywood's favorite symbols of *specifically* white humanity, the very animalistic qualities usually ascribed to non-whites. *Planet* thus destabilizes white racial identity. And in a move that echoed the post–Tet offensive feelings of the time of its release, in *Planet* the white Western hero has finally fallen.

Coming at the close of the sixties, in the middle of an increasingly hopeless war, *Planet of the Apes* coincided with the end of the era of Kennedy and Johnson, whose campaign slogan had promised "leadership for the sixties," and it challenged the hoped-for resolution of the politics and the motion pictures of the New Frontier. Its apocalyptic vision depicted, perhaps even predicted, the unthinkable: the victory of nonhuman over human, East over West, non-white over white.

Of course, this depiction of the Western hero's failure was in fact a manifestation and exploitation of the possibility and fear that were latent in the New Frontier politics and films all along: if there had been no threat to the white hero's supremacy, the New Frontier epics, and indeed the New Frontier itself, would not have been necessary.[58]

Thus Jacobs, Abrahams, Shaffner, Wilson, and company used Heston's image to critique its own mythic charge. Critic Pauline Kael observed:

> The picture is an enormous many-layered black joke on the hero and the audience, and part of the joke is the use of Charlton Heston as the hero.... Physically, Heston, with his perfect, lean hipped, powerful body, is a god-like hero; built for strength, he's an archetype of what makes Americans win. He doesn't play a nice guy; he's harsh and hostile, self-centered and hot-tempered. Yet we don't hate him, because he's so magnetically strong; he represents American power — the physical attraction and admiration one feels toward the beauty of strength as well as the moral revulsion one feels toward the ugliness of violence.... Franklin Schaffner uses the Heston of ... "The Naked Jungle" — the man who is so absurdly a movie-star myth. He is the perfect American Adam to work off some American guilt feelings or self hatred on, and this is part of what makes this new violent fantasy so successful as comedy.[59]

Those guilt feelings and self-hatreds are worked out on the figure of Heston's body as an icon of American civilization. The abuses visited upon his body by the apes include shooting, beating, burning, stoning, gagging, and the threat of castration — abuses which have historically been visited upon non-whites by whites. The threat of castration by apes, who were traditionally associated with darkness, sexuality and, by extension, femaleness, suggests that there was also a crisis of masculinity built into *Planet* and Heston's other sixties epics — a crisis that had to be continually combatted in film after film through the defeat of anything dark, bodily or feminized by the white, intellectual, and masculine.[60] A combat which Heston finally loses in *Planet*. (Indeed, the final shot of the film shows him fallen in front of a giant woman who is both darker and stronger than he.)

Zaius' threat of lobotomization, which would destroy Taylor's "identity," echoed the identity crisis of the West. The loss of Heston's identity, the image of him helpless, trapped in a world run by a "lower" order of life, spoke to the anxiety caused by Third World self-assertion and the West's fear of losing its identity as the dominant force in world affairs.

Heston, who as an image of strength came to represent the inevitability of victory of white over non-white, is abused mercilessly by this non-white horde. At one point as Taylor attempts to escape from the ape city, he comes across a group of gorillas, chimpanzees, and orangutans who start to stone him. The scene alternates between Taylor's point of view and the apes' point of view. Thus the audience becomes both the punished and the punisher. This spectacle of abuse is a dual signifier giving expression to an anxiety-reducing release of guilt feelings over American racial oppression and an anxiety-provoking depiction of revenge for those abuses. (This same dual meaning is part of the violence of *Conquest* as well. There the violence is even more intense, however.)

Planet's success can be attributed in part to the fact that without "platforming" its political content, it tapped into some of the major cultural confusions of its time. During a time when the United States was plagued by a crisis of identity and of confidence, *Planet* took the image of Charlton Heston as the man who defends Western culture from the encroachment of savages and removed him from any recognizable context. He is temporally and spatially dislocated, cut off from his society. The civilization he strives to defend has been dead for centuries. Its only remaining outpost is this time not a fort or a stronghold of power, but a cave full of decomposing artifacts — eyeglasses, false teeth, prefabricated heart valves — which, as Taylor points out, all speak to humanity's weakness and fragility.

As Taylor, Charlton Heston, an icon of Western civilization, does not know where he is in space or time. Nor does he know where or in what condition the civilization is that he is supposed to represent, although he assumes that it has disappeared. Early in the film he declares to astronaut Landon with a certain amount of satisfaction that "time's wiped out everything you ever knew — it's all dust."

Taylor is adrift spatially in that, until *Planet's* surprise ending, he and the audience along with him assume he is lost in space hundreds of light years from Earth. Having conveyed his spiritual dislocation in the opening monologue and depicted his temporal dislocation by the references to the time passage which establish that his ship crashed in 3978, the film proceeds to show Taylor's spatial dislocation. The astronauts wander aimlessly in the barren desert. They are frequently filmed from far away, dwarfed by the landscape, and they witness freak electrical storms and meteorological anomalies which they cannot fathom.[61] As the review in *Daily Variety* pointed out, the shots of the astronauts lost amid the "desolation and grandeur of an indifferent mother nature matches perfectly with the desired story setting of the results of an insolent human nature."[62] It is as if mother nature has punished human nature—quite a statement of fear, and of guilt. As the astronauts set out to explore the planet, Dodge asks Taylor in which direction they should go. Taylor arbitrarily gestures and says, "that way." "Any particular reason?" Dodge asks. "None at all," answers Taylor. Not only does he not know where he is, Taylor, like much of the United States at the time, does not know where he is going.

The problem of the war against Vietnam and the larger "problem" of the failure of Western colonial adventures are heavily present in these opening scenes. The sense that the United States had blundered into an confusing and unwinnable war is recalled by the U.S. astronauts crash-landing and their directionless wandering. As they are about to set out exploring their new find, Landon plants a tiny U.S. flag in the soil. Seeing this, Taylor starts laughing uncontrollably and walks away as his laughter echoes off the mountains of barren rock. The laughter seems totally out of proportion to the actual humor of the image and seems more a response to Landon's insistence on claiming the planet in the name of a dead empire. The film here literally makes a joke out of Western empire-building. And the film's vision of racial and nuclear apocalypse argues that such efforts will end in ruin. This mocking of U.S. imperial ambitions expresses the sense of the instability of the dominance of Western empires engendered by anti-colonial movements throughout the world from Algeria to Vietnam.

In the same vein, Taylor's disastrous initial encounter with the apes is a rebuke to Western colonialism. Having come across the tribe of mute humans, Heston, that icon of Western imperial privilege, looks them over and declares arrogantly that "if this is the best they've got around here, in six months we'll be running this planet." Seconds after this announcement of imperial ambition, he is hunted down by an army of gorillas.[63]

As noted earlier, in the course of the 112-minute film, Heston, so often depicted as invulnerable, is stripped, hunted, shot, made mute, beaten, burned, tied up, and gagged, and barely escapes emasculation and lobotomization. Although other movie heroes have endured similar perils, usually they are rewarded at the end of the film. Here the hero's reward is the bombed-out remains of his own self-destroyed civilization, obviously not a satisfying reward for a hero's sufferings. A culturally stable icon was utilized to convey a sense of profound cultural destabilization.

As Taylor, Heston is trapped between the opposing symbolic poles of human and ape and despises both. Taylor is representing and defending a civilization and a species in which he has no belief and for which he holds no love. His only assurance of humanity's worth is that humans are better than animals, hardly a reassuring assurance, especially when, in fact, the film argues that humans are by definition no better than the animals from which they descend and which may succeed them. Reviewer Joseph Morgernstern recognized this and commented that "the film catches us at a particularly wretched moment in the course of human events when we are perfectly willing to believe that man is despicable and a good deal lower than the lower animals."[64]

The very use of Heston as the symbol of humanity speaks to certain cultural assumptions of racial and gender realities. The woman in the crew is found dead within the first few minutes of the film. Soon after, the African-American man in the crew is killed, stuffed, and displayed as an oddity, an inanimate object. Thus any possible gender or racial competition for the status of representative of humanity (and the concomitant status of fully human) is eliminated and a white man goes on to represent all of "civilized" humanity. For the filmmakers and presumably for much — if not all — of the audience, the use of a white-skinned man as the representative of all humanity was acceptable. White stood as the unquestioned standard for and embodiment of human.[65] We must ask if U.S. audiences then — or now — would have accepted, for instance, an African or an Asian man or woman as the symbol of humanity?

Taylor has dual meaning as both symbol of and critic of civilization. In the opening scene, Taylor rhetorically asks, "does man, that marvel of the universe, that glorious paradox that sent me to the stars, still make war against his brother, keep his neighbor's children starving?" As symbol, Taylor himself embodies this particular problem: he waxes superior about humanity's lack of compassion, but he is merciless in ridiculing his fellow astronaut Landon. And as both symbol and critic, Taylor embodies the problem of "civilization" alienated from itself. His concern is one of the film's main concerns — the tension between humanity's capacity for "civilization" and its capacity for "animal" brutality. This tension, which for the sake of discussion I shall call "the human paradox," is central to the film's most important issues: humanity's destructive potential and that potential's racialized manifestation in the conflict between the impulses for racial peace and racial war.

While the ape society is threatening to Taylor, it is not monolithically evil. In fact, some aspects of race relations in the ape society surpass those of the United States. For example, while there is considerable prejudice and evidence of discrimination among the ape races, there is no evidence of violent domination akin to slavery among the apes.

Furthermore, the cardinal rule of ape society in *Planet* seems to be the imperative laid down by an ancient orangutan religious figure known as the "Lawgiver" that "Ape shall not kill ape." And all the members of ape society follow that rule to the letter. (The breaking of that rule in *Battle* occasions a considerable crisis.) There is no evidence that the apes engage in race wars against each other. In contrast, however, there are no people of color

among the human tribes in *Planet*, which raises the question of whether the
other races had been wiped out by white humans before the apes came to
power. The African-American astronaut, Dodge, is such an oddity to the
apes that he is stuffed and prominently displayed in a museum.

As Zaius says in Serling's script, "We apes have no death wish," and
this fact of ape society introduces one of *Planet*'s ironies: while humans
have the appearance of civilization and the customs of brutality, the apes
have the appearance of "brutes" yet are in some fundamental ways more
"civilized."[66] The use of a number of British or British-sounding actors
(Roddy McDowall, Kim Hunter, Maurice Evans) to play the apes may have
emphasized this point because British accents often code "civilization"
in U.S. popular culture. The filmmakers rehabilitate apes in order to critique humans. If the "savage" ape can in fact become like the "civilized"
human, human beings are not inherently superior to apes and may in fact
be just the same. As Winthrop Jordan said, "to liken human beings to beasts
is to stress the animal within the man."[67]

Even the menacing Zaius is a somewhat sympathetic antagonist. He
hates humans because he fears them. And he fears them because they are
destructive. Given what he seems to know about human history, his fears
are not just the exaggerated fantasies of a bigot. Zaius' critiques and fears
of humanity echo Taylor's criticisms, which probably resembled those
made by much of the audience.

To make his point regarding the danger of humanity, Zaius has Cornelius read from the apes' Sacred Scrolls, the religious scripture written by
the Lawgiver:

> Beware the beast man, for he is the devil's pawn. Alone among God's
> primates he kills for sport or lust or greed. Yea, he will murder his brother
> to possess his brother's land. Let him not breed in great numbers for he
> will make a desert of his home and yours. Shun him. Drive him back into
> his jungle lair — for he is the harbinger of death.

While Taylor does not like what he hears, he cannot argue with it. Even
the reference to murdering brothers recalls Taylor's earlier critique of people making "war against [their] brother[s]," and the reaction shot of Taylor
when Cornelius mentions "brother" tells us that the irony is not lost on him.
Furthermore, Zaius condemns humanity for exactly the same reasons that
Taylor did, because of its competing instincts towards civilization and
brutality. When Taylor asks why Zaius fears and hates him, the response
again is a familiar indictment of the human paradox: "Because you're a man.
And you're right — I have always known about man. From the evidence, I
believe his wisdom must walk hand in hand with his idiocy. His emotions
must rule his brain. He must be a warlike creature who gives battle to everything around him — even himself." For viewers in the midst of the Vietnam

War, political assassinations, and race riots, who were primed to believe that humans were "despicable and a good deal lower than the lower animals," this critique may have hit very close to home.

However, though Taylor, and presumably much of the audience, recognize some truth in Zaius' critique of humanity, he is still a racist (or speciesist) and the film does not endorse his genocidal intentions. While acknowledging the frailties and fears out of which racism arises, the film calls into question racism camouflaged as self-protection or even as "law and order."

In fact, the film questions whether Zaius is more concerned about the threat human beings pose to ape survival or the threat they pose to the position of ape superiority. Zaius knows that apes grow up with the belief that they were created in God's image. The inferiority of the human is a necessary precondition of the superiority of the ape. Zaius rabidly argues the superiority of apes, yet he is panicked by the appearance of Taylor precisely because the presence of a human being of equal intelligence, and the possibility that there may be more, threatens his most cherished notions of order and his own social position. Humanity therefore poses a psychological and physical "threat" of which Taylor is made a symbol.

Zaius knows that apes evolved from humans, and his fear is very likely the fear of the human that remains within the ape. Conversely, the oppression of apes by humans in *Conquest* is shown to stem from the fear of the ape that remains within humans. In ape society, as in human society, the hated racial other is constructed as a symbol of society's fear and, perhaps most importantly, the source of its vulnerability, and a system of racial oppression is built out of that fear. Similar fears have fueled bigotry throughout the world from the American frontier to the plantations of Virginia to the death camps of Europe. And, sympathetic though Zaius may be in some regards, his fear still leads him to the final solution attempted so many times in human history: "man is a nuisance," Zaius declares, "the sooner he is exterminated the better. It's a question of simian survival."

In his incisive commentary on United States film, *The Devil Finds Work*, James Baldwin observes that "the obligatory fade out kiss, in the classic American film, did not really speak of love, and, still less, of sex: it spoke of reconciliation, of all things now becoming possible. It was a device desperately needed among a people for whom so much had to be made possible."[68] *Planet* recognizes the need for such reconciliation and laments its absence. Yet in another of the film's inversions, in *Planet* the sign of the kiss underscores the impossibility of such reconciliation.

In the novel, Merou and Zira are overcome with emotion and are about to "kiss like lovers." At this point Zira forces him away, the taboo against interspecial/interracial love apparently proving too strong. When reflecting upon that encounter later, Merou (and perhaps Boulle?) concludes

The apocalyptic image of the West's aspirations laid waste by its destructiveness became the *Apes* series' most memorable scene and one of the most powerful images of sixties cinema.

that "the emotions that came to life between us had no name on Earth or in any other region of the cosmos. The separation was essential."[69]

Near the end of the film Taylor, about to escape from Zaius, asks Zira and Cornelius to come with him. They decline. Indicating Zaius, Cornelius states simply, "his culture is our culture." Cornelius is here perhaps aware that the rules of U.S. movies (and the rules of U.S. history?) state that cultural divides—racial and sexual divides—may be negotiated or even narrowed, but they cannot ultimately be bridged. After shaking Cornelius' hand—at least some kind of friendship may be possible—and advising Lucius to keep flying "the flags of discontent," Taylor tells Zira that he'd like to kiss her goodbye. "All right," she replies, "but you're so damned ugly!" Minutes later he is gone. Zaius returns to suppressing knowledge of history while Taylor, like so many U.S. heroes, rides off on his horse to meet "his destiny." In the film the kiss takes place with none of the tabooed passion hinted at in the novel, but with the same underlying message: the separation is essential.

Taylor faces that destiny in the film's final scene, which presents one of the most powerful images in sixties cinema: the half-buried, weather-beaten Statue of Liberty looming over the pathetic figure of the fallen Taylor. In this moment Taylor and the audience finally know where in time and space he actually is. Seeing the statue, he dismounts his horse and says, "Oh my God. I'm back. I'm home. All the time it was—We finally really did it!" Then as he realizes the full magnitude of the sight before him, Taylor falls to the ground, pounding the beach in anger, yelling, "You maniacs! You blew it up! Oh, damn you! God damn you all to hell!" The sense of desolation conveyed by the scene is encapsulated well by the following lines spoken by Prime Minister Witte in *Nicholas and Alexandra*, another Franklin Schaffner film: "Everything we fought for will be lost, everything we loved will be broken. The victors will be as cursed as the defeated. The world will become old and men will wander about lost in the ruins and go mad." The scene appears to suggest that there is indeed nothing left for Taylor to do but "wander about lost in the ruins and go mad."[70]

In late December 1964, Serling wrote that scene to have astronaut Thomas find the statue and then go off to find his fellow human beings and optimistically begin history anew. Two weeks later, in early January 1965, any glimmer of hope was removed and the scene had Thomas gunned down, dead on his feet before the statue. While the film's actual ending was not that final, a sense of despair had taken the place of the earlier hopeful vision, a vision that would not resurface until the end of the series.

The American hero fallen before the decomposing statue is a further critique of U.S. ambitions. The image hit theater screens precisely when the country's poisonous racism at home and disastrous militarism abroad, epitomized respectively by the assassination of Martin Luther King and the Tet offensive, both within weeks of *Planet's* release, had led to a public questioning of the image of the United States as the land of the free and the home of the brave — precisely the image that the statue had come to symbolize both for those at home and those abroad. The statue scene juxtaposed a bright shining myth with a corroded reality.

But the scene also speaks to the futility of giving into cynicism, of "dropping out" as Taylor tried to do. Not only a protest against the powers that be, the scene also critiques those who had given up on rehabilitating the nation. After all, it is not just an imperialist who is rebuked here, but also a cynic who, declaring that "somewhere in the universe there has to be something better than man," tries to evade the pressing problems of his society. Yet his plans for an escape to the stars literally come crashing to the ground, a ground where the problems of the past and present must be confronted. Because of his lack of courage, Taylor is no doubt as culpable for the corruption of society and the destruction of the world as the masters of war whom he chastised.

Yet the film is trapped in the same dilemma in which it traps Taylor, unable to rise above its own pessimism. Around the corner lies not hope, only emptiness and despair. The statue of the giant woman in front of Taylor and Nova is symbolic not only of U.S. history but also of mother nature. No hope for a new beginning in an idyllic paradise is offered because a pitiless nature has wiped out its mistake and the apes have risen to take over. Nature itself is not valorized as innocent, however, for it is the biological core of humanity that *Planet* presents as the root of human civilization's evil. Thus both nature and civilization stand as damning and damned.

Taylor and Nova do not get to play the expected roles of Adam and Eve and begin the rebirth of the human species. By encountering the statue just as they have begun their journey to start a new life together, they discover the evidence of the fall from grace before they even reach the garden. Taylor and Nova cannot start a new paradise, for humanity is still in exile. The message of the Statue of Liberty is here inverted from "come in" to "stay out." They cannot start again because the destruction in front of them would ultimately be their end. History is taken for destiny, and the new humanity is stopped before it even begins.

In *Planet of the Apes*, the voyage into outer space leads not to "the final frontier" as "Star Trek" was then promising, but rather to a wasteland, a societal graveyard where the wages of the sins committed on the earlier American "frontiers" have been paid in full.

In the closing shot, Taylor, unable to escape either his contentious time, the flaws of his biology, or the faults of his civilization — for such is the fate of symbols — has fallen to his knees before the fallen Statue of Liberty. The indifferent waves crashing around his body provide a powerful vision of humanity's aspirations defeated, laid waste by its destructiveness.

Two

Return to
the Planet of the Apes

Planet of the Apes can be seen as containing a double allegory regarding race. One allegory codes white humans as white humans, with Taylor as their representative, and codes black humans as apes. It may be objected then that by showing the apes as the practitioners of racial oppression, the responsibility for racism is being symbolically displaced onto African-Americans. African-Americans are thus scapegoats for the racism of European-Americans.

This interpretation is weakened, however, by the fact that the apes themselves, rather than being depicted as racially undifferentiated, are depicted as separate, mutually antagonistic races. A closer examination reveals that the film puts weight on the second, more complex, allegory, which codes white gentile humans as orangutans, white Jews as chimpanzees, and African-Americans as gorillas. The configuration of conflict is not just between human and apes, but humans with some apes and some apes with other apes. No particular race is therefore scapegoated. Responsibility for racism is displaced, however, onto biology.

In *Planet* we can see the beginnings of the *Apes* series' first theory of the origins of racial oppression. Here racism is biologized—it is figured as part of our genes, part of our biological constitution. The key to this construction was the depiction of apes as racist against each other and racist (or speciesist) against the humans. Depicting racial bigotry and oppression among the apes—from whom we descend and who, in the film, descend from us—without providing information about the history of ape society and conflict locates racism as an evolutionary problem. *Planet* thus shows racism as endemic to primates, rather than as a historical or cultural problem arising from the political and moral choices of particular people, groups, or societies. While Taylor's assertion that "Man was here first, you owe him your science, your culture, whatever civilization you've got" acknowledges the possibility of a historical explanation for the apes' racism

55

(they learned it), in the absence of exploring that possibility, the film puts more focus on nature than on nurture (they inherited it).

This look to the genes as the source for human problems was fairly common and not surprising given the country's mood. By the end of 1969, as APJAC was in preproduction on the second *Apes* film, the revelation of the My Lai massacre, an event utterly inconsistent with U.S. citizens' self-image as the righteous rescuers of Vietnam, but depressingly consistent with the logic of the large scale war of attrition, had further shocked an already dismayed U.S. public. The years of domestic and international violence had produced the sense that the very "nature" of the U.S. was somehow "tainted" and "the idea that events were driven by some form of collective insanity, a congenital flaw in the American 'national character' that produced an irrational 'propensity to violence,' gained currency and credence."[1]

While *Planet* generally received very positive reviews, this pessimistic view of human nature and biology was one of the most frequently made critiques. Critic Judith Shatnoff, for instance, in *Film Quarterly* argued that *Planet* was "scored by Queen Victoria" and was

> a negative utopia drawn from a Darwinian nightmare. It may be set in the future but it never left the nineteenth century in its fixed morality and its inability to imagine life in other terms developing other values, as if the *logic* of evolution — not just the *history* of evolution — moves life in only one direction. So, allegorically, the past is the future. The apes repeat all of man's mistakes. . . . They haven't eliminated violence, just repressed it — sometimes [emphasis added].[2]

If humanity's future looks like its past, then devolution must be our fate; although we may have learned to walk upright and mastered the flame and the wheel, we are basically beasts by nature. In taking up this issue, *Planet* echoed the nature-nurture debate which was raging at the time among scientists interested in primate studies.[3]

In a film dealing with racial conflict, the film's biological determinism has important implications. *Planet* suggests that there is something inherent in the evolutionary stock — which precedes specific human races, cultures, and power struggles — that predetermines human racial animosity and conflict. The logical — and quite dreadful — implication of this theory, possibly overlooked by the filmmakers (at least consciously), is that if racism is a biologically inherited characteristic, part of "human nature," then we cannot change it. And if in fact we cannot change our nature, it follows that we cannot really be held accountable for it. Human beings — in the case of the United States in particular, white human beings — are thus paradoxically both *off* and perpetually *on* the hook: exonerated of any responsibility for racial oppression yet doomed by their very "nature" to commit it.

While human beings and apes appear as similarly doomed by "the logic of evolution," there is an essential—and essentialist—difference asserted in *Planet*. The violence of the apes is extraspecies, not intraspecies as in the case of humans. (One of the chimpanzees in the *Apes* television show derisively comments that a human is "the only animal on Earth that wars on its own kind.") As we have noted, while the apes discriminate against each other, they do not kill each other. The law of "Ape shall not kill Ape" is obeyed. This is the primary demarcation between ape and human, and it is extremely important throughout the series. The apes' Sacred Scrolls condemn human beings as homicidal. In *Escape*, Cornelius stresses that "one of the reasons for man's original downfall is your peculiar habit of murdering one another. Man destroys man, apes do not destroy apes!"

This difference is the apes' mark of superiority over the humans. Still living before the fall, they have not committed the sin of Cain. In this respect, the apes are figured here as "noble savages," and indeed the myth of the noble savage is the article of faith that Zaius, as chief defender of the faith, chiefly defends. "We apes have learned to live in innocence," he proclaims in *Beneath*, "Let no creature, be it man or some other form of life, dare to contaminate that innocence!" But by the end of the series, the filmmakers did indeed contaminate the innocence of the apes and substantially challenged *Planet's* theory of the origins of racial oppression, the implications of that theory, and Zaius' myth of choice.

Planet of the Apes was not made with a sequel in mind, but after *Planet* began breaking box-office records, the idea caught on.[4] As he was walking across the Twentieth Century–Fox lot with Mort Abrahams one day, producer Stan Hough (who later produced the "Planet of the Apes" television series) suggested that Abrahams make a sequel. Abrahams took the idea to Jacobs, and within two months of *Planet's* release they were working on a second *Apes* film. The history of the second *Apes* picture's development is revealing for what it tells us about the direction in which the producers wanted to take the *Apes* story at that time.

In an initial idea submitted by Rod Serling, Taylor finds the remains of a human city, some weapons, and an old airplane which he uses to fight off the apes. Just as it looks as if Taylor will be defeated, another spaceship from the past arrives and prevents his death. Having the chance now to return to his own time, Taylor chooses a woman astronaut from the ship's crew as his mate and decides to stay to rebuild humanity in the apes' time. Significantly, this story would have rehabilitated the image of the Heston hero as the invincible defender of civilization and would have gone even further by depicting him as humanity's savior.[5] After this proposal and two other Serling concepts were rejected, Jacobs approached Pierre Boulle who, after initial skepticism, was enthusiastic about writing a sequel.[6]

Boulle's screenplay was entitled *Planet of the Men* and was completed in July of 1968, five months after the release of the first film. The script begins with Taylor and Nova starting a colony of humans. Taylor eventually teaches them to talk, to protect themselves against the apes, and to raid ape outposts for food.

The scene shifts to the apes' city, 12 years after the close of *Planet*, where Cornelius, having served a prison sentence for heresy because of his theories of apes evolving from human beings, runs for political office. He is supported by a small group of radical chimpanzees. Competing with Zaius for the post of minister of science, Cornelius presses the apes to "without prejudice, stretch out [their] hands to the humans and help them to better their miserable condition. It would be a task worthy of apes." In effect, he proclaims an ape-man's burden.[7]

In contrast, Zaius warns of "a human tide which comes to submerge us and which would be the end of all civilization on this planet."[8] His language echoes that of Western proponents of scientistic racism and eugenics in the early twentieth century like T. L. Stoddard, who warned of a "rising tide of color against white world supremacy."[9] Playing on the racial fears of the ape population, Zaius easily wins reelection (just as Stoddard and his allies in the United States won legislation restricting the immigration of non–Nordics into the United States). Along with gorilla Field Marshall Urus, Zaius plans to launch a war of extermination against the humans. Zira, Cornelius, and Lucius go to Taylor's camp to warn him.

Taylor's son Sirius hates all apes, and when the attack comes he disobeys Taylor's orders to take prisoners. He offers the apes no quarter and exhorts the human troops he leads to kill all the apes. Sirius and his troops slaughter the ape army and then set out to conquer the ape capital and wipe their "wicked" city "from the face of the planet" because "only fire can purify this foul place."[10] Taylor, dismayed that he helped bring about a reassertion of humanity's thirst for destruction, is killed by the other humans while he is trying to protect Cornelius and Zira. As the apes go insane and revert to their primitive animal state, Zira and Cornelius kill themselves in order to die with dignity. In the final scene, Zaius, who has lost his advanced intelligence and been reduced to a circus ape, is given a lump of sugar and dumbly applauds himself after struggling to stammer "Z . . . Zaious" for the human audience.

Boulle had opposed the idea, introduced in Serling's *Planet* script, that war had destroyed humanity and thought the cause of ape ascendancy should have remained biological. With *Planet of the Men*, Boulle was trying to refocus the material back onto the issue of human regeneration he had stressed in the original book. The novel's main character, Ulysee Merou, is convinced that he was "brought to this planet to be the instrument of human regeneration" and to be "the new savior of this human race in decline."[11]

Like Serling's sequel story, Boulle's script would have, to a degree, rehabilitated the traditional Heston hero by having Taylor serve as the protector of humanity. But Boulle had a tendency to raise hope in his stories only to dash them with surprise downbeat endings. In fact, the *Men* script underlined the failure of the Heston hero by depicting his new breed as vengeful and unscrupulous.

With *Planet*, Jacobs and company did not exploit the possibility, latent in the *Apes* material, of embellishing an old theme in U.S. racial mythology: the move away from civilization back to a prehistoric wilderness in which the race could be revitalized and symbolically reborn through racial violence against a blood enemy.[12] Boulle expanded on that theme in his *Men* script and showed that rebirth as nothing more than a replication of the human character flaws that led to humanity's initial downfall. Indeed, the logic of *Planet* precluded such a regeneration and revitalization. Since humanity's flaws are presented as the function of nature and not nurture, the move back to nature offers no promise of noble rebirth.

Despite Boulle's efforts, the rebuilding of humanity was apparently not a story APJAC productions was interested in telling: Jacobs rejected the script, finding it "wasn't cinematic."[13] Interestingly, despite both the series' continued moving away from Boulle's themes and Jacobs' assessment of the quality of the script, *Planet of the Men* prefigured much of what was to come in the later *Apes* films, including the repeated failure of appeals for racial reconciliation seen throughout the series, public unrest led by radical chimpanzee youth (seen in *Beneath*), a plan by Cornelius and Zira to kill themselves (alluded to, although not enacted, in *Escape*), their death in each other's arms (*Escape*), a revolt by the oppressed species leading to the reversal of racial domination (*Conquest* and *Battle*), the vengeful excesses of that revolt (*Conquest*), a debate over the proper means and goals of racial revolution (*Conquest*), and a gorilla-led and a human-led race war both waged with the pledge of "no prisoners" (*Battle*). In fact, one crucial element from *Men* did find its way into *Beneath*: General Ursus (derived from Field Marshall Urus) does lead a war of extermination against the humans, a war with disastrous results.

In another sequel idea entitled *The Dark Side of the Earth*, which shares elements of both Serling's and Boulle's proposals, Taylor and Nova find the remains of a twentieth century town inhabited by thinking, talking humans. They join the humans and enjoy their pastoral, carefree lifestyle until another U.S. spaceship crashes, with one astronaut surviving. In time, the second astronaut, like Sirius in *Men*, leads the humans on an attack against the apes just as the hawkish apes led by Zaius plan to exterminate the humans. As in Boulle's screenplay, the humans take over and the apes revert to a primitive pre-articulate state. But Taylor is not killed in this story. Rather, remembering a bomb he found in the humans' arsenal and disgusted by the carnage, prejudice, and hatred he has witnessed, Taylor decides to destroy everything so that God can try it all over again. He crashes the ship into the city, igniting a nuclear holocaust which leaves nothing except the reproductive imagery of a flower and a bee.[14]

While this ending does contain a seed of hope, we can see in the development of the first *Apes* sequel an increasing sense of nihilism. The producers went from Serling's hopeful vision of humanity reborn to Boulle's more pessimistic *Planet of the Men* to *The Dark Side of the Earth* and *Beneath* in which Taylor decides that all life is so corrupt he must destroy it so a new beginning can take root.

Following the rejection of the above proposals, in the fall of 1968 APJAC hired British poet and screenwriter Paul Dehn to work on a script for a *Planet of the Apes* sequel. Dehn, who had counterespionage experience during World War II, made war and the threat of nuclear weapons a recurring motif in his writings. Dehn shared a best-screenplay Oscar with James Bernard for the 1950 film *Seven Days to Noon* which focused on an atomic research scientist's plot to force nuclear disarmament by threatening to detonate a bomb in London. A similar problem was at the heart of his screenplay for *Goldfinger*, in which James Bond must prevent the villain from using a nuclear device to contaminate the Fort Knox gold supply.

These themes dominated a book of Dehn's poetry entitled *Quake, Quake, Quake: A Leaden Collection of English Verse*. Illustrated by Edward Gorey, known for his macabre Victorian-style artwork, *Quake, Quake, Quake* consists of a number of short poems, some of them adapted from popular children's rhymes, that deal with war and nuclear desolation. Filled with images of maimed soldiers, mutated children, the ravages of radiation, cancer research on animals, nuclear wastelands, and poisoned environments, *Quake, Quake, Quake* displays a deeply held apprehension about the threats to health and survival in the nuclear age. The title alone expresses the depth of Dehn's anxiety over these threats. The themes of Dehn's earlier work made him exceptionally well suited for the *Apes* project, and Dehn's political concerns and apprehensions greatly impacted his work on the *Apes* films, particularly *Beneath*.

Dehn, who became the main *Apes* writer, wrote a treatment entitled *Planet of the Apes Revisited*, submitted in September 1968. This story has some of the same thematic concerns as *Men* and is similar to the one finally chosen for *Beneath*, but ends with the destruction of both the ape army and the mutants by an atomic bomb in the underground city. Afterward Taylor and Nova reunite with Zira and Cornelius, return to the ape city, free the humans, and begin a new age of racial togetherness symbolized by the birth of a half-human, half-ape child. Interracial sex, however, while a historical fact, was still a public taboo. (In fact, at one time the production code of the Motion Picture Producers and Directors of America, Inc., explicitly forbade portraying miscegenation.) And it was a taboo that the producers were not willing to violate. (It had only been a few years since the Supreme Court had overturned Virginia's antimiscegenation laws in *Loving v. Virginia*.) The ending was eventually dropped; apparently it would have been too controversial to depict that pinnacle of U.S. cultural no-no's: an interracial child. Dehn recalled that "it was thought that Man-Ape miscegenation might lose us our G certificate!"[15] Another ending had radiation-scarred gorillas emerging after the explosion to continue the violence.

The *Planet of the Apes Revisited* treatment was typical of the body of Dehn's later *Apes* work in that both sides eventually emerge as reprehensible. It differs, however, in that the destructive elements in both the ape and the human community destroy each other, leaving the apes and humans of goodwill to build peace together. This is the last time Dehn would script a "surgical strike" of this kind. In his final script, no good-hearted survivors are left to sow the seeds of reconciliation. And as foreshadowed by his scene of the mutated gorillas arising from the earth to destroy the promise of peace, Dehn's vision for the *Apes* series became a never-ending cycle of race wars.

The Serling story, *Planet of the Men*, and *Planet of the Apes Revisited* all envisioned the possibility of the rejuvenation of human beings and a racial rebirth, *The Dark Side of the Earth* left open the possibility that some kind life might survive, and the *Revisited* treatment even envisioned the achievement of racial peace. As we have noted, however, human regeneration was not an issue of interest for Jacobs' APJAC productions, and racial harmony was not a prospect for which the series allowed much possibility. (It was not until the last film in the series that such a prospect was depicted as even a faint hope.) Again displaying an increasing sense of nihilism, no doubt fed by events like the Tet offensive, the My Lai massacre, the King and Robert Kennedy assassinations, and the violence at the 1968 Democratic convention, all of which occurred between the making of *Planet* and the making of *Beneath*, every one of the above concepts was ultimately rejected in favor of a story that depicts the escalation of racial tensions to the point of the annihilation of both human and ape and of the entire planet.

Even more than *Planet*, *Beneath the Planet of the Apes* expresses a sense of dismay over the Unites States' involvement in the Vietnam War. It merges that concern with the problem of racial conflict and implicitly makes the connection between the racism of the United States at home and its racism abroad.

In *Beneath*, a power shift is underway. The strength of the gorilla military, under the leadership of the hawkish General Ursus (James Gregory), is on the rise. Ursus exploits the growing threat of famine and the disappearance of 11 army scouts in order to justify invading the Forbidden Zone. Zaius, Zira, and Cornelius (played by David Watson due to scheduling

conflicts with Roddy McDowall), and, it is intimated, the rest of the orangutans and chimpanzees, are against Ursus' plan but are unable to stop it.
While Zira was giving orders to gorillas in *Planet*, she is superseded by
Ursus' authority in *Beneath*. When she tries to protect Brent (James Franciscus) and Nova by selecting them for study, she is denied them by Ursus,
who has marked them for target practice.

The takeover is also depicted imagistically—the gorillas on screen far
outnumber the chimpanzees and orangutans who, in fact, barely appear in
the film at all and are largely irrelevant to the main story. "The trouble with
us intellectuals," Cornelius laments, "is that we have responsibility but no
power." Later, as Cornelius watches the gorilla army led by General Ursus
embark on its expansionist war, he tells Zira defeatedly that "we chimpanzees are too few. How can we take initiative when they are in control?" The
chimpanzee's mournful expressions as the gorilla war machine marches on
must have resonated with many on the left, who saw their influence marginalized by the power of the right as the Vietnam War ravaged on and Richard
Nixon took the presidency. In *Beneath*, the rising influence of the gorillas signals that the racial and political balance of power is changing for the worse.

The power shift is evident in the first image of the ape city—General
Ursus delivering a speech to the apes "Citizens Council." The term "Citizens Council" recalls the racist "White Citizens Councils," prominent in
the sixties, which fought against desegregation and "employed economic
sanctions, held rallies and used intimidating rhetoric to instill fear in local
blacks."[16] Audience expectations having been cued by the term, it should
have come as no surprise that Ursus' ideology is one of racial supremacy.
The first words we hear Ursus speak—"I'll tell you one thing every good
soldier knows: the only thing that counts in the end is—Power! Naked,
merciless force!"—are emblematic of gorilla temperament in the series. In
the screenplay, Ursus' rationale for going to war reads like a pastiche of
racist expansionist ideologies from U.S. history:

> What I saw when I became your Army Commander,—broke my heart. I
> saw our country imprisoned on one side by the sea, and by the north and
> south and west,—by naked desert. And inside our country, we found
> ourselves infected by those enormous parasites which we call Humans . . .
> by parasites who devoured the fruits that *we* had planted in a land rightly
> *ours*; who fattened on the fertility of fields that we had made green with
> wheat; who polluted the pure and precious water of *our* lakes with their
> animal excrement; and who continued to breed in our very midst like
> maggots in a once-healthy body. What should we do? How should we
> act?—I know what every good soldier knows: the only thing that counts
> in the end is—Power! Naked, merciless Force! Today the bestial Human
> herds have at last been systematically flushed from their feeding grounds!
> No single Human Being has escaped our net. They are dead. Or if not
> dead, they are in our cages—condemned to die.

I do not say all Humans are evil simply because their skin is white. But our Lawgiver tells us that never will they have the Ape's divine faculty for distinguishing between Evil and Good. Their eyes are animal, their smell the smell of the dead flesh they eat. Had they been allowed to live and breed among us unchecked, they would have overwhelmed us. And the concept of Ape Power would have become meaningless; and our high and splendid culture—would have wasted away and our civilization would have been ravaged and destroyed. Because the only good Human is a dead Human. And those lucky enough to remain alive will have the privilege of being . . . *used* . . . by our revered Minister of Science, Dr. Zaius . . .

We will never lose our sense of purpose. We will never degenerate. We will never become weak and hairless. Because we know how to purify our own people—with *Blood*! The Forbidden Zone has been closed for centuries. And rightly so. But we now have evidence that that vast, barren area is inhabited. By whom or by what we do not know. But if they live—and live they do—then they must eat. We must replenish the land that was ravaged by the humans with new, productive feeding grounds. And these we can obtain in the once Forbidden Zone.

So, now it is our holy duty to enter it, put the mark of our feet and wheels and guns and flags upon it!—To *expand* the boundaries of our ineluctable power! To kill our enemies—known and unknown—like so many lice! And to *invade*—INVADE, *INVADE*—! [Emphasis in original.][17]

Not all of the above speech made it into the film's final cut, but the film-makers' conception of Ursus and of the conflict he escalates is filled with historical resonance. The fact that Ursus refers to the humans' white skin color, as opposed to defining them as, for example, hairless or straight-backed, suggests that his view of skin color as a primary marker of difference is modeled on the human understanding of race.[18] The reference to "Ape Power," though it did not make the film's final cut, in its resemblance to the then current slogan "Black Power" seems the first semiovert connection made between apes and African-Americans. This, coupled with the disparaging reference to humans as "white" expresses the common misunderstanding that those wanting "Black Power" were by definition necessarily "anti-white."

Other racial themes and invocations of Western, and in particular North American, cultural memory pervade the speech. Ursus' rhetoric depicts a community "imprisoned" by the sea on one side and by a desert, a type of "wilderness," on the other, a community faced with the encroachment of "bestial herds." Ursus' construction of the problem and the "necessary" response to it recalls the ideology behind both the extermination of the Native Americans and imperialism: a beleaguered community must assert military might and genocidal violence in order to prevent "degeneration."[19] And his exclamation that "the only good Human is a dead Human!" is adapted from U.S. General Sheridan's genocidal curse that "the only good Indian is a dead Indian."

Ursus' construction of the racial "other" as a parasite threatening the health and purity of the body politic also recalls the racism of early twentieth century nativists and eugenicists who claimed that the "inferior" genes of Italians, Jews, Slavs, and other non–Nordics would contaminate the racial purity of the United States. These arguments were instrumental in bringing about racist U.S. immigration restrictions in the early 1900s and helped usher in the era of the Nazis' attempts at ethnic "purification."[20] (Similar arguments against non-white immigrants can still be heard today.)[21] Ursus' concern over a rising tide of whiteness resonates both with the Western paranoia of the "yellow peril," "first world" fear of the "third world population explosion," (human overpopulation was also Zaius' rationalization for genocide), and the threat to Western dominance posed by the "rising tide of color."

Ursus' zealous machismo and imperialist program echo, among other things, Theodore Roosevelt's call to the "strenuous life" and the ways in which a country's "manliness" is often constructed as a function of its ability and willingness to commit violence.[22] Roosevelt feared that the absence of a frontier would lead to the deterioration of the leadership stock of the United States, and he saw it as his duty to call those of his class "to renew their virility and to save the class from leisured inanition [by taking up] the challenge of empire."[23] Likewise, Ursus sees ape society in danger not only because of the presence of human "maggots" but because it is weakened by indecisive orangutan politicians and chimpanzee intellectuals. Thus, like Roosevelt, Ursus comes along with the invigorating mettle of the warrior class to save ape "culture" and "civilization" by exhorting the apes to "purify our own people with blood! . . . and to *invade*—INVADE, *INVADE*—!" Ursus' call for national and racial regeneration through violence would have likely qualified him to be a good Indian fighter or defender of "manifest destiny." He does not even know what race he will fight in the Forbidden Zone, but he knows that "whom" or "what" he will fight is different and therefore necessarily both inferior and threatening, and thus worthy of extermination.

Ursus even manages to receive the sanction of the ape religious leadership. An orangutan minister prays for a blessing for the army on the eve of a "holy war" against an enemy who has been denied the apes' divine gifts of "spiritual godliness and bodily beauty." Ursus' bored expression during the minister's speech suggests that he does not believe the religious rhetoric, but he is nonetheless able to manipulate and secure the sanction of the religious establishment.

Indeed there is reason to suspect that Ursus' justifications for war are somewhat fabricated. He cites the threat of starvation as a principal cause for invasion, yet in the home of Zira and Cornelius, who are now married, Zira is preparing to bake a cake with chocolate icing, and a full basket of fruit sits on their table. These are not the signs of a society facing famine. Ursus also attempts to inflate slightly the number of ape scouts lost in the Forbidden Zone in order to gain support for invasion. Ursus' tactics recall the Tonkien Gulf incident and other episodes in which the U.S. government also used deception to win public support for the war against Vietnam.

Thus *Beneath* portrays a society poised for a war into which it has been misled, a war against an unseen enemy in an unfamiliar wilderness. It is a war which the intellectuals and liberal youth oppose, but the politicians, some of them reluctantly, and members of the conservative establishment support it. And once in the war, it proves to be far more difficult to win than they anticipated. Seen from this perspective, *Beneath* was about the Vietnam War and critiqued the United States' role in that war as motivated by imperialist racism rationalized and sold through deception.

As we have seen, Ursus' racial and military ideology had long-standing precedents in U.S. ideology and history. Yet the critique is not just leveled at the United States.[24] The name "Ursus" is Latin for "bear," which links the ape general to the symbol of the Soviet Union and thus extends the critique to the Eastern bloc nations as well as the West, bringing both together in one reprehensible figure. As in other films influenced by the confusions of the Vietnam War, the clear distinctions between "us" and "them" are here broken down. Thus both warriors in the cold war are critiqued as militaristic and brutal in a film that, consciously or unconsciously, replicated some of the major conditions and tensions of the war, while displacing its political concerns into another time and place.[25]

If "we" resemble "them" to such a degree that the same figure can represent both, then we are our own enemy.[26] If this is the case, what hope is there to extricate ourselves from the destructive morass we are in? The film offers none. While the military of both the United States and the Soviet Union are pointedly represented by the most brutish of the apes, those who would oppose the masters of war are themselves represented by the chimpanzees, the most marginalized and powerless of the apes.

Cornelius' exclamation of liberal intellectual powerlessness is followed by a display of that powerlessness—the crushing of a chimpanzee peace protest. The young chimpanzees stage a sit-in in front of the advancing army and chant slogans such as "Love yes. War no!" "No more war," "No more lies," "We want freedom, we want peace." The protest is broken up by the army, to cries of "gorilla brutality!" and filmed with hand-held photography that evokes nightly news footage of sixties human protests. *Beneath*, like *Planet*, invoked the generation gap and the racial gap, as well as the political cleavages those gaps marked. After the protestors are carried away, the scene ends with a shot of the military wagons rolling over the peace signs as the army marches off to war. Again arguments for racial peace fail to sway those in power, and again this has dire results.

The racial sensibilities of the mutant human beings living beneath the planet of the apes both resemble and contrast those of the apes. Like Taylor, the mutants return the apes' hatred, describing them as "slobbering, monstrous [and] materialistic," "hideous creatures," and surmising that "either their skulls [are] too thick, or they really [know] nothing at all." (The irony of the mutants worshiping an atomic bomb while calling the *apes* materialistic seems woefully lost on them.)

While the racial realities of the mutant population are fairly ambiguous, the mutant high command is somewhat more egalitarian than that of the apes. It is composed of three white men, including the mutant leader Mendez, one white woman, and one black man. A diverse look, what Abrahams called a "United Nations" type feeling, was deliberately written into the script. (Even size diversity was a goal: the film had a heavy-set character named "Fat Man" and early drafts of the story featured a dwarf.)

Further, there are signs that the notion of white supremacy has disappeared in the mutant society. The African-American character, named simply "Negro" in the screenplay and credits, would have produced for many a visual association with the racially oppressed. However, while definitely subordinate to the white leadership, Negro's presence in the high command and Negro's position on the dais in the church with the other high command leaders suggest that he is one of the mutant city's five most important members.

A more ambiguous indication of the mutants' racial sensibilities is the rubber masks they wear to hide their faces, which have been malformed after nearly two thousand years of exposure to radiation.[27] The masks give them the appearance of "normal" humans, but when they are removed, their malformed faces are exposed. Dehn's original treatment for the film stated that the mutants should be "a serious prophetic warning against the Mis-Shape of Thing[s] to Come."[28] Based on anatomy diagrams, the makeup for the mutants was designed to simulate what a human being would look like without skin and therefore without what we commonly see as the primary marker of racial difference. When the masks are removed in a religious ceremony, the mutants' flesh appears to be monochromatic — without the masks there is no visible color difference. Thus, when the mutants remove their masks to "reveal their inmost selves," their inmost selves are all the same color, without racial difference as we understand it.

Some notion of racial difference, though not necessarily racial hierarchy, may exist however. Although without the masks the mutants are all the same color, and although the same color masks could have been worn by everyone, the fact that some *chose* to wear black masks suggests that white skin was not regarded as superior and that citizens of African as well as of European ancestry wanted to retain their color.[29] Thus the mutant society, at least as regards its own members, appears to have accomplished the difficult task of harmonizing the recognition of similarity with an appreciation of difference.

An alternate reading of the mask color issue could argue that white supremacy has prevailed, that the white population did not want the racial differentiation blurred, and so ensured that the black mutants wore dark masks so that they could be identified and pure blood lines and racial hierarchies could be maintained. However the racially integrated high council and religious service—led by Mendez a popelike religious and political figure—lends weight to the argument that mutant society has achieved some kind of racial harmony.

But the mutant society is by no means a benign utopia. Like their enemy Ursus, the mutants also bring together characteristics of the United States and its Communist adversaries into one symbolic figure. The mutants' extraordinary mental and telepathic powers allow them to create fantastic and convincing illusions—huge walls of fire, a bleeding statue of the ape lawgiver—and to create severe pain in Brent's mind, force information out of him, and compel him to act against his own will. The depiction of the mutants thus recalls the then prevalent fear of Communist, and particularly Asian Communist, torture and brainwashing.[30]

And the mutants also resemble U.S. citizens. Not only in the obvious fact that they inhabit the remains of Manhattan, but also in that their illusions fail to bring them victory over their racial "inferiors" and their ultimate weapon is their bomb. Thus the mutants situation parallels that of the United States, which also had based its strategy in Vietnam on illusions, false images, and distorted facts: a misunderstanding of Vietnamese political culture and unrealistic hopes for counterinsurgency, surgical strikes, and the war of attrition. Although the United States found an enemy more formidable than had been expected, its nuclear weapons were impractical, at best, to use. Thus the film allegorically criticizes all sides in the Vietnam War as cruel, hostile, and determined to fight a war that could only exact a brutally high price on both sides.

Both the apes and the mutant humans are so reprehensible to Brent that he refuses to help either side. "Go ahead, annihilate each other," he defiantly tells the mutant interrogators. His disgust resembles that of the U.S. public at the time, faced with a political landscape very much like Pauline Kael's description of the filmic landscape in which there was "no longer a right side to identify with and nobody you really felt good about cheering for," and in which the choice was "a matter of preferring the less gross and despicable characters to the total monsters."[31]

The mutant's bomb-worship is a fascinating inversion of Christian belief and ritual. Recalling Jesus' statement that he was the "Alpha and the Omega," the bomb has those very greek letters on one of its fins. Moreover, its role in the mutants' religious mythology is similar to that of Jesus in

Can a planet long endure half human and half ape? The advertisement art for *Beneath* suggested a world literally split between hostile races. A warning of the mis-shape of things to come?

Christianity: the mutants hold that the bomb should be venerated because one of its "ancestors," an earlier bomb, had made the mutants what they were. As a later-model bomb, the Alpha and Omega bomb was metaphorically the descendant of their maker. Thus the Alpha and Omega bomb was the "child" of their god and its presence and power could usher in the final apocalypse.[32] (The rationale for the mutants' bomb worship was not fully explained until *Battle*.)

The mutant hymns and liturgy, with their references to "the blessing of the bomb almighty and the fellowship of the holy fallout," were adapted from texts used in Christian observance. The bomb even looks like an upside down cross (with obvious phallic connotations). Taylor sardonically explains that the bomb, built "in the sweet name of peace," can "burn the planet to a cinder, how's that for your ultimate weapon?"

The worship of the doomsday bomb as "a holy weapon of peace" is perhaps the ultimate extension of the nuclear deterrence theory that envisioned mutually assured destruction as the greatest protector of life. It is also a monument to self-delusion: the mutants possess the most powerful weapon in the world, yet have managed to convince themselves that they are vulnerable and defenseless. Frederick S. Clarke noted that the mutants represented a "reprehensible trait within us, our rationalization in socially acceptable terms of our own innate hostility and aggressiveness."[33]

The very notion of a "weapon of peace" is emblematic of the human paradox. This conflict and racial hostility combine in Taylor to bring about Earth's destruction. At the end of the film, the apes have embarked on a race war against the humans and reached the city. The human leader Mendez, rather than have the humans' sacred space defiled by apes, orders the citizens to kill themselves, and the bomb is aimed at the ape city. The gorillas invade, killing Brent and the remaining mutants and shooting Taylor. When the wounded Taylor asks Zaius for help, Zaius characteristically responds, "You ask me to help you? Man is evil capable of nothing but destruction!" Taylor, here embodying the human paradox, mutters, "you bloody bastard," and with his remaining strength proves Zaius right by detonating the bomb and destroying the Earth.

In its final scenes, *Beneath* returns to the familiar ground of the Heston race-war epic: Heston, as Taylor, again protects a stronghold of white civilization — pointedly, in this case, the remains of St. Patrick's Cathedral, here transformed into the church of the bomb — from the onslaught of another non-white horde. Like *Planet*, however, *Beneath* is critical of this traditional role. In what seems a pointed barb at, and warning about, the extent to which the United States might have gone to avoid defeat in Vietnam, rather than see the rising tide of color engulf him, Taylor, the representative of the white West destroys the whole world.

As Taylor's hand slowly slips off the firing mechanism, the color fades from the scene and a white glare grows increasingly brighter until it obliterates the picture and the screen goes white. *Beneath* then ends with the following nihilistic narration: "In one of the countless billions of galaxies in the Universe lies a medium-sized star. And one of its satellites, a green and insignificant planet, is now dead."

This ending is devastatingly pessimistic: it is not enough that nature has wiped out its mistake and destroyed human civilization as we saw in *Planet*. *Beneath* showed apes as also capable of militarism and evil. Thus the whole of primate evolutionary stock is so polluted that it must be wiped out — indeed all life must be destroyed root and branch. This can be seen as an act of the mutants' God, or an act of Taylor's God, as a corrective act of nature or of destiny, or the culmination of the human paradox and humanity's death wish. Seen from any perspective, the judgment is "guilty" and the sentence is death.

The effect of the juxtaposition of and connection between a Vietnam allegory and a nuclear holocaust delivered an impassioned statement

Rather than be engulfed by the rising tide of color, the representative of the white West destroys the whole world.

against the war. And the juxtaposition of and connection between a race war and the annihilation of the world delivered an impassioned warning about the evils of racial hatred. *Beneath*'s end is an indication of the importance placed on these issues. In one of the *Apes* series' strongest cautionary statements — made as the United States itself was engaged in racial warfare abroad and at home — the capacity for barbarity despite the desire for peace and the propensity for racial conflict reach their ultimate climax and destroy all life on the planet.

After they had destroyed the planet of the apes, it seemed rather unlikely that the filmmakers could continue the *Apes* series. Yet science fiction often is about the unlikely, and the *Apes* saga was just getting started. Much to Dehn's surprise, after *Beneath* opened, he received a telegram saying, "Apes exist, sequel required."[34] Dehn then began work on the screenplay for what was originally titled *Secret of the Planet of the Apes* but was eventually renamed *Escape from the Planet of the Apes*. In the third *Apes* film, a reporter asks presidential science adviser Otto Hasslein what he expects to experience from the historic first meeting of human beings with intelligent apes. "Fear" is his response. And although *Escape* initially has a lighter tone than the first two films, and although Director Don Taylor saw the film as a love story and "didn't try to hammer the sociological overtones," fear is exactly what comes to pass.[35]

In *Planet*, Taylor and the audience were faced with the results of a racial apocalypse with no way of knowing its cause. By bringing representatives from that time of racial apocalypse back into the audience's time, *Escape* began the process, continued in *Conquest* and culminated in *Battle*, of supplying the history of that racial apocalypse and making racial conflict the series' main political concern.

Escape stands out as a turning point in the series that laid the groundwork for the more highly political nature of the last two films. With *Escape* the filmmakers shifted the political focus of the series from "foreign" affairs to domestic racial conflict. The physical landscape of the films is no longer the strange ape civilization, the radiation-twisted mutant society, or the eerie deserts of the Forbidden Zone. It is now a major modern U.S. city. The time is no longer the fortieth century, but the imminent present (1973).

Granted there is still some displacement. It is telling for instance that the film set closest to the audience's time is also the least explicitly political and the least violent of the *Apes* films. However, while on the surface the least political entry in the series, *Escape* in fact upped the stakes of the series' conflict by locating the threatening racial "other" in the middle of contemporary society. In setting, time, and plot, *Escape* brought the *Apes* series home.

This shift makes it possible to identify *Escape* as a marker dividing the series into two parts: the first consisting of *Planet* and *Beneath*, in which race is one of a number of issues of concern, and the second consisting of *Escape*, *Conquest*, and *Battle*, in which race increasingly takes the center stage as the series' main political focus. This move also laid the groundwork for turning the *Apes* series into a more direct comment on the domestic politics of the day—for delivering a warning that the potential for a real racial cataclysm loomed over the racial conflicts of the late twentieth century United States.

Having shown the failure of U.S. imperial ambitions through the misadventures of Colonel Taylor and having shown the gorilla's expansionist "foreign war" end in nuclear annihilation, the *Apes* series had largely exhausted the themes of Western colonialism, the cold war, the Vietnam War, and nuclear destruction. What more can you say about international political tensions once you have destroyed the entire Earth? Therefore, in order to continue the series, it made sense to shift the political focus to race, a topic which had already been integral to the constellation of issues at the heart of the first two films. Indeed, since the problems of both colonialism and the Vietnam War were a function of racism, the more direct confrontation of racial conflict in the second half of the series can be seen as a logical progression away from the manifestations and toward the "core" of the problem.

In *Escape*, the chimpanzees lose their original racial connotations and, as representatives of the soon-to-be-enslaved apes, become symbolic of African-Americans in their struggle with whites. Unlike *Planet* and *Beneath*, in which the white humans were the main protagonists, once the series becomes a more pointed allegory of domestic racial conflict, the apes become predominantly the sympathetic characters, while the human villains are all white, and after *Escape*, whites are never again major protagonists.

Because it takes place in a technologically advanced society, *Escape* is closer, in some respects, than the original film to Boulle's novel and to Serling's early *Planet* script. In many ways *Escape* also inverts the plot of the first film: in *Escape*, Zira, Cornelius (again Roddy McDowall), and chimpanzee scientist Dr. Milo (Sal Mineo) go back in time and land on a planet of human beings; the apes do not talk at first; they are befriended by two human doctors; the leader of the scientific establishment interrogates them about their origins, comes to fear them as a threat to the survival of his civilization and wishes to destroy them; and they have to flee from the city and eventually are killed. (Zira even discovers a stuffed gorilla in a museum much like Taylor discovered Dodge.)

Despite its similarities to earlier *Apes* films, *Escape* marks a significant shift in the series' handling of racial conflict. In the first half of the series, human racial strife had been allegorized in two ways — both as conflict between apes and humans and as conflict between different races of apes. In *Escape, Conquest,* and *Battle,* the latter strategy is almost entirely dropped. The racial differentiation between orangutans, chimpanzees, and gorillas is de-emphasized as all the apes become stand-ins for African-Americans. The later films intensify the allegory, moving away from the conflict between ape *races* (gorillas, chimpanzees, and orangutans) and focusing instead on the conflict between *species* (humans and apes). Apparently the terms of the series' original allegory were deemed no longer adequate for conveying the depth of racial division and hostility in the U.S. — it was as if the film-makers saw the alienation between races as so vast that it could best be allegorized as alienation between species.

When Hasslein (German actor Eric Braeden, born Hans Gudegast) interrogates Zira and Cornelius, he calmly assures them that "this is not an interracial hassle." The conflict is precisely an interracial hassle, however, right down to one of the C.I.A. examiners derisively calling the apes "monkeys," knowing that the apes see the term as offensive (perhaps even as a racial slur). Cornelius' racial pride is wounded, and in response he chastises the humans by saying that "one of the reasons for man's original downfall is your peculiar habit of murdering one another. Man destroys man, apes do not destroy apes!"

Hasslein pays no attention to the possibility of humanity's self-inflicted destruction; his concern is to prevent the domination of humanity by apes. The internal threat is ignored in favor of focusing on the external threat. He has Zira and Cornelius explain to him the history of ape development on Earth: a plague wiped out dogs and cats and left humans without pets. "For man this was intolerable" Cornelius says sarcastically. "He might kill his brother but he could not kill his dog." Apes were taken into human homes as pets and later trained to perform tricks, which then developed into services and then into slavery. After two centuries, the apes

> became alert to the concept of slavery. And, as their numbers grew . . . [they became alert] to slavery's antidote, which of course is unity. . . . They learned the art of corporate and militant action. They learned to refuse . . . at first they just grunted their refusal . . . but . . . there came [an ape who] did not grunt — he articulated. He spoke a word that had been spoken to him, oh time without number, by humans — he said "No."

Eventually the apes turned the tables on their masters and reversed the domination.

What Cornelius described the apes doing in preparation for their liberation was what African-Americans were in fact doing at the time: engaging in corporate and "militant" action to resist exploitation. Thus this scene was a pivotal part of clarifying the *Apes* series' allegory into one of black-white conflict.

Hasslein sends the president's Science Commission transcripts of Cornelius' and Zira's testimony regarding the development of ape civilization and the eventual destruction of the Earth, a cataclysm he blames on the apes, despite the fact that they had no weapons capable of such destruction. The commission concludes that the apes' progeny could prove an increasing threat to the human race and "conceivably end by dominating it." It therefore recommends that the birth of Zira's child be prevented and that both apes "humanely be rendered incapable of bearing another."

It is telling that those in power do not frame the problem as a dilemma caused by one race oppressing another and thus creating a situation that provoked retaliatory oppression. In such a case, the obvious solution would be to prevent the enslavement of the apes, thereby eliminating both the source of the apes' resentment and their desire for retribution. But the humans in power are not opposed to racial domination in principle, they just want to be the dominators. The problem, as Hasslein and his colleagues see it, is that the apes will one day turn the tables and dominate the humans. The humans demonstrate a depressing lack of imagination: they cannot envision and therefore they cannot create racial peace.

The "solution" they choose is to extinguish the possibility of ape intelligence, and thus resistance, in order to enable continued domination by human beings. In fact, preventing the enslavement of apes would be *more* likely to prevent the later domination by the apes because in ape history as related by Cornelius, it was ape enslavement that was the precursor to ape revolt and the revolt leader had no connection to Zira and Cornelius, who of course were not yet born. It would have been a safe bet that, even if Zira, Cornelius, and their child were killed, a talking ape could independently rise to lead an ape revolution as Cornelius described. Thus eliminating slavery, rather than eliminating Zira and Cornelius and their child, would have offered the best chance of avoiding racial domination. The humans' strategy—destroying those who oppose the problem rather than destroying the problem—resembles the U.S. government's attempts to smash African-American efforts at dissent and opposition rather than eliminating the injustices which led to those efforts and is a classic case of addressing a symptom rather than confronting a cause.

When Zira and Cornelius escape from their human captors, they take refuge in "Armando's Circus." Their baby, named Milo after their deceased traveling companion, is born among the straw-filled cages of the circus. The birth of the ape child in this modern manger creates a tableau reminiscent of a simian "holy family" modeled on the Christian one.

Significantly, Armando (Ricardo Montalban) is Latino. This casting choice once again repeats the structural feature of the oppressed helping the oppressed. *Escape* associate producer Frank Capra, Jr., recalls that Armando was specifically conceived as non–Anglo. Unlike most of the film's Anglo humans, the apes' befrienders Stephanie Branton (Natalie Trundy) and Lewis Dixon (Bradford Dillman) excepted, Armando is opposed to the humans' domination of apes. Similarly, Armando's response to the possibility of ape domination is directly opposite that of the European-born Hasslein. In fact, he declares that he hates "those who try to alter destiny, which is the unalterable will of God. And if it is man's destiny one day to be dominated, then, oh, please God let him be dominated by such as you."

Like his ape counterpart Dr. Zaius, Dr. Otto Hasslein is in certain

Oh, come let us adore him. In the ape nativity scene, the ape holy family welcomes the simian savior in a modern manger.

regards a sympathetic antagonist. He wrestles with at least some of the moral issues involved in the treatment of the apes. When asked by the president (played by white actor William Windom) if, given the power to change the future, they had the right to use that power, Hasslein responds: "I don't know. I've wrestled with this, Mr. President. I just don't know. How many futures are there? And which one has God, if there is a God, chosen for man's destiny? If I urge the destruction of these apes, am I defying God's will or obeying it, am I his enemy or his instrument?"

Although Hasslein is ambivalent, he is also determined. His German name and accent might have raised associations with Nazi fascism, an association made appropriate when Hasslein advocates genocide. The president, however, is more circumspect. Reluctant to murder three innocents to change what is merely a prophesied future, he comments that "Herod tried that, and Christ survived." "Mr. President, Herod lacked our facilities," Hasslein coolly responds. The president points out that Herod "also became very unpopular. Historically unpopular. And we don't want that to happen do we?" The president later expressly forbids Hasslein to kill the apes. Despite the president's orders, Hasslein shoots Zira and the baby she is holding and is then killed by Cornelius, who in turn is shot by the police.

Having established chimpanzees as political dissidents in *Planet* and *Beneath,* in *Escape* the filmmakers portray Zira and Cornelius as threateningly radical. They criticize humanity's habit of self-destruction, speak out against sexism ("A marriage bed is made for two," Zira tells the Bay Area Women's Club "but every damned morning it's the woman who has to make it!"), are appalled by men beating each other up for profit in a boxing match, and are even vegetarians. The apes do not just threaten human domination, they oppose human values.

Calling the film "rather splendid, rather encouraging," *New Yorker* critic Penelope Gilliatt observed that Zira carried a "left-wing carpetbag that looks as if it must be full of pamphlets and wheat germ health foods." Rather taken by Zira and Cornelius, Gilliatt enthusiastically wrote that the couple were

> obviously . . . the most intelligent and radical beings ever depicted on a screen. No film about, say, Mme. Curie or Einstein could hold a candle to this. . . . The chimps . . . are destined to write broadsides, and sit down as pacifists outside embassies, and quietly dominate the thought of mankind. The chimp[s] . . . look extremely like Bertrand Russell — especially the wife.[36]

Exactly one year later, a *Time* magazine article for which Dehn was interviewed would make similar observations: "The chimpanzees . . . are like Bloomsbury intellectuals. . . . 'They're all terribly like Bertrand Russell, my chimpanzees,' muses Dehn, in what is presumably a compliment to both sides."[37]

Symbols of nature, racial and gender equality, anti-exploitation, and pacifism, the apes are killed by a repressive state just as the conservative backlash was gaining force against a counterculture that espoused many of the same values as Zira and Cornelius. The film echoed real life attempts to maintain the traditional order by neutralizing dissent: *Escape* was on the country's movie screens around the same time killings at Kent State were on the country's television screens.

Appeals for racial harmony having again failed, the film ends in violence and blood, the two chimpanzees dead in each others arms, the murdered baby thrown in the water. The baby that is killed, however, is not Milo but a newborn chimpanzee taken from Armando's circus; Zira had secretly switched Milo with him in order to protect her child. The final shot is a hopeful one of the intelligent ape child speaking his first words.

Critic Frederick S. Clarke noted that *Escape* "poses a fascinating question — will baby Milo be the cause of the reversal of the natural order or, having his origins in the future, will he somehow change the course of history so as to avoid enmity between apes and men and the future destruction of the Earth?"[38] In addition to this textual question, *Escape* begins a shift in the thematic direction of the series by asking an important question. Faced with three possibilities—racial domination, the reversal of dominative relations, or nondominative relations—how should one respond? This question is taken up in *Conquest* and is paramount in *Battle*.

After *Planet*, the sequels *Beneath* and *Escape* both extended and explored the conflicts of the first film in ways that, while self-conscious, were not always overt. With *Conquest* came a major break in the style of the *Apes* movies as the filmmakers brought the political concerns of the series to the forefront. *Conquest* and *Battle* complete the shift in the series' focus to the struggle for racial dominance.

THREE

Urban Riots and
Ape Revolution

In the introduction we noted similarities between the *Apes* movies and scientific primatology that enabled the filmmakers to address many of the same issues as did the scientists. While these similarities were substantial, there were also critical differences between the films' underlying ideological charge and that of the primate texts produced by scientific primatologists.

Haraway demonstrates that in the sixties primatology texts like *Miss Goodall and the Wild Chimpanzees* placed Western blond female scientists in proximity to apes as a symbolic reunion with nature from which white Westerners had been recently separated both by decolonization and "the cold war nuclear culture."[1] Haraway notes: "In all these stories humans from scientific cultures are placed in 'nature' in gestures that absolve the reader and viewer of unspoken transgressions, that relieve anxieties of separation and solitary isolation on a threatened planet and for a culture threatened by the consequences of its own history."[2]

The *Apes* series did precisely the opposite. In fact, in direct contrast to other popular primate texts, in *Planet* the blond woman is dead on arrival, denied the opportunity to perform the mediating, soothing function of a Diane Fossey or Jane Goodall. Indictment of humanity's transgressions is a constant refrain in the *Apes* series. Separation and isolation are here intensified into genocidal hostility, and the consequences of history are both unmerciful and inescapable.

Haraway argues that in these works

> the animals are (colored) surrogates for all who have been colonized in the name of nature and whose judgement can no longer be repressed. . . . Black people *were* the beast; it is written into the history of lynching and into the history of biology. It is their accepting touch, coded back onto the animals, that was so ardently sought in the ongoing western narrative of threatened apocalypse [emphasis in original].[3]

78

But primatology can both alleviate and exacerbate Western anxieties. This point is borne out by the fact that the *Apes* films offer much grimmer prospects for negotiating racial estrangement. Taylor in *Planet*, and Stephanie Branton and Louis Dixon in *Escape*, are granted Zira and Cornelius' accepting touch in the form of a handshake and a kiss. As we have seen, however, in each case the touch precedes and underscores the characters' ultimate separation from each other.

Moreover, each of these characters who receives that touch is an individual who is alienated from his or her own people. Zira and Cornelius are also renegades from their society; therefore whatever reconciliation is achieved is strictly personal, not collective. The desired gesture of reconciliation and collective absolution was precisely the gesture that most of the *Apes* films denied. And even in *Battle*, when reconciliation between human and nature, human and ape, and white and black are possible, it is only barely so, and the reality of decolonization (the newly liberated apes) and the threat of nuclear devastation (the nuclear irradiated humans and their doomsday bomb) remain powerfully present.

The *Apes* films for the most part did not serve as symbolic mediators for the Western "crises" of separation, loss, guilt, and anxiety brought on by decolonization and the black liberation movement. The *Apes* movies typically figure this estrangement as unresolvable. Nowhere is the sense of racial alienation more evident in the *Apes* series than in the violent *Conquest*.

In 1965, as Arthur Jacobs was struggling to get *Planet of the Apes* made, Malcolm X predicted:

> The "long hot summer" of 1964 in Harlem, in Rochester, and in other cities, has given an idea of what could happen — and that's all, only an idea. . . . You name the city. Black social dynamite is in Cleveland, Philadelphia, San Francisco, Los Angeles . . . the black man's anger is there, fermenting. . . . In this year 1965, I am certain that more — and worse — riots are going to erupt, in yet more cities, in spite of the conscience-salving Civil Rights Bill. The reason is that the *cause* of these riots, the racist malignancy in America, has been too long unattended [emphasis in original].[4]

Historian Harvard Sitkoff writes that between 1965 and 1968 three hundred race-related disturbances and race-related violent confrontations, usually referred to as "riots," gripped the nation, involving an estimated half million African-Americans, a number equivalent to the number of U.S. soldiers serving at the time in Vietnam. The battles resulted in over eight thousand casualties.

Set off by a scuffle between Los Angeles police and the mother of a drunken driving suspect, the most famous of these confrontations occurred in the summer of 1965 in Watts, a Los Angeles black ghetto. It lasted six days and involved fourteen thousand National Guardsmen and fifteen hundred law enforcement officers battling an estimated fifty thousand African-Americans. In 1967 alone there were almost 150 disturbances in cities all over the country, including Boston, Chicago, Dayton, Detroit, San Francisco and New Haven. The far right advocated that whites arm themselves against a Communist-inspired black insurrection.[5]

The Kerner Commission assigned to investigate and report on the country's numerous civil disorders starkly concluded that the United States was disuniting and "moving toward two societies, one black and one white — separate and unequal." In a nation as multiracial and multiethnic as the United States, the complexities of racial inequalities and conflict go beyond issues of black and white. It is in terms of black and white, however, that racial difference is most often perceived and discussed. And the two nations metaphor, while incompletely accounting for the racial, ethnic, class, and gender complexities of American life, accurately described the political *perceptions* of and — even more importantly here — *the cultural response to* the country's racial alienation.

As the *Apes* series implied that blacks and whites were so alienated from each other that they required symbolic representation as entirely different species, many saw the domestic conflicts between blacks and whites as analogous to a war between two nations. African-Americans and European-Americans alike characterized the urban violence with words such as "siege," "revolt," "insurrection," and "pacification" — the rhetoric and terminology of the Vietnam War.

Typical of this comparison was the article "Trigger of Hate" in the August 20, 1965, issue of *Time* magazine, which stated that "the atmosphere reminded soldiers of embattled Saigon"[6] and invoked five war-related terms, "war weary," "pitched gun battle," "white flag," "regroup," and "battleground," in one single paragraph to describe the riots. The article also quoted California Governor Pat Brown referring to the Watts riots as a war.[7]

It was not just the white press and white politicians who were comparing the racial conflict at home with that abroad; respected African-American leaders like Robert Moses, for example, had drawn the same analogy. An anonymous leaflet distributed in Chicago, presumably by a non-white person, during the violence that erupted after a speeding fire truck accidentally killed an African-American woman, linked U.S. urban riots to a worldwide battle of white against non-white and framed the riots as defiance against "the same rulers who are making war on working people throughout the world in Vietnam, the Dominican Republic, and the Congo."[8]

And the traditional association of non-whites with apes and monkeys was invoked to explain the Watts riots when Los Angeles Police Chief William Parker likened those who took part in the riots to "monkeys in a zoo ... throwing rocks."[9]

Concurrent with the increasing urban violence, the black liberation movement was engaged in confrontational rhetoric and increasingly hostile action. Along with the rise in the call for Black Power came an increased push for black autonomy of groups working for black liberation. Asserting the need for black self-determination, groups that previously had strong white liberal support, such as the Student Non-violent Coordinating Committee, excluded their white members. The call of "We Shall Overcome" was challenged by the cry of "We Shall Overrun." These developments and the often misunderstood call for "Black Power" made many whites, including many who had been supportive of black liberation, nervous about the future of U.S. race relations. The assassination of Reverend Doctor Martin Luther King, Jr., was a further blow to the efforts to maintain progressive, nonviolent, transracial political alliances. In the midst of these turmoils, the apocalyptic *Planet of the Apes* and its sequels transferred the racial turmoil of the times into a less threatening science fiction context.

Sitkoff writes that in 1966, "hardly a day seemed to pass without the evening news showing film of surging black mobs breaking windows, smashing cars, ransacking stores, putting the torch to white businesses, and hurling bricks at embattled police and firemen."[10] In 1972, American audiences would see those same scenes of racial explosion repeated on movie screens across the nation.

Given the common linkage of issues of race to discourses about apes and monkeys and the fact that the Vietnam War was quickly and repeatedly invoked as an explanatory metaphor for the urban riots, it is not surprising that the *Planet of the Apes* series, which had allegorized Vietnam, would later be used to address these very riots. *Conquest of the Planet of the Apes* was "absolutely based on the Watts riots"[11] and is the centerpiece of the *Apes* saga's racial allegory.

Since the release of *Planet*, the *Apes* films had been recognized by audiences and critics as commentary on U.S. race conflict. *Conquest* intentionally mined and developed that theme more extensively. As we have noted, the sharpening focus on domestic racial conflict was a logical progression in the series. Change in the series may also be seen as a predictable characteristic of a serial format. As in any series or genre, repetition eventually allowed the *Apes* filmmakers to bring out what was originally latent. Revisiting source material invites, indeed may demand, innovation and variation in order to differentiate later works from the original and avoid redundancy. Consequently over time, in order to keep the material fresh and interesting to the audience and to themselves, artists may shift focus or explore different possibilities within the original framework. Thus as Jacobs embarked on his fourth *Apes* production and Paul Dehn wrote his third *Apes* screenplay, the production process and the movies became more self-consciously political.

Conquest introduced another significant element into the thematic development of the *Apes* property. With *Conquest*, J. Lee Thompson took over the series as director. Known for his action pictures like *Guns of Navarone* (1961) and the original 1962 *Cape Fear*, Thompson had worked with Jacobs early in the difficult process to obtain financial backing to produce *Planet*. Thompson believes that concern over the potential political content was one of the reasons that Jacobs had difficulty securing studio funding for *Planet*.[12]

Thompson had been kept from directorial involvement with the series due to other commitments, but he stayed interested in the series. Thompson says he recognized early on the potential racial themes of the Apes films, and once he came back to the material, he foregrounded its racial content and brought a major shift to the character of the *Apes* saga.

A recent article by Andrew Asch reports that Thompson was "riveted to his television during the 1965 Watts riots. He felt that the mayhem he saw on TV could be a precursor to a larger race war . . . and felt that it was important to depict the rage that exploded in the Watts riots." According to the article, Thompson kept this "dream alive . . . [and] recalls suggesting a Watts riot allegory to . . . Paul Dehn." Thus, unlike *Escape* director Don Taylor, who had sought to underplay the "sociological overtones" of the series, Thompson focused on those overtones and unabashedly moved racial conflict to the forefront.

This more explicitly political tone is a significant difference between the first three films and the last two. No longer is racial conflict delicately handled. As their titles suggest, *Conquest* and *Battle* deal with the issue openly, brutally, even disturbingly, and indicate an increased sense of crisis. In each previous *Apes* film, racial hostility cannot be contained and erupts in violence. In Thompson's two installments, the violence is even more intense. In addition to the urban violence of the proceeding years, *Conquest* is also an expression of and a response to the anxiety evoked by the rise of the "Black Power" slogan and the changes in the black liberation movement.

As *Conquest* was being made, *Conquest* screenwriter Paul Dehn commented in an interview: "It's a very curious thing that the *Apes* series has always been tremendously popular with Negroes who identify themselves with the apes. They are Black Power just as the apes are Ape Power and they enjoy it greatly."[13] It is difficult to know precisely what Dehn meant by the last sentence or if his assertion of African-American identification with the apes is accurate. Regardless of the ways African-Americans actually experienced the films, however, Dehn's comment is sufficient evidence of at least three important facts: first, that by at least the time of *Conquest*, Dehn, who had also written the scripts for *Beneath* and *Escape*, was aware of and spoke on the record about the racial content of the *Apes* saga; second, that he was convinced that black (and perhaps white?) viewers were aware of the racial content as well; and third, that, even if no one else was, Dehn *himself* was associating the apes with blacks.

That Dehn was consciously associating the apes with blacks and constructing the *Conquest* screenplay as an allegory of United States white-black conflict is absolutely clear in his original *Conquest* story outline. In the outline, Zira and Cornelius' son, now renamed Caesar, is evading the authorities by masquerading as a human named "Caesar the Monkey-Faced Boy" in Armando's circus. When the government begins to suspect that he is not a human "freak" but an ape, he runs away on Armando's suggestion.

Meanwhile, a plague accidently brought back to Earth by astronauts, which is harmless to humans, kills off all the dogs and cats. Apes are taken into human homes as pets, later as servants, and then as slaves. Caesar is eventually captured and sold into bondage. Once enslaved, he starts teaching the other apes to resist. Caesar later meets Wayne, one of the astronauts who brought back the plague. Feeling guilty both for the animal deaths caused by the germ he was carrying and for the resulting ape enslavement, Wayne dedicates himself to ape liberation. Caesar reveals his identity and parentage to Wayne, who then buys Caesar from his cruel master. Eventually, as in the final film, Caesar leads the apes in a revolution that frees them from captivity.

Dehn's outline is filled with explicit comparisons of the oppression of apes to the oppression of Africans. He explains that "an Ape Slave Trade has developed, and [apes] of the three main species are being shipped and freighted from Africa and South America to be sold at public auction like the Negroes of old" and notes that Caesar is "whipped as the Negro slaves were."[14] Dehn also linked the plight of the apes to that of African-Americans in the twentieth century United States when he specified that apes "travel (in the *back seats* only) of buses" (emphasis in original).[15] And the outline unambiguously demonstrates that Dehn was basing the story on the tensions between black "radicals" and white "liberals." Dehn notes that "under harsh treatment . . . Caesar becomes embittered and militant." "Militant" was and is still a catch-all term used to express disapproval of blacks rightly or wrongly considered "extreme." Similarly, the human characters in the story note that the previously "diffident, more docile" Caesar is developing "a hint more pride and fanaticism." The human's reaction to Caesar's uncompromising demands for ape liberation was modeled on the discomfort many whites felt about the political positions of black radicals.

That the tensions between white liberals and black radicals and the anxiety provoked by the term "Black Power" were inspiration for *Conquest* is further evident when Dehn describes the interaction between Caesar and Armando when Caesar and Wayne come to recruit his help. "We begin to suspect that Caesar is being nice to Armando because he wants to *use* him [emphasis in original]. Does he feel the same way about Wayne? (Compare a black man 'using' a liberal white for the same end.)" Dehn then notes the increasing estrangement between Wayne and Caesar: "Both were previously in favor of peaceful demonstrations. Now Caesar is for violence. Wayne works for ape liberation; Caesar, for Ape Power."[16]

Although there were occasional comparisons to real-world events in previous *Apes* outlines and scripts, never before had the political inspiration of the films been so noticeably integral to the story development of an *Apes* picture. The ruptured relationship between white liberals and black radicals and the apprehension over Black Power were at the heart of the story outline's conflict, and it is significant that despite major story changes these anxieties remained central in the final film.

Given the ominous connotations in Dehn's use of the term "Ape Power" in the Ursus speech from *Beneath* and the negative context in which he uses the term in the *Conquest* outline, we could expect that Dehn held a similarly negative view of Black Power. However, even though Dehn's reaction to the term "Black Power" suggests that he too mistook the slogan as a synonym for reverse racism, *Conquest* is the first film in the series in which the darkest apes, the gorillas, are sympathetic characters.

While we cannot be as certain as Dehn about African-American response to the films, *Conquest of the Planet of the Apes* does share some of the appeal of the "blaxploitation" action films that were directed toward African-American audiences in the early seventies. As in the blaxploitation films, *Conquest*'s main protagonist is non-white and as in the blaxploitation films, *Conquest* shows non-whites defeating White Power. According to Thompson, "White audiences saw this as a genre movie, but Black audiences understood the politics of *Conquest* immediately and cheered for it."[17] A British magazine about the *Apes* films noted this affinity and even asserted that the series' racial overtones were "quickly noted by Black Americans, cheering with plenty of 'Right On' cries, for the apes against whitey. The series therefore indirectly spawned the recent black movie thriller genre."[18] These assertions of audience reaction are unverifiable, and the claim of causation is simply incorrect. However, while no direct connection might have been intended, it is more than coincidental that *Conquest* came out at the height of the blaxploitation genre's popularity.

The year prior to *Conquest*, one of the most widely acknowledged classics of the genre, Melvin Van Peebles' *Sweet Sweetback's Baadasssss Song* was released along with the popular *Shaft*. The year *Conquest* was released, 1972, also saw the release, among others, of *Superfly*, *Shaft's Big Score*, *Blacula*, the Westerns *Buck and the Preacher* and *The Legend of Nigger Charley*,[19] *Come Back Charleston Blue*, a sequel to *Cotton Comes to Harlem* (1970), and *The Man*, written by *Planet* co-writer Rod Serling based on Irving Wallace's best-seller, about the first African-American president of the United States.[20]

Some important countercultural films showing Native Americans in a more sympathetic light were also contemporary with the *Apes* movies, including *A Man Called Horse* (1969), *Soldier Blue* (1970), *Little Big Man* (1970), *Billy Jack* (1971), and *Return of a Man Called Horse* (1972). Like the blaxploitation and Native American films, the *Apes* series, especially *Escape* and *Conquest*, could only have been possible during a historical moment that produced not only a greater interest in films starring non-whites but also a willingness among some audiences to see the traditionally accepted valence of racial heroism reversed, or at least challenged. Responding to the country's political currents, movies no longer assumed that cowboys were by definition the good guys; and the nation's stock racial villains, Native Americans and African-Americans, could now be shown heroically or at least more sympathetically.[21]

While *Conquest* is akin to the blaxploitation genre in some of the pleasures it offered, there is a fundamental difference: *Conquest* allows the expression of impassioned resentment of and violent resistance to the racist police state, but the trade-off is to keep the expression of these resentments and resistance safe by denying them to the African-American characters and by displacing political radicalism onto the apes.

However, this strategy did not—and was not intended to—totally obscure the issues at hand. Reviews of the film indicate that racial oppression and resistance were recognized as *Conquest's* core issues. For instance, the June 14, 1972, review in *Daily Variety* noted that "minority group injustices and civil rebellion comprise the plot line, with quite obvious parallels to contemporary society" and stated that Caesar "has to Uncle Tom his way through the prevailing slave environment."[22] And an article which appeared shortly before the release of *Conquest* in *Time* magazine noted that

> All the pictures have had deliberate racial overtones that are far from flattering to whites; the oppression of the apes has been equated with the denial of civil rights to U.S. blacks. In *Conquest*, the racial parallel will be explicit. The climatic uprising, says Dehn "is a little bit like the Watts riot."[23]

Thus, even before the film was released, the expectation was that *Conquest* would more directly address the political implications of the *Apes* material. More recently, Vivian Sobchack has noted that *Conquest* "continues the racial themes of the earlier films with more insistence."[24]

The political, and in particular the racial, dimensions of the *Apes* saga were indeed more explicitly highlighted in *Conquest* than in the previous films. Thompson's description of the film's production offers some insight into the way that race was coded both as species and as color:

> Both the stylistic and the thematic concept is that the film should give a feeling of a state that is under domination by a growing dictatorship. The people, the ordinary civilians, in the film are very colorless; the only colorful people in the film are the apes who wear red, green, and yellow. . . . The people do not wear colored clothes. It is in this respect that we give it this cold, dehumanized look.[25]

Thus the humans in the film were, in fact, dehumanized. And, deliberately, the most human of them was an African-American and therefore literally and metaphorically the most "colored." This racial concept pervades the entire film. In fact, while the *Time* article is correct in stating that all the *Apes* films had been "far from flattering to whites," *Conquest* is the only film in the series in which there are absolutely no sympathetic white characters.

Armando is interrogated in the office of the oppressive white Governor Breck (Don Murray). The office has an engulfing stark white look, thereby associating the room's relentless whiteness with the governor's ruthless malevolence. Thus conflict in the film was conceived and presented as a struggle between the noncolored and the colored. And with its uprising of ape slaves imported from places such as Africa and Indonesia, *Conquest* depicts a "third-world" revolt by a colored horde laying siege to the command post of a white Western power. All the film needed was Charlton Heston to defend the fort.[26]

One of the principal strategies used to emphasize *Conquest*'s political implications is a different orientation to time. While each film is set in the audience's future, *Conquest* continued *Escape*'s dramatic shift of concern from possible future to actual present, precognition to recognition, and made the implicit explicit.[27] In all five of the films, time, history, and memory are important concerns. But the first three films are all primarily concerned with humanity's potential future. *Planet* and *Beneath* envision that future, and *Escape* depicts Hasslein's attempts to change it. *Conquest* is a break with that fixation — concern is here with the immediate situation in the film. *Conquest*, though textually oriented toward the future, subtextually referenced the audience's past to address the audience's present.

With their constant shifting of time frames, the *Apes* films' relation to time is somewhat complicated. In *Conquest*, Caesar is aided in his struggle to attain freedom for his fellow apes by MacDonald, the governor's African-American assistant. Now here is where it gets tricky: the film was released in 1972, and in it Caesar's present (nineties) is set in the audience's future (nineties) and resembles MacDonald's past (mid–sixties to early seventies) which was in fact the audiences present. So while the film was set in the future, that future most directly resembled the audience's present. The series' temporal displacement therefore results, in this installment, in bringing attention directly to, and anchoring it to, the audience's present.

The second part of the *Apes* series is no more dystopian than the first,

Conquest's advertisements resembled those of Heston epics such as *Ben-Hur: A Tale of the Christ* and *El Cid*, thus signaling that like these films, *Conquest* was about racial battles and the falling and rising of empires.

but there is a crucial difference. In the first two films, the dystopian cataclysm depicted exists only in the imagination and is set far in the future. However, by reflecting more directly the conditions of contemporary U.S. society and by modeling the later films more closely on cataclysms in the audience's memory such as the Nazi holocaust and the urban racial violence of the sixties, the filmmakers brought the films closer to home and conveyed a more intense feeling of relevance and danger. *Planet* and *Beneath* take place in the aftermath of a racial apocalypse in which human characters ask, "How did this happen?" *Escape* and *Conquest* showed what happened to bring on that apocalypse — and what led to the cataclysm on the planet of the apes looked a lot like what was actually happening in the United States. In the latter two films of the series, the characters' questions change from "what happened" to "what is happening and where will it lead?" The *Apes* series warns that racial domination must stop lest it result in revolt and reversal.

Conquest's first dialogue establishes the importance of both time and the identification with a particular time frame. Armando and Caesar (Roddy McDowall) have flown to a major city by helicopter to promote Armando's circus, which is traveling in the area. Their identity cards are checked by two "state security officers." Armando proudly mentions that Caesar is the only ape "ever to have been trained as a bareback rider in the entire history of the circus." "Circuses are *past* history," one of the officers caustically replies. "Not while I live and breathe," is Armando's determined response. Armando here is temporally bracketed and linked to another time, a time when apes were not enslaved, when they were still the objects of benevolent, albeit paternalistic, amusement and affection. Even the name of his circus, the site of continued compassionate treatment of animals, reflects the importance of this time orientation. In *Escape*, it was simply "Armando's Circus." In *Conquest*, it is called "Armando's *Old Time* Circus" (emphasis added). The name shift emphasizes that Armando and his values are out of their time. Armando's earlier appearance in *Escape*, his selfless assistance to Zira and Cornelius, and the fact that this appearance was set in the audience's time (early seventies) would presumably link him with the audience and make it more likely that audiences would identify with him.

Armando is also spatially set apart from the slave state. His circus, we find out later, travels in the outlying provinces, which presumably, not being major centers of production and consumption, are free of the institution of slavery. He is thus out of place in the oppressive city. Armando's values, symbolized by his admiration of Saint Francis of Assisi for Francis' love and kind treatment of animals, are also of another time and place and are the opposite of the values of the racist police state.

Armando's defiant declaration that circuses will not be "past history" as long he "lives and breathes" foreshadows his death. His death is important for the story's progression because it is after he is killed that Caesar begins planning the ape revolt. That is, when Armando, the symbol of the treatment of apes as pets, as objects, is destroyed, so is that option for apes. When Armando dies, so does the possibility of apes remaining in obsequious deference or subordination. Deference and subordination were the same conditions then being rejected by African-Americans. Following Armando's death, Caesar could not, even if he wanted to, go back to being objectified as a pet, just as he would not allow himself to remain a slave. Through Armando's death the film limits the possibilities for apes to either enslavement or freedom.

While there are crucial shifts from the rest of the series, *Conquest* is by no means totally disjunctive from the other *Apes* movies in its treatment of time, history, and memory. Whether characters such as Cornelius and Hasslein seek to uncover the past, or, as in the case of Zaius, seek to obscure it, knowledge and memory of the past are presented as the key to understanding and controlling the present and the future. *Conquest* itself is an attempt at influencing the present and future by referencing the past.

As we have seen, cultural products work by accessing our cultural memories. This is especially the case with parts in a series, in this case with film sequels, where memories of earlier films are relevant as characters, conflicts, and storylines established in the original are continued, developed, even altered, in subsequent installments. *Conquest*, although no longer directly chronicling the lives of the main characters of the first three films, relies on the audience's memory of several elements from those films, including the constant animosity between apes and human beings, the alliances formed by "good" apes and "good" humans, the prediction of ape enslavement and revolt, the continual alignment with chimpanzees, the affiliation with Zira and Cornelius, and the hope for apekind and subsequent "threat" to humanity posed by their child. Thus even though *Conquest* introduces an almost entirely new set of characters, the film is intertextually bound with the earlier *Apes* movies which retain a presence here, just as it is extratextually bound with the societal pressures which helped produce it.

In addition to these internal references, *Conquest* establishes the terms of its conflict by playing on the audience's memory of extratextual historical references. A carefully constructed world is built around references to recent historical episodes of racial oppression. The most important reference is to the racial violence that shook the United States during the years preceding the release of the film.

As Thompson has confirmed, *Conquest* was based on the Watts riots. The images of the ape revolt, a sort of simian version of Nat Turner's insurrection, included destruction of stores, several fires, and altercations between dark-skinned "rioters" and light-skinned armored police officers — all of which recall vivid scenes of similar rage and destruction that rocked urban areas in the mid- to late-sixties. Watching the destruction in the film evokes memories of the then-prevalent call to "Burn, Baby, Burn." Even the hand-held photography in the ape revolt scenes conveys the visceral sense of confusion, danger, and fear reminiscent of television news footage that audiences would likely have seen of race riots across the country. Watching a sequence of similar events, the causes and anxieties of the original conflicts which the film resembles would have been in the audience's memory.

Interestingly, the screenplay makes no specific reference to the Watts riots as a model, although the script's stage directions refer to the rebelling apes as "rioters" and the script does compare the ape uprising to the Attica prison rebellion, an event which also had significant racial dimensions. Also of note is that Hari Rhodes, who portrayed MacDonald, recalls no discussions on the set concerning *Conquest*'s racial themes.[28] This may be because the racial content was obvious enough not to require any comment. It may also be that the themes of racial oppression and revolution with which the film deals were too difficult and threatening to discuss openly. This may in fact be one of the reasons that a film about the Watts riots had to be disguised as a film about an ape revolt. Indeed, as we will discuss, the film does attempt to gain a safe psychological distance from the core subject matter by disclaiming its actual intentions. After all, we are to believe that *Conquest* is not a statement about black uprisings, but a science fiction story about talking apes. In fact, this disclaimer seems to have worked so well as to convince even some who were substantially involved with the film's production. Frank Capra, Jr., who served as associate producer on the last three *Apes* films, while acknowledging that it is possible that the political concerns of the time might have "subliminally" affected the development of the film, saw no racial content in the film and feels that *Conquest* "didn't intentionally try to draw off the Watts riots or any other riots."[29] There is no reason to assume that Capra was deliberately lying. Rather, this disagreement between Capra on the one hand and Dehn and Thompson on the other demonstrates that films are collective efforts and that those involved in making a film may have very different understandings of it and may be unaware, at least consciously, of just what it can mean. Again, artists' intentions do not control meaning.

In addition to the violent racial clashes of the sixties, *Conquest* is constructed around a constellation of visual and historical references to other instances of racial conflict and resistance to oppression. In the depiction of slavery and the low-status occupations that the apes are assigned—for example, janitors, shoe shiners, bus boys, domestic servants, and window washers—the enslavement and continued exploitation of African-Americans are recalled, as is the status of other racial minorities such as

In *Conquest*, numerous images of enslavement link ape slaves to African-Americans.

Latinos, albeit less directly. The abusive treatment of the apes by the state security forces recalls police brutality against African-Americans. The ape slave auction and the importation of ape slaves from Africa are both allusions to the American slave trade. And all of this was presented at a time of great interest in the historiography and legacy of slavery.

In addition to the revolt scenes, the film refers to the racial strife of the time through numerous allusions to recent political conflict: a protest by human waiters who have been displaced by ape slave labor, recalling the tensions of white blue collar workers with racial minorities and immigrants; an unauthorized gathering of apes refusing to disperse, similar to sit-ins in the sixties; a scene of a tired ape female being shocked by police with a cattle prod for sitting on a humans-only bench, reminiscent of sit-ins, of police use of cattle prods against civil rights demonstrators, and of Rosa Parks' refusal to go to the back of the bus; and Caesar's final speech, which bears a resemblance to the confrontational rhetoric of black nationalism. When he is sold as slave labor to the governor and forced to hide his ability to speak, Caesar's experience also echoes that of many African-Americans, who have donned the mask of supplication in order to hide the face of rebellion. He becomes a "house slave" in order to tear the house down.

And with its seemingly omnipresent security forces' uniforms resembling those of the Nazi gestapo, its chimpanzee armbands resembling those worn by prisoners in the ghettos and Nazi murder camps, and Breck's entrapment in an underground command post reminiscent of Hitler's bunker, the authoritarian human state bears striking resemblances to the Nazi Third Reich and the Nazi holocaust. One scene juxtaposes the Nazi-looking troops with a government announcement that the ape revolt can be controlled if the police are given "complete freedom of movement." The scene thereby critiques the prevalent conservative discourse of "law and order" by linking it to fascism. Although set nineteen years in the audience's future, the film invoked and mobilized painful memories of both the audience's distant and recent past and its current crises to provoke a response.

The film not only references particular conflicts of U.S. history and culture, but also employs religious motifs three thousand years old. As this was to be a film about a people rising up from slavery, Caesar bore resemblances to a powerful archetype of that theme: Moses. We have previously noted the parallels in the depiction of Caesar and the depiction of the Christ: Caesar's place of birth resembles a twentieth century manger; his parents are hunted by Hasslein as Jesus' parents were by Herod, to whom Hasslein is compared; he is figured as a mystical presence with uplifting powers for his people; and the religious mythology of the apes later explicitly names Caesar as a savior sent by their god.

But the resonances with Moses and the Exodus tale are even more extensive: as was the case with Moses, Caesar's birth and destiny are prophesied; attempts are made to kill him as a baby; he is hidden and raised in the home of one of the dominant group; he grows up unaware of his true identity and the enslaved condition of his people; when he becomes aware of these things, he infiltrates and joins them; he commits violent acts against the masters, who attempt to eliminate him; and he leads the exodus from enslavement, is established as leader and, as we see in *Battle*, never quite reaches the promised land. The application of the narrative elements of the Exodus tale to *Conquest* is an attempt to underscore the themes and deepen the meaning of the film's story by setting it within a sacred precedent.[30] *Conquest* replays the biblical paradigm so that the audience more readily appreciates who are the good guys, who are the bad guys, and just what is at stake.

In the role of Pharaoh is Governor Jason Breck. Unlike Zaius and Hasslein, he is an entirely unsympathetic antagonist. Obsessed with security and possessing high political ambitions, he presides over a tightly monitored slave society. Masters are held accountable if their apes are found in the wrong place. The right of human labor to assemble and bargain collectively is controlled and may be repealed by the government. (Undoubtedly the threat of replacement by ape labor would be a tool used to control worker demands.) Armando, held in custody without being charged, is read no rights, given no legal counsel, and is compelled to deliver a confession against his will.[31]

Obsessed with rising ape I.Q.'s and disobedience, Breck rhetorically asks how many apes there are "all burning with resentment, waiting for an ape with enough will, with enough intelligence to lead them. Waiting for an ape who can think, who can talk?" Breck's fear that an ape who can talk might have the intelligence to lead the other apes recalls the fear of talking humans expressed in *Planet* (Taylor notes that his appearance has sent Zaius into "a panic") and *Beneath* (Cornelius warns Brent that if the gorillas "catch you speaking, they will dissect you, and they will kill you, in that order") and the fear of talking apes in *Escape*. This fear is a constant concern in the first four films.

The preoccupation, especially in *Conquest*, mimics the intense fear of slave literacy and the need to suppress it in order to maintain a racial power imbalance favorable to whites.[32] Not unlike the way we view literacy, speech in the *Apes* films is seen as perhaps the most important expression of intelligence and is attributed an almost magical power to empower one to understand and control one's circumstances. Also, like literacy and education, speech in the *Apes* films is one of the most crucial boundaries between the enslaver and the enslaved. Thus Zaius and Governor Breck are terrified by, respectively, the prospect of a talking human or a talking ape and attempt to conceal knowledge of and destroy that threat.

Likewise, Breck's obsession with the rising I.Q. of the apes is an inverse mirror image of the obsession of many whites with "proving" the low intelligence and inferiority of African-Americans, Jews, Eastern Europeans, and other "non–Nordics" by using suspect I.Q. tests. Skewed, specious, and questionably interpreted "intelligence testing" has been a common device for promulgating racist claims of the inferiority of "non–Whites" and has been effectively used by eugenicists and nativists to shape social policies, including immigration restriction and forced sterilization of the genetically "inferior" and "undesirable."[33] These perverse pronouncements, no matter how questionable the conclusions, no matter how many times their methodology is debunked and their motives discredited, are ritually resurrected whenever the comforting shibboleths of white supremacy need reassuring.[34]

Breck's heart having been hardened, he is obsessed by his fear and hatred of the apes and seems to take a cruel pleasure in subjugating them. He is paranoid about disobedient "servant" apes and is determined to "crush them once and for all." As the apes attack his headquarters, Breck rages: "If we lose this battle it's the end of the world as we know it. We will have proved ourselves weak—inferior. And all those groveling cowards who are alive when the battle is over will be the weakest of all. This will be the end of human civilization and the world will belong to a planet of apes."

On the one hand we know that he is right. It is precisely the beginning of ape rule that the audience has come to see. Yet his rantings somehow still seem melodramatic and unlikely to elicit sympathy. Breck's one humane moment is when he decides not to subject Caesar to additional torture once he has forced Caesar to reveal that he can talk. He says, almost pityingly, "he's not responsible for what he is." But that brief moment of sympathy is negated in the next line when he malevolently continues, "but looking at him . . . it's like seeing a deadly bacillus . . . and knowing you've got it bottled up at last."

The intensity of Breck's hatred and paranoia seem totally incomprehensible until we are afforded a glimpse into his racist psychology and see why the apes pose such a threat to him. Following the apes' takeover of Breck's command post, Caesar asks Breck why human beings enslaved apes. Breck's response is delivered with a classic mixture of self- and other-hatred:

> CAESAR: Tell me, Breck . . . how do we differ from the dogs and cats you and your kind used to love? Why did you turn us from pets into slaves?
>
> BRECK: Because *your* kind were once our ancestors. Man was born of the ape and there's still an ape curled up inside of every man. The beast that must be whipped into submission. The savage that has to be shackled in chains. You are the beast Caesar. You *taint* us. You poison our guts. When we hate you, we're hating the dark side of ourselves [emphasis in original].[35]

On its face this may seem only dialogue from a science fiction movie. It is, however, in fact a rather insightful statement about the dynamic of fear and projection underlying the racism of white against non-white in which "the other is not seen for what it is but for what it evokes."[36] A similar ideology has influenced white attitudes toward Native Americans. Richard Slotkin points out that Puritan writers saw Native Americans as the embodiment of "devilish propensities inherent in sinful flesh" and "romantic writers from Cooper to Melville had seen dark-skinned peoples as incarnations of the 'dark side' of human character, embodiments of both the creativity and the erotic peril of the libido."[37]

Winthrop Jordan, replicating the voice of a white racist, illustrates a similar combination of paranoia and hypocrisy: "We do not lust and destroy; it is someone else. We are not great black bucks of the fields. But a buck *is* loose, his great horns menacing to gore into us with life and destruction. Chain him, either chain him or expel his black shape from our midst, before we realize it is ourselves" (emphasis in original).[38] Breck's explanation of the psychological underpinnings of slavery may not be kind or even fair, but it is at least honest and does resonate with other attempts to justify racial oppression. Note how closely Breck's anxiety and irrational rationalization resemble those of the early twentieth century eugenicist T. L. Stoddard:

> Each of us has within him an "Under-Man," that primitive animality which is the heritage of our human, and even our prehuman, past. This Under-Man may be buried deep in the recesses of our being; but he is there, and psychoanalysis informs us of his latent power. This primitive animality, potentially present even in the noblest natures, continuously dominates the lower social strata, especially the pauper, criminal and degenerate elements — civilization's "inner barbarians."

And so to maintain the "stability" of society, and even the "stability" of those of "the noblest nature" in whom the "Under-Man" potentially still lurks, both the outer barbarians swelling in the "rising tide of color" and those "inner barbarians," "paupers," and "degenerates" in "the lower strata" must be brutally repressed, for

> The social revolution is now in full swing. Such upheavals are profoundly terrible. . . . [They are] "throwbacks" to a far lower social plane. The complex fabric of society, slowly and painfully woven, is torn into tatters; the social controls vanish, and civilization is left naked to the assaults of anarchy. . . . Not only is society in the grip of its barbarians, but every individual falls more or less under the sway of his own lower instincts. For in this respect the individual is like society. When society's dregs boil to the top, a similar process takes place in individuals, to whatever social level they belong. In virtually every member of the community there is a distinct resurgence of the brute and the savage, and the atavistic trend thus becomes practically universal. . . .[39]

Stoddard was a favorite of Adolph Hitler, who based his Nazi eugenics courts and forced sterilization law on models put forth by *U.S.* eugenicists. By the time Stoddard visited Germany's eugenics court in 1940 (when he called one man who came before the court "ape-like"), the court had sterilized 375,000 and would eventually sterilize two million human beings. Nevertheless, Stoddard described the court as "truly humanitarian" and even expressed concern that it was "too merciful."[40]

It is important to bear in mind that Stoddard was *not* dismissed as some kind of racist lunatic. Quite the contrary, Stoddard, a Harvard-educated historian and lawyer, was highly influential in U.S. intellectual, cultural, and political circles, as were a great number of his colleagues.[41] Despite the acceptability that his ideas were granted, his ravings are rather explicit evidence of James Baldwin's observations that the problem of identity involves "a terror as primary as the nightmare of the mortal fall" and that an identity is questioned when it is menaced, "when the wretched begin to rise"—as, for instance, in the "rising tide of color against white world supremacy"—when "the stranger's presence [makes] you the stranger, less to the stranger than to yourself."[42]

Even after the Nazis carried his ideas to their deadly logical conclusion, the influence of Stoddard's language and ideology still registered in the public debate over race during the height of the sixties' racial violence. In 1965, for example, *Time* magazine printed a letter about the Watts riots from a reader in New Mexico who hoped that the riots would "serve to convince some Northerners what Southerners have always known—that the majority of nigras are unstable, subhuman savages. When the riot scratched the fragile 'civilized' crust of [a black biochemistry graduate in an earlier *Time* article] the despoiler and murderer of the Belgian nuns in the Congo was revealed."[43]

The letter, which could have been written by Stoddard himself, reiterates an "underman" argument: Blacks are by nature savage, lurking beasts waiting to rise up, rape, and ruin the "civilization" to which they are unassimilable. The assertion that within the seemingly "civilized" educated black man lies murderers from the Congo is an essentialist claim mystifying race and suggesting that all black people are identical and can be simplified and abstracted into a savage essence. The pernicious slander of Stoddard and his ilk is, like a tenacious virus, with us still.

Thus while Governor Breck's ideology is unreasonable, it is not at all unprecedented and was—and is—a part of the nation's shared political and cultural vocabulary. Breck's language of "taint" and "poison," for instance, recalls both the dogma of racial "purists" and the pollution language of Ursus in *Beneath*. His fixation on order and his dread of apocalyptic social change is a filmic embodiment of age-old ideologies of racial superiority and subordination. And Breck employs the "solution" that Stoddard himself advocated, the solution that the apes of *Planet* and *Beneath* used for their human problem, the solution that has been employed so many times throughout history: absolute, brutally violent, self-mortification through the persecution of a constructed "other," created in one's own image, onto whom is projected one's own insecurities, fears, and ultimately one's own guilt.[44]

As we see in the film, and in history, that persecution is directly proportional to the fear of the "crisis," internal or external, that must be overcome. Concerned with the "rising tide of disobedience" (Stoddard's concern, remember, was with a "rising tide of color"), Breck orders all apes on his "Achilles list," a list of all apes reported for acts of disobedience within the previous year, taken into custody as threats to state security. As the apes get closer to fulfilling Cornelius' prophecy from *Escape*, that they would become aware of their enslavement and its antidote in corporate and militant resistance, Breck tightens the reins of social control. Likewise, during the sixties and seventies, as African-Americans grew more insistent on being treated with full dignity, local and federal governments grew more repressive. The Achilles list is reminiscent both of Nixon's enemies list and of the Federal Bureau of Investigation's obsessive surveillance and harassment of African-American leaders and organizations.

Breck employs the same methods to control the apes that were advocated and used by conservatives to control black political resistance. For instance, Breck tries to forestall a revolt by destroying the talking ape, the only one with "enough intelligence to lead" the others. In much the same manner, white conservatives had advocated the repression of "black radicals" and a number of African-American political leaders — Medger Evers, Martin Luther King, Jr., and Fred Hampton among them — were killed by white Americans during this time. Breck's order to "shoot to kill" the rebelling apes also echoes the order of Mayor Richard Daley of Chicago for dealing with African-Americans during the riots.[45] *Conquest* argues against these types of measures by showing their failure to solve either the problems of oppression and racial strife or the retaliatory violence to which they lead.

Breck's fear of ape intelligence and speech, the fear of slave literacy, is in fact the fear of the self-assertion of a victim's humanity and identity and is a corollary to the dependent relationship he has established with his external and internal "beasts."[46] As Baldwin noted:

> That victim who is able to articulate the situation of the victim has ceased to be a victim: he, or she, has become a threat. . . .
> Once the victim's testimony is delivered, however, there is, thereafter, forever, a witness somewhere: which is an irreducible inconvenience for the makers and shakers and accomplices of this world. These run together, in packs, and corroborate each other. They cannot bear the judgement in the eyes of the people whom they intend to hold in bondage forever, and who know more about them than their lovers. This remote, public, and, as it were, principled, bondage is the indispensable justification of their own: when the prisoner is free, the jailer faces the void of himself.[47]

Without the myth of an inferior, the myth of the superior cannot be sustained. Faced with an ape as intelligent as himself, Breck is deprived of his cherished myths and, shorn of their protective veil, Breck indeed cannot "bear the judgement" in Caesar's eyes. After delivering his speech, Breck turns away from Caesar and is left only with the "dark side" — and the void — of himself. Ironically, Breck is on his knees as he delivers these lines, thus, like Zaius in *Planet*, he is forced to look up at his racial "inferior." The last shall be first, and the first shall be last.

A trace of the fear of such a racial apocalypse is embedded in the film's title, in which liberation of the oppressed is referred to as a "conquest," as if a revolution from within is more properly seen as an invasion from without. Similarly, some white Americans saw the civil rights movement as a Communist-backed attempt to weaken the United States, while some whites in the South saw civil rights efforts like the "Freedom Summer" as external interference by Northern liberal "troublemakers." In a way, Caesar could be seen by the whites in *Conquest* as an outside invader because he was raised by a non-white person, came from outside the community, and went on to lead the revolt.

Conquest is partly about the coming of age and initiation of its Moses figure. As noted, Caesar had been cloistered in "Armando's Old Time Circus," traveling in the outlying provinces. His journey to the capital city is his first exposure to the horrific reality of ape enslavement. Within a short time, he is the leader of the revolution that topples the government. Both spatially and politically he moves from periphery to center, and so from ignorance to knowledge, disconnection to responsibility, false freedom — through bondage — to actual freedom. The story of his ascendance takes place when he is eighteen, an age we commonly associated with male coming of age. When Breck, after purchasing Caesar, gives him the opportunity to choose his own name from a book of names, he picks the same name Armando gave him. Now, however, "Caesar" ceases to be just a name given to him by another. "Caesar" and its related meaning of "king" becomes an identity which he chooses for himself, for he does in fact become a king.[48]

Caesar even learns of love and sex when he falls in love with the demure chimpanzee Lisa but is sent to the breeding annex to mate with a voluptuous and eager female chimpanzee. (Even in the ape world it seems women's roles are divided into the stereotypes of either virgin or whore.) The scene also recalls the years of enslavement in which African-American sexuality was co-opted into the system of slave production.

Caesar's conflict with the slave state is a return to one of the themes in the original Pierre Boulle novel: the conflict of the superior being with the inferior society. This conflict is the occasion for his coming of age and the development of his latent capacities. Seen from this perspective, the film is a tale both of becoming aware of racial identity and societal position and of claiming political self-determination and responsibility.

Conquest is primarily concerned with the status of blacks in the United States and with the nature of the black struggle for liberation. This concern, implicit in the previous films, is here made explicit. One of the earliest indications of this shift is the presence and function of a large number of both major and minor black characters.

In each of the preceding films, there had been only one African-American character of note: Dodge in *Planet*, Negro in *Beneath*, and an African-American member of the presidential commission in *Escape*. (Although this unnamed character's role in the narrative is negligible, his position in the power structure is noteworthy.) Each of these men is cordoned off, segregated if you will, from the main action and conflicts of the film. They are not major players, and their absence would result in interesting but not very significant changes.

This is not the case in *Conquest*. African-Americans here have an increased quantitative presence and increased qualitative importance. African-Americans are visible throughout the film; they are shifted to the center of the conflict and are now visually, narratively, and thematically indispensable. This central placement of the black American in both *Conquest* and *Battle* was used to indicate the centrality of racial conflict, most specifically black-white conflict, to the latter part of the *Apes* series.

Despite the central positioning of African-American characters, the series is ostensibly about apes, and *Conquest* must preserve that focus in order to maintain its status as fiction. Therefore the film both moves toward the issue of race and distances itself from that issue at the same time.

This connection and separation are established in the first shot of the film. *Conquest* begins with a shot of a staircase and the superimposed title "North America 1991." This creates a safe distance between the audience and the events of the film. Immediately, at least on a surface level, the film is spatially and temporally displaced out of the audience's frame of reference. The first shot establishes that the action, and therefore the problem, of the film is somewhere in North America but not necessarily in the United States, and takes place in 1991, not 1972, even though the film was precisely concerned with life in the United States in the seventies. Deniability for the audience and the film is thus established from the very first moments.

Into the shot walks a gorilla wearing a red jumpsuit. Race is introduced from the outset: the first figure in the film is both visually and, as we see in a matter of moments, figuratively black. (The ape makeup appliances used in *Conquest* had a darker tone than those used in the previous films, with the gorillas going to a darker brown that on first sight looks black. Caesar's skin tone is dark enough to resemble the color of many mixed-race and "light-skinned" African-Americans. The effect is perhaps most significant in the nighttime revolt scenes in which the gorillas are the most numerous of the apes and look literally black.)

The camera pans to the left to include more gorillas, and into the shot comes an African-American slave-handler wielding a truncheon. The association of ape slave and black handler is crucial for establishing and disclaiming the film's concern. The film strives to tell the audience that its concern is not about black Americans, primarily through the roles they play in the society envisioned by the film. For instance, MacDonald's ability to serve as a top assistant to the white governor is a sign that relatively higher levels of political power are available to blacks — at least to black men, for there are no African-American women of note in the film.

Early in the film there is a brief scene that appears trivial but is in fact quite significant. In it we see the dining room of a restaurant in which two African-American men are discussing business opportunities. The casting of two black actors in these parts was no coincidence. Dehn's script specifically refers to them as "Negro tycoons" and has one argue that the "real future is in hydroponic farming," while the other maintains that "the big money's in synthetic alloys."[49]

In Dehn's screenplay for *Escape* he wrote that a section of VIP's "could include Negroes."[50] Dehn thus opened up the possibility of increased importance for African-Americans but did not expressly designate the "VIP's" as black or give them any dialogue.

Dehn's scripting of these two "Negro tycoons" in *Conquest* differs on both counts from his *Escape* script. Although their screen time is less than a minute, the fact that they were deliberately written as "Negro" and "tycoons" and that they were given dialogue discussing "big money," indicates that the filmmakers, or at least Dehn, wanted to signal specifically that black males have attained fairly high economic and business positions in the society depicted.[51] Greater power and prestige for blacks is suggested, and the relationship of blacks to the rest of society is figured as nonproblematic.

The relationship of blacks to apes, however, while it appears nonproblematic to the blacks in the film, is in fact very important. "Ape Management," the organization in charge of the slavery apparatus, is responsible for the training, electrical conditioning, sale, and discipline of the slaves. It is staffed predominantly by African-Americans. In fact, the Ape Management supervisor is African-American, signaling black achievement of considerable administrative responsibility and Black co-option into oppressive structures.[52]

The placement of African-Americans throughout Ape Management is open to varied interpretations. On the one hand, since, like a prison guard, an ape-slave handler has power over others without having high authority or prestige, this may be taken as evidence that the majority of blacks are still in relatively menial jobs and undesirable positions. While this may in fact be true, the film at least allows for the possibility of an improved political and economic position; African-Americans are no longer relegated to the lowest level of society because apes have taken that place. This development mimics the history of ethnic progression in the United States, recalling the irony in the changing racial dynamics as one group moves up and more recently arrived immigrant groups take their place at or near the bottom.

More interesting is the fact that what emerges visually in the scenes of apes being trained to make beds, clean floors, and serve drinks by blacks is the image of former slaves training new slaves. A visual irony, but not an illogical development. It is precisely former slaves whom one would expect to be most qualified to train new slaves. (Tellingly, after Caesar is bought by Breck, of all Breck's assistants it is the African-American MacDonald who trains him to mix drinks.) The scenes of blacks training apes also sustains the firm association, indispensable to the film, between the two groups and their respective enslavements.

That African-Americans in the film have become part of a system of domination and exploitation by which they had once been victimized is a key to one of the main themes of the *Apes* series. That we learn to enslave by being enslaved, that oppression is the surest teacher of oppression, is one of the subtler points of the *Apes* series. The series also argues that oppression has no color. One might marvel that, save for MacDonald, the African-American characters do not show sympathy for the apes nor see any irony in their own treatment of them. Indeed, the handler who leads Caesar around by a chain in front of the bidders at the slave auction is an African-American, as is one of the potential bidders. And repeatedly much of the business of enslavement is conducted by former slaves. Thompson wanted the keepers and handlers to be black partly to reflect the irony he saw in black men serving as prison guards being "unkind to their own people,"[53] that is, being unkind even to those with whom one is ostensibly connected by race or previous condition of servitude.

Having African-Americans run the slavery apparatus is another signal that, on the surface, the condition of blacks and black-white relationships are sufficiently nonproblematic that the blacks involved see no problem with being part of the master class in relation to the apes and have no difficulty with participating in the subjugation of another race. Establishing that textually nonproblematic relationship, while keeping it subtextually ironic, was one of the strategies employed both to hold off and engage the issue of the oppression of black Americans.

The film could do both because the *Apes* series had been self-consciously produced and presented as both entertainment and social commentary. The producers thus brought attention to the fact that the *Apes* films, like all movies, can function both on a level of text and subtext. Focusing on both dimensions is necessary to understand the films. Figuring the black American as part of the apparatus of enslavement, as oppressor rather than oppressed, is an obvious role reversal and an inversion of audience associations and expectations regarding black Americans. This inversion sends two messages. On a textual level the message communicated is "this film is not really about blacks."

However, numerous images of enslavement in *Conquest* link the ape slave to the African-American human, an iconic representation of slavery and economic exploitation whom the audience would know was still in an oppressed condition. Again the film's temporal inversion is crucial: since the filmic future directly addressed is the actual present indirectly addressed, the visual linkage of a racially oppressed person of the future with one of the present thematically equates them. Thus the second, subtextual, message is "this film is really about blacks." The positioning of the apes and black humans in relation to each other in the first shot and then throughout the film continually deflects attention away from and simultaneously refocuses that attention back onto the issue of race.

At the same time that the film disavows this concern through the social positioning of black Americans, it affirms that concern with the character of MacDonald. MacDonald, like the other defenders of the racially oppressed in the series, is a mediating figure. Like the chimpanzees of *Planet* and *Beneath* and the Latino Armando in *Escape*, he is part of the dominant racial class, in this case humans. But he had formerly been discriminated against by the racial elite and is at odds with it. His position is top assistant to the governor, yet as a descendent of slaves, he sympathizes with the apes and opposes the governor's oppressive policies. Thus the film positions MacDonald as a liminal figure, on the borders of two worlds, but not fully a member of either. Because of the more violent nature of the conflict in this chapter of the *Apes* saga and its more explicit resemblance to the time of its production, MacDonald's role as a mediator is even more crucial than the roles of other mediating figures in the series. MacDonald is a kind of liberal wish fulfillment: both outside and inside the system he can subvert the power of the elite while keeping the force of the revolution in check.

We are introduced to MacDonald when he comes to the defense of an ape messenger who is being beaten by white police officers. He angrily orders them to stop, tells them to sedate the ape, and then leaves. When an officer asks who MacDonald is, another officer informs him that he is the governor's top assistant. "What's the matter? He loves apes?" the first officer resentfully asks. "Don't it figure?" the second officer answers, a statement that both acknowledges the logic of MacDonald's sympathy and insults him with the age-old charge that Africans are apes. Thus, within the first few moments of his appearance, the film establishes and comments upon the expectation that because he is a black man, MacDonald will be compassionate towards the apes. Caesar, the film's hero, nods his head in approval of MacDonald's good dead, a visual cue for the audience likewise to approve of him. MacDonald's admirability is reinforced by the way in which he is filmed. He is consistently framed from low angles, thus the audience must always look up to him, literally as well as figuratively.

MacDonald recognizes that as slaves the apes have a connection to his own past. After Breck buys Caesar at the auction, displaying a gross historical insensitivity by having MacDonald do the bidding, Caesar masks his superior intelligence by spilling soda water. "It seems he's not so bright after all," Breck triumphantly observes. "No," MacDonald resentfully agrees, "but then brightness has never been encouraged among slaves." "Don't be so touchy, Mr. MacDonald. All of us were slaves once, in one sense of the

word or another," Breck says glibly. MacDonald then argues against sending Caesar back for reconditioning and strokes his hand to soothe him.

Caesar also understands the historical link between his experience
and MacDonald's history, and realizing that MacDonald does as well,
Caesar uses that connection. Breck, suspecting that Caesar is the child of
Zira and Cornelius, orders him turned over to State Security Chief Kolp
(Severn Darden). MacDonald is resistant and lies to the governor, telling
him that he has just sent Caesar out on an errand. Taking him out of the
command post, MacDonald eventually realizes that he cannot keep Caesar
hidden from Kolp for long:

> MacDONALD: I wish there was some way we could communicate, so
> you'd understand that I —
> CAESAR: I understand, Mr. MacDonald. Yes. I'm the one they're
> looking for.
> MacDONALD: I never believed it. I thought you were a myth.
> CAESAR: Well, I'm not. But I will tell you something that is — the
> belief that human beings are kind.
> MacDONALD: No Caesar. There are some —
> CAESAR: Oh a handful perhaps, but not most of them. No, they
> won't learn to be kind until we force them to be kind. And
> we can't do that until we are free.
> MacDONALD: How do you propose to gain this freedom?
> CAESAR: By the only means left to us. Revolution.
> MacDONALD: But, it's doomed to failure!
> CAESAR: Perhaps — this time.
> MacDONALD: And the next.
> CAESAR: Maybe.
> MacDONALD: But you'll keep trying?
> CAESAR: You above everyone else should understand. We cannot
> be free until we have power. How else can we achieve it?
> MacDONALD: (*Pause as he hears the footsteps of the security police*) Go!

Here MacDonald has embodied the *Apes* series' theory of racial alliance,
a theory that Caesar counted on him understanding. By exposing himself
and stressing that above all people MacDonald "should understand," Caesar
took a leap of faith that MacDonald's affinity with Caesar as an oppressed
creature would overrule his affinity with humans, black or white. Caesar's
gamble pays off, for, like the previous racial defenders we have seen in the
series, MacDonald risks his own life to defend the victimized. The shot
structure of the scene reinforces the thematic issues. Caesar and MacDonald are initially framed together in the same shot. But as they argue the
merits of revolution, they are framed separately in tight close-ups, a visual
emphasis of their ideological separation. When MacDonald tells Caesar to
go, he leans over and touches him, and both figures, their differences overcome, are again framed together. This shot structure is repeated in the final

debate between the two at the film's conclusion, yet here the ideological gap is larger and is not bridged visually.

The series suggests that a common history of oppression should form the foundation for political alliances. Identity and affinities are not here determined by biological but by situational factors, an idea further developed in *Battle*. Thus in *Planet* and *Beneath* Zira and Cornelius can oppose the other apes; in *Escape*, Stephanie, Louis, and Armando can defy the humans; and in *Conquest*, Armando and MacDonald can challenge the racist state.

While chimpanzees racially have more in common with orangutans than with humans and African-American humans have more in common with European-American humans than with apes, the films argue that this should not determine their political actions. In this regard, environment is privileged over heredity as an ideological motivator. The oppressed helping the oppressed emerges as a conditioning motif throughout the series; the motif shapes the plots of the films and seems intended to shape the audience's political sensibilities as well.

With MacDonald, as with the mediators in the earlier films, past or present experience of discrimination provides an intellectual, emotional, and moral imperative behind his sympathy with the oppressed that overrules his stake in remaining in a privileged position. Similarly, in *Escape* Louis Dixon, who as a WASP male presumably has not suffered discrimination, still acts out of a sense of integrity and compassion that compels him to resist racial domination.

The mediating figures throughout the series oppose the racial violence of the master race, even though their opposition holds little short-term personal benefit and great personal risk. Zira, Cornelius, Branton, Dixon, Armando, and MacDonald are models of and for resistance to oppression. They point towards a resolution of society's racial problems (those of the fictional apes and those of the real humans) and towards a future reformulation of society on nonracist grounds.

MacDonald and Caesar are linked visually again after Kolp captures Caesar. Taken to the Ape Management complex, he is wired to a shock table designed as a conditioning device to induce a Pavlovian association of pain with the word *no* which is shouted at the apes as they are given an electric shock.[54] Breck and Kolp use the shock table to force Caesar to talk. He is repeatedly subjected to high levels of voltage as the command "Talk!" is piped into the room through a loudspeaker.

With his arms strapped down extending in either direction from his body, the scene resembles an electric crucifixion of the apes' savior. Eventually the pain becomes unbearable and after his screams subside, Caesar looks up at MacDonald, who is in the observation room, and cries, "Have pity." MacDonald gets the message, quietly leaves the room, and shuts off the power supply to the shock table. When the decision is made to kill Caesar by electrocution, no electric charge comes through. Caesar feigns death and is later able to escape. MacDonald's acts of mercy twice save Caesar's life and enable him to pursue his struggle. Caesar's rising after being "electrically crucified" further constructs him as a simian Christ-figure.

The film maintains what may be called a liberal disposition towards Caesar's struggle, and embodies and plays out a liberal tension regarding it, and the struggle it was meant to represent. The film simultaneously reflects support for the black liberation movement and concern over its tone and direction. While the film (and perhaps the filmmakers) appears supportive of the struggle, maybe even of a degree of violent confrontation, it still seeks a role in shaping the response to oppression.

As we see at the film's conclusion, MacDonald is supportive of that struggle, but does not want to see it go too far. The final scene, which takes place after the apes have revolted and captured the governor's command post, emphasizes visually the power reversal and emphasizes thematically some of *Conquest*'s most pressing social concerns. Visually the scene reverses the film's opening shot of apes descending a staircase and depicts the victorious Caesar having just ascended the staircase outside of Breck's seat of power. The fallen Breck, shackled and pinned down by gorillas, is at the bottom of the staircase. The mediating MacDonald, placed fittingly in between them on the staircase, observes the carnage with dismay. We see him looking around, and the film cuts to a shot of an African-American man lying dead with a rope around his neck. This shot likens the apes to a lynch mob, and it is after seeing this sight of a lynched black man that MacDonald protests the mob justice and killings.

> MacDonald: Caesar, this is not how it was to be!
> Caesar: In your view or mine?
> MacDonald: Violence prolongs hate, hate prolongs violence. By what right are you spilling blood?
> Caesar: By the slave's right to punish his persecutors.
> MacDonald: Caesar, I, a descendant of slaves, am asking you to show humanity.
> Caesar: But I was not *born* human.
> MacDonald: I know the child of the evolved apes...
> Caesar: Whose children shall rule the earth.
> MacDonald: For better or for worse?
> Caesar: Do you think it could be worse?
> MacDonald: Do you think that this riot will win freedom for all your kind? By tomorrow—
> Caesar: By tomorrow it will be too late. If a tiny, mindless insect like the emperor moth can communicate with another of its kind over a distance of eighty miles—
> MacDonald: —an Emperor ape might do slightly better?

CAESAR: Slightly? What you have seen here today, Apes on the five
               continents will be imitating tomorrow.
MACDONALD: With knives against guns? With kerosene cans against
               flamethrowers? [Emphasis in original.][55]

A significant cultural debate is played out here. The debate in this and in
the earlier quoted scene between Caesar and MacDonald recalls the
debate among African-Americans in the sixties on the proper direction of
the liberation struggle. Caesar's insistence on achieving power through
violence is meant to reflect a black "radical" position, while MacDonald's
countering arguments about the futility of violence seem crafted to echo
black "moderates." Throughout the scene Caesar and MacDonald are
framed separately in close-ups, the visual nonrelation again reinforcing
their ideological estrangement. The question the film is posing is "which
character and whose ideology is the proper model of and for a revolutionary
leader?"

It is equally likely, and perhaps more so, however, that MacDonald is
not meant to embody the views of black "moderates" as much as act as a
surrogate for white "liberals." On the textual level at least, the debate is not
between members of an oppressed group. It is between a member of the
subordinate group struggling for emancipation and a sympathetic member
of the dominant group. Thus the scene visually resembles a debate between
black radicals and white liberals.

In that debate the dominant group member gives his support and
assistance and therefore feels entitled to help direct the movement and
determine its character, while the dominated group member insists on
self-determination for his people's struggle. Similar conflicts were occur-
ring between black leaders and their white allies as African-Americans
demanded more autonomy and control of their struggle. Thus MacDonald's
situation parallels quite closely that of many white liberals during the late
sixties and early seventies: he is supportive of the cause of liberation, but
concerned about its tone, and he fears that his own influence, either in
society at large or within the movement, is at risk.

Because of the way MacDonald is written and filmed, the film can be
interpreted as privileging him and his perspective. A number of facts suggest this. In all the *Apes* films up through *Conquest*, the racial reconciliation
message is privileged, it is advocated by the protagonists with whom we are
supposed to be aligned, and it fails to convince those in control of societal
power. Likewise, *Conquest* makes MacDonald the advocate of the reconciliation message, uses the techniques described above to align the audience with MacDonald, and has MacDonald fail to convince Breck and later
Caesar. In the absence of evidence suggesting that *Conquest* was meant to
deviate from the pattern established by the earlier *Apes* movies, *Conquest*
appears to support MacDonald's position.

MacDonald has in his past gone through an experience similar to Caesar's. As a politically active African-American man roughly in his forties in 1991, he very likely would have been involved in the black liberation struggles of his youth in the sixties and seventies — struggles which, as we have seen, were portrayed as having had considerable success by 1991. All the *Apes* films privilege historical knowledge as the key to understanding and influencing present and future. MacDonald probably has knowledge of a history of racial oppression and struggle. His firsthand experience would, from the perspective established in the *Apes* series, grant him authority to speak on how to conduct successful social struggles.

Furthermore, regardless of the actual political beliefs of the hundreds of people involved in making the *Apes* films, it is a liberal view that is most frequently embodied in the series. And the Kingesque advice MacDonald gives would have been closer to the sentiments of most progressive whites than the angrier separatist vision articulated by Caesar. Thus, considering all of these factors, the film appears to favor MacDonald as the best model of and for leadership. In fact, just as MacDonald is like liberal whites, the film *itself* seems like MacDonald: trying to secure a position of influence by not offering unqualified support, but rather by linking that support to a particular vision of proper strategy.

Avoiding the myopia of mere propaganda, however, both MacDonald and Caesar are sympathetic characters who have valid arguments. We can make a case that the film favors Caesar and his ideology as the preferred model. *Conquest*'s director J. Lee Thompson attributes the Watts riots to the feeling on the behalf of black Americans that "nothing was being done to help them — then violence came about."[56] The film may not be expressing liberal anxieties about the direction of the black liberation movement but rather, or additionally, frustration that genuine progress towards racial equality was not being achieved. The film is, and wants the audience to be, aligned with the apes, and the violence of the apes does not seem disproportionate to the crimes committed against them. Nor does the violence seem excessive in view of the apes' need for liberation from enslavement.[57]

In fact it is significant that the apes' move towards violence seems like a natural progression, given what the filmmakers showed in the first three films. *Planet, Beneath,* and *Escape* all established that appeals to the powerful in the name of racial peace will fail. Indeed, in Caesar's case, his own parents were brutally murdered despite the fact that they bore no hostility to the humans. Since Governor Breck is dismissive of MacDonald's counsel against further repression, no mediated negotiation seems likely. And because Caesar cannot speak without endangering his own life, direct negotiation is not possible. In the face of this kind of opposition to justice, violence is framed as the most rational recourse. Many of those who "rioted" in the sixties may have similarly seen violence as the only means available to oppose discrimination, economic exploitation, and police harassment. Therefore, while *Conquest* argues that violence should not be used to oppress the former oppressors, the entire series up to this point has set up the expectation that "they won't be kind until we force them to be kind" and *Conquest* may be seen as endorsing violence as a means of destroying oppressive structures.

As originally filmed, however, by the movie's end Caesar is planning to repeat the crime of racial oppression and enslave the humans. Thus despite the sympathy with the apes and their need for freedom, the original version of the film challenged the traditional notion that a burst of "redemptive" violence will produce a fundamentally just social order. In any case, the film did not seek, or at least did not achieve, ideological closure and left open questions regarding the strategic and moral appropriateness of violence.

It is likely, however, that when the original cut was presented, Twentieth Century–Fox balked, thinking the film was advocating violent racial rebellion. It was not until a prerelease screening in Phoenix, Arizona, that Fox realized, as Thompson put it, that "they had a very controversial film on their hands." In a significant change from the previous year, when a sneak screening of *Escape* in Phoenix had garnered 92 percent "excellent" ratings from the audience, parents had taken their children out of the *Conquest* screening, complaining about its violence, and the studio feared that the film would be "too volatile." (Given the paranoid and insulting fear that the milder violence in Spike Lee's 1988 film *Do the Right Thing* might incite African-Americans to riot, Fox's reaction to *Conquest* is not surprising.) Meetings at Fox ensued, and although Jacobs and Thompson argued for leaving the film unaltered, the studio ordered it toned down. Thompson, who had already altered the violence to get a "PG" rating from the Motion Picture Association of America, further edited the film and made significant changes in the crucial final scene.[58]

In the original scene, in response to MacDonald's question about the likelihood of knives and kerosene cans prevailing against flamethrowers, Caesar makes the following impassioned speech:

> Where there is fire, there is smoke. And in that smoke, from this day forward, my people will crouch and conspire and plot and plan for the inevitable day of man's downfall: the day when he finally and self-destructively turns his weapons against his own kind. The day of the writing in the sky, when your cities lie buried under radioactive rubble, when the sea is a dead sea, and the land is a wasteland out of which I will lead my people from their captivity! And we shall build our own cities, in which there will be no place for humans except to serve our ends. And we shall found our own armies, our own religion, our own dynasty. And that day is upon you now!

This apocalyptic vengeful crescendo was to conclude the film. (And as *Conquest* was written so it could serve as the last film, should the producers or the studio choose not to continue the cycle, these could have been the final words of the *Apes* series.) Following the pessimistic pattern of the first three films, *Conquest* was intended to end with MacDonald's call for mercy going unheeded and the apes planning to reverse the system of domination, envisioning, indeed plotting, humanity's destruction in a fanatical vision of racial nationalism.

But after the order came down from Fox, Thompson took a shot of a distraught Lisa, Caesar's romantic interest, looking at the carnage and then back up at Caesar, and dubbed over it a voice-over of her stammering "n-n-n-n-no!" The word that Cornelius prophesied in *Escape* would be spoken to protest human domination, is here redirected to protest planned ape domination. This is a considerable inversion of the expectations set up in *Escape* and foreshadows the apes themselves becoming enslavers. Caesar, apparently convinced by Lisa's appeal for mercy for the humans, then makes the following speech, also added in the dubbing studio:

> But now, now we will put away our hatred. Now we will put down our weapons. We have passed through the night of the fires. And those that were our masters are now our servants. And we who are not human can afford to be humane. Destiny is the will of God. And if it is Man's destiny to be dominated, it is God's will that he be dominated with compassion, and understanding. So — cast out your vengeance. Tonight we have seen the birth of the planet of the apes!

At the utterance of the last line, the apes start a chorus of shrieking and cheering as the soundtrack brings up a striking piece of music from Jerry Goldsmith's score for *Planet*. While it is plausible that Lisa's protest could have "soothed the savage beast" (women in films are often portrayed as opposing the violence of men),[59] the dissonance in tone between the two parts of the speech is noticeable. And one can observe that during the entire length of the second speech, we see reaction shots from MacDonald, Lisa, and the other apes, and close-ups of Caesar's eyes, but only two shots of his mouth moving, shots which are slightly out of sync with the dubbed-in vocals.

The difference in the final scene is significant because it is a difference that makes a difference. The changes blunt the critique of Caesar, and the film ends with a much softer tone. While Caesar still plans for human beings to be the apes' servants, he is not as strident in his hopes for humanity's self-destruction. Rather than end on plans for war and punishment, the final words speak of compassion and understanding. The change allows the film to depict the successful managing of one of the crises it addresses — the changing tone of the black liberation movement. MacDonald's view, the black "moderate" or white "liberal" view, prevails over that of Caesar, the black "militant nationalist" position. Even in the reedited ending, however, it is not MacDonald, but rather Lisa, who succeeds in convincing Caesar to be merciful. The change in the direction of the apes' revolt is self-determined, not a result of outside advice. Thus while it is unclear if Mac-Donald can secure the influence he seeks, his perspective prevails because it is put into the mouth of one of the apes.

This is one of the few moments in the series when a crisis is success-fully managed, and it is significant that if the filmmakers' original concep-tion had prevailed, this moment would not have happened. It is equally significant that it is not the advocacy of the mediating race that makes the difference, but rather the advocacy of a member of the dominant race that results in change.

As much of the audience, and probably the majority of the white audi-ence, would have supported MacDonald's view, the alteration to the final scene may have very well made the film more palatable, and thus more marketable, to those white audiences. In fact, the last scene is as important for what it did not show as it is for what it did show. While in the released version Breck's fate seems dire, it is nonetheless ambiguous. The shooting script in contrast was much more explicit. The screenplay called for him to be strung up and flogged by the apes, his "twitching body finally fall[ing] limp and motionless under the lash," as the screeching apes beat the remaining humans in the square. The final shot was to be a "ZOOM IN on the Apes' dark, demented faces in the glow of firelight. Their eyes gleam maniacally. The sound of their screaming intensifies, growing louder and louder, until it reaches a PEAK . . . and ends in an ABRUPT BLACKOUT and SILENCE."[60] This somewhat disturbing, and quite reactionary, scene uses the racist stereotype of maniacal dark devils screeching by firelight.[61]

Moreover, this was the only *Apes* film so far written to conclude with the title card "The End" on screen. Coming after scenes that replicated violent episodes across the nation's cities, those who felt threatened by that violence might have connected the words "The End" with the fear of the end to which the actual violence could lead. If intended as a warning that extraordinary oppression will result in extraordinary retaliation, the end-ing, and the vengeful tone of this scene in particular, might have backfired. It may have destroyed the audiences' sympathy and caused in many viewers a reactionary backlash against the apes and the cause the apes metaphorically represented.[62] Even liberal whites who wished — and wish — to see racial inequality eliminated would not — and do not — want to be punished, or even be held accountable, for their profit from it.

Of course, it is possible that the film was originally designed to convey the conservative message that repression is needed to quell the rising tide of color and prevent the apocalyptic "end." The changes at the end there-fore may represent not a shift from a radical to a liberal message, but a shift from a reactionary to a liberal perspective. If the ending was intended to communicate reactionary alarm, or even if it might have unintentionally sent such a message, it is better that it was changed. While a reactionary response is less likely given the changes, even as amended the ending may present a variety of messages.

To the filmmakers' credit, the film does not offer monolithic or unnegotiable conclusions. Unlike propaganda, *Conquest* takes somewhat seriously the various dimensions and possible answers to the questions it poses. As we have discussed, the film assigns more credibility to its own viewpoint, but the fact that it raises more questions than it definitively answers also sets it apart from mere propaganda.

The tensions are explored, and the questions seem deliberately left open. The answers are negotiable, and the film allows one to take a variety of messages and supply one's own answers. The film allegorizes the tensions and conflict between three racial ideologies: white supremacy (represented by Breck), integrationism (MacDonald), and Black Nationalism (Caesar). Reactionaries, reformists, and revolutionaries of various persuasions and races could likely find a pertinent message. One viewer might experience *Conquest* as a radical fantasy in that the system is not changed through reformist methods, but rather is quickly overthrown. Another might view *Conquest* as liberal wish-fulfillment because the revolution is pulled back short of total destruction. Conservatives or reactionaries committed to the status quo could also take various messages from the film: either that Breck's tactics were too oppressive and caused a situation destined to explode, or that he was not repressive enough to maintain the social control and forestall the ape conspiracy, or even that the black middle class cannot be trusted.

The film does not offer much support or comfort to conservatives, however. Through Caesar, radicals are able to achieve vicariously in the surrogate world of movies what they had been unable to achieve in the real world: the decisive overthrow of an exploitative racist power. MacDonald and Lisa, the liberal characters, achieve in the film what had eluded the liberals in politics: the simultaneous triumph over a reactionary regime and the managing (or controlling) of the impulses towards racial nationalism and destructive confrontation. On the other hand, the reactionary characters, Governor Breck and Inspector Kolp, are overthrown and left with neither material nor symbolic victory.

Regardless of the film's ideological complexity and regardless of the particular interpretations by different audiences, one point remains clear and consistent with what we have seen in the other *Apes* movies: in *Conquest* racial conflict cannot be contained and results in violence.

Of all the films in the series, *Conquest* deals most with the meaning of "ape" as a verb. Apes are trained to be slaves by aping former slaves;

Caesar infiltrates and then apes the other apes to evade detection by the state; and in the revolt, apes mimic black Americans—thus simultaneously capitalizing on and turning into a somber pun the use of the word "ape" as a racial slur.

This film has an opposite valence to that charter myth of American racist cinema, *Birth of a Nation*, in which a community is formed by the racially oppressive through reinforcing their domination over dark-skinned masses. To the contrary, as Caesar states, this film is about "the birth of the planet of the apes," a film in which a community of dominated, oppressed, dark-skinned masses unites to overthrow those who have abused and exploited them. *Birth of a Nation* is concerned with the maintenance of an oppressive system, while the birth of the planet of the apes is about the overthrow of an oppressive system and about what might follow.

Here again the notion of aping obtains. Boulle's novel and Serling's original *Planet* script underscored the fact that the apes were imitators who developed their society by mimicking human beings. *Conquest* does indeed depict the birth of the planet of the apes, and it is here that we begin to see where the apes of *Planet* and *Beneath* got the idea for a racially discriminatory society—they copied it, they aped it from human beings.

The film tells us that racial oppression comes from racial oppression—one of the underlying and more subtle implications of MacDonald's seemingly clichéd insistence that "violence prolongs hate and hate prolongs violence." MacDonald's statement is yet another element of the film with multiple possible meanings. If directed to a white audience, it could be a chastisement and a call to them to stop subjugating people of color. If directed to a black audience, it could be a warning that they should not do unto others as had been done unto them (as *Conquest*, in fact, shows blacks doing to apes and apes planning to do to humans). This is one of oppression's hazards: the sins of the master may be visited upon the slaves, only to be visited by them upon the new slaves, who may, in fact, be the former masters. (As my college professor Jerry Watts once succinctly put it, "oppression does not breed ethics," and this is no less a hazard to the slave than to the master.) *Conquest* argues that we learn to abuse by being abused. "All of us were slaves once," Breck says, perhaps not so glibly after all.

This recursive nature of brutalization is what Baldwin discussed when he considered T. E. Lawrence's *Seven Pillars of Wisdom*, upon which was based the movie *Lawrence of Arabia*. Baldwin's observation is a keen insight into the psychological needs served by Breck's brand of racism, a racism reflecting the desire to control one's own "dark side":

> The necessity, then, of "those lesser breeds . . ." —those wogs, barbarians, niggers—is this: one must not become more free, nor become more base than they: must not be used as they are used, nor yet use them as their

abandonment allows one to use them: therefore they must be civilized. But, when they *are* civilized, they may simply "spuriously imitate [the civilizer] back again," leaving the civilizer with "no satisfaction on which to rest" [emphasis and brackets in original].[63]

The threat is everpresent that seeds of oppression, exploitation, and abuse, have always, will always, and must always bear the fruit of oppression, exploitation, and abuse. You will reap what you sow.

We can see this potential developing in Caesar's determination to create a society in which "there will be no place for humans except to serve our ends." The apes appear destined to replicate the mistakes of their masters. This is perhaps always the danger with slaves and masters, for, as Baldwin asks, "how can one . . . dream of power in any other terms than in the symbols of power?"[64] Now that they have learned the arts of civilization, which are all too often the arts of brutalization, there is no reason to think that the former slaves will not practice them with the same horrific skill as the former masters and no reason, as Thomas Jefferson suggested, to expect that "the almighty has [any] attribute which can take side with us in such a contest."

Thus there is an acute tension in *Conquest*. Of all the *Apes* movies, it is the one that is most explicit in its support for the black liberation struggle, yet at the same time it expresses considerable nervousness about it. The film registers both heightened concern for black liberation and heightened anxiety about the possible price of that liberation for whites.

Will the apes, in fact, as Zira put it in *Escape*, "turn the tables on their owners?" Will the system of domination be overthrown or merely overturned? These questions, and the fears behind them, are very much a part of the last two *Apes* films. "For better or for worse?" *Conquest* urgently demands. *Battle* takes up that question.

FOUR

"Ape Has Killed Ape"

Planet, Beneath, and *Escape* established a thesis: racial domination. *Conquest* introduced an antithesis: revolt against domination, and even reversal of it. *Battle for the Planet of the Apes* depicted the difficult struggle to achieve a synthesis: racial equality, and even racial harmony.

In June 1972, around the time of *Conquest*'s release, an article in *Time* magazine stated that the projected fifth *Apes* picture was to show "how the apes, like the humans who preceded them, began to ruin the world." The article's phrasing was apt, for the worldview Paul Dehn offered in his *Apes* scripts depicted an ineluctable drive towards ruination, the only variable being who occupied the driver's seat. The article quoted Dehn as saying that "up to now . . . the blame has been entirely on the humans. But I think now the apes are going to share it."[1] Dehn then proceeded to write a treatment for *Battle for the Planet of the Apes* in which Caesar enslaves the humans and denies them all rights. Dehn's storyline was not used, but his core theme remained, and the next film shares the blame by showing how the apes, do indeed, become "like the humans who preceded them."

In Dehn's story outline of *The Battle for the Planet of the Apes*, thirteen years have passed since the ape revolt. Caesar rules as emperor, and the apes have reversed the power relations of *Conquest* and enslaved the humans. MacDonald serves as Caesar's personal servant and fears that the apes will exterminate the humans when they are no longer useful. He asks the ape ruling council, made up of three chimpanzees, three gorillas, and two orangutans, to allow human representation. A chimpanzee council member named Pan supports the idea, but he is overruled.

Ninety percent of humanity is under ape domination. The apes control the territory to their south, but there are still human rebels in the north. One of the human rebel leaders, Nimrod, is a former U.S. Army general. His real name is General Mendez, and he is the ancestor of the mutant leader Mendez in *Beneath*. Nimrod sends a representative to the apes' capital with an ultimatum: set the humans free or Nimrod will destroy the apes' city with a nuclear bomb. The messenger is killed, and Caesar assembles the apes in shelters, allowing a limited number of humans with useful skills into the shelters. Nimrod's airplane pilots drop the bomb and level the city.

Eventually the survivors emerge from the shelters and begin to rebuild the apes' city. Nimrod and his followers, scarred and mutated by the nuclear radiation, later shell the rebuilt city. The apes counterattack, fighting on horseback against humans in restored automobiles, and they force the humans to retreat. Nimrod fires a projectile, which falls just short of the ape army. The humans explain that the projectile will soon explode and emit nerve gas that induces sterility in those who inhale it — Dehn described it as a "genocide bomb."[2] Fearing the destruction of their reproductivity, the apes retreat, designating the land that will be affected by the bomb the "Forbidden Zone." It is then revealed that the projectile was empty, a bluff to frighten off the apes. The story ends with human children releasing a baby chimpanzee, who had earlier been taken captive, declaring that the young ape can do nothing with the humans but "pine and die" and that "he belongs with his own kind."[3]

In Dehn's outline, the threat of genocide, even though an empty one, is ironically the only thing that saves the humans from extermination. Expressing a narrow sense of possibility, in Dehn's story, MacDonald, who advocates equality and peace, and Caesar, who is poised to alter his oppressive policies, are killed by Aldo, while conservative politicians and the military go on to dominate society. A brittle détente based on a policy of mutually assured destruction and a cold war based on mutual enmity substitute for real peace. In Dehn's vision the bottom line remains separation of the races, each keeping to their "own kind."

As an exercise in cautionary fiction, Dehn began with the ideology and cycle of the "savage" war, of the race war — atrocity countered by atrocity countered by atrocity ad nauseam — and then intensified it and projected its culmination in utter destruction and misery for both sides. Dehn either could not or would not extricate his characters from that compulsive cycle. Justice, peace, and reconciliation were denied a place in his *Apes* stories. It took two other writers, John William Corrington and Joyce Hooper Corrington, to introduce even a meager glimpse of hope into the series.

According to Thompson, after *Conquest*, Fox wanted no more surprises and ordered him to make a "kids' picture."[4] This is perhaps a reason why Dehn's story was not used. Consequently, the political content of *Battle for the Planet of the Apes* is less explicit than that of *Conquest*, but nevertheless it is still extremely important. In *Battle*, the balance of racial power has shifted once again. The apes have not yet overcome the problem of racial domination, for while humans are not exactly slaves, they have been made a servant class. The film seriously considers the prospect, and expresses the fear, that the civilized beasts "may simply spuriously imitate the civilizer back again, leaving the civilizer with no satisfaction on which to rest."

Battle attempts to evoke ambivalent reactions and problematize easy audience identification. Presumably the audience should feel glad that the apes have achieved their freedom, yet dismayed that humans now exist in a subordinate status. Characters whom audiences are prepared to respect from seeing *Conquest* (Caesar, Lisa, and MacDonald) are at times allied with and at other times opposed to each other. *Battle* differs structurally from the other *Apes* movies in that in the first four films the main identification figure enters the film's social space from the outside: Taylor in *Planet*, Brent in *Beneath*, Zira and Cornelius in *Escape*, Caesar in *Conquest*. Thus the audience is aligned with outsiders and the racially dominated. But in the fifth film, we do not follow the action from the perspective of a new member of the community (while a narrator introduces and concludes the film, his narrative voice does not distance the audience from the action). Without the distancing luxury of being the outsider, the viewer is more like a member of the community and is more directly implicated in the film's action and dilemmas. The audience is also denied the ease of identifying primarily or solely with either the humans, as in the *Planet* and *Beneath*, or with the apes, as in *Escape* and *Conquest*. Good and evil are more evenly distributed among the species.

Having been approached by APJAC to write the fifth *Apes* film, Joyce Hooper Corrington and John William Corrington wrote a story entitled *Epic of the Planet of the Apes* in September 1972. *Epic* was the basis for the last film, *Battle for the Planet of the Apes*, which responded to a desire to look past the fractious times of the sixties and early seventies towards a time of reconciliation, a reconciliation the United States sorely needed after ten years of assassinations, wars, and intensified racial violence abroad and at home.[5]

Before there can be reconciliation, there must sometimes be reformation, and reformation is an integral concern in *Battle*. Discussing studies of the social behavior of apes and monkeys, Haraway notes that "there is a constant refrain drawn from salvation history; primatology is about primal stories, the origin and nature of 'man,' and about reformation stories, the reform and reconstruction of human nature. Implicitly and explicitly, the story of the Garden of Eden emerges."[6]

This is very much the case in *Battle for the Planet of the Apes*. In preparation for writing the fifth *Apes* movie, the Corringtons viewed prints of the first four *Apes* films at Fox. Joyce Hooper Corrington recalls that they thought that so far in the series "humans represented all the bad things that we'd done [but] the apes were . . . before the fall . . . before Adam and Eve . . . without original sin."[7] The Corringtons thought that the apes had been constructed as "noble savages" in this regard and wrote a screenplay that depicted the apes' fall from grace.

Battle contemplates the apes' ability to reverse that fictional fall as a way of considering the potential for human beings to reverse their own actual fall. In the first four films, the apes seem to have undone the sin of biblical Cain: they do not kill each other. This is the border that separated ape from human. *Battle* would show this border being crossed and then contemplate the possibility of crossing back.

Thus, as Corrington puts it, "playing with the innocence of the apes and the fall from innocence," the Corringtons built the screenplay around the story of Cain and Abel. The message the Corringtons were trying to get across was that "you're living in the Garden of Eden but . . . the evil is there waiting to overwhelm you and you have to be able to deal with it and change history. You have to be able to change human, or ape, nature so that ape nature is different from human nature or you're going to create the same situation again and blow up everybody again." The story of the apes in *Battle* was deliberately about the origin and reconstruction of "human nature."

In order to take this theme seriously, the last two films in the series move away from the biological determinism of the early films. *Conquest* and *Battle* argue that racial violence is caused by violent experiences and oppressive conditions, not by tainted genes. Conquest shows that the biologically created "human nature" posited in *Planet* is in fact historically created. And coming at the end of the *Apes* cycle, *Battle* finally opens up the possibility that "human nature" might be historically altered.

The film opens with a shot of a forest and the title "North America 2670 A.D." The camera pans to the right past trees, boulders, and a river as a narration commences: "In the beginning, God created beast and man so that both might live in friendship and share dominion over a world at peace. But in the fullness of time, evil men betrayed God's trust, and in disobedience to his holy word waged bloody wars—not only against their own kind, but against the apes—whom they reduced to slavery." On "slavery" the pan ends, revealing the Lawgiver, who has been reading the narration from a scroll. The Lawgiver continues over footage from *Escape* of Zira and Cornelius' deaths, and from *Conquest* of ape enslavement and the ape revolution:

> Then God in his wrath sent the world a savior—miraculously born of two apes, who had descended on Earth from Earth's own future. And man was afraid, for both parent apes possessed the power of speech. So both were brutally murdered. But the child ape survived. And grew up to set his fellow creatures free from the yoke of human slavery. Yet, in the aftermath of his victory, the surface of the world was ravaged by the vilest war in human history. The great cities of the world split asunder and were flattened. And out of one such city, our savior led a remnant of those who survived, in search of greener pastures, where ape and human might forever live in friendship, according to divine will. His name was Caesar—and this is his story in those far-off days.

Here the filmmakers show the transformation of secular events into religious myth. As interpreted in ape religion, 700 years after the fact, Zira and Cornelius go from refugees from Earth's nuclear holocaust to the bearers of God's wrath, Caesar moves from revolutionary leader to holy savior, and racial equality is elevated from political ideology to divine mandate. The "historical" events of *Escape* and *Conquest* are crystallized and reformulated as a mythic narrative that, like human myths, "recapitulates [a] people's experience in their land, rehearses their visions of that experience in relation to their gods and the cosmos, and reduces both experience and vision to a paradigm."[8]

Many elements of the scene signal that what follows is a morality tale. The orangutan Lawgiver is placed in a natural setting; the script employs the language of "God's trust" and "holy word"; the story is related by the Lawgiver, a religious figure in *Planet* and *Beneath*; and John Huston, director, star, and narrator of the 1966 film *The Bible*, is cast as the Lawgiver. And the ape myth of origins recalls creation stories from the Bible by its primordial opening, its recounting of disobedience leading to a fall from grace, an Edenic state destroyed through the betrayal by a human Cain of a simian Abel, its rescued baby, its divine wrath, its tale of a hunted slave liberator, and its recollection of an exodus to a promised land.

The film in fact does have a biblical tone—*Battle* is concerned with topics such as the will of God, the way in which that will can be obeyed and disobeyed, the fate of those that oppose it, and the challenge of following it. And, like the biblical Jacob, the apes wrestle with divine will. *Battle* thus brings to the series an even further magnified sense of the importance of its issues by using biblical motifs and religious language to lift race relations out of the political sphere of right and wrong and re-present the issue in the religious realm of good and evil.

After the Lawgiver's introduction, *Battle*'s plot unfolds in what is essentially an uninterrupted, unnarrated flashback. Although the Lawgiver states that the story is about Caesar, *Battle*'s narrative begins with the gorilla general Aldo. When the film shifts from the Lawgiver's sermon to the actual story events, it is Aldo that the camera focuses upon and follows during the credits.

Thompson's use of credit sequences was distinct from the pattern established in the early films. In the first three films, the credit sequences were used to orient the audience to the space in which the story begins. Franklin Schaffner's credit sequence in *Planet* featured shots of spaceflight that grew increasingly abstract and impressionistic in order to convey the displacement of time and space and ended with a simulated passage through the Earth's atmosphere just before Taylor's crash-landing. In *Beneath*, Ted Post had the credits appear over shots of barren desert to convey the feeling of isolation and desolation confronting Taylor in the wake of his discovery of humanity's destruction. Don Taylor used *Escape*'s credits to show the passage of Cornelius, Milo, and Zira from freedom to confinement as they are transferred from the spaceship, transported on military vehicles, and then caged, and to indicate the shifting of the series narrative focus back onto the contemporary United States. But Thompson went a step further than using the credit sequences to convey mood and setting. He additionally used them to introduce the central problem that must be overcome in the film. The opening shots of ape servitude in *Conquest* establish the problem as enslavement. In *Battle*, the problem is the dark-skinned ape.

Corrington explains that Aldo was "the Cain figure, the one who was tending toward violence, who couldn't live in the state of nature, whose natural proclivity was toward violence and power." In *Battle*, Caesar asserts that "when you get to know and trust a person you cannot help but like him," and he has become a nascent integrationist. Aldo, meanwhile, has taken the role held by Caesar in *Conquest* as the representative of "Black Nationalism." Corrington maintains that *Battle* "was not . . . meant to be a racial treatise." She acknowledges, however, that "one could not help but put in a little bit of what [was] going on in the world with . . . 'Black Power' and stuff like that. It was too prevalent." She recalls that "there was a fear at that time of black militancy" and says that the gorillas were "reverse racists to a certain degree. I think that was probably on our minds as we did it."

Aldo in fact resembles a caricature of "black militants"[9] and "Black Power" advocates. He is a caricature born out of a lack of understanding of the various meanings of the Black Power slogan. "Black Power" was a term that meant many things to many people and ranged from black economic development to black control over black community institutions to Stokely Carmichael's advocating "killing the honkies" and his declaration that Black Power "will smash everything that Western civilization has created."[10] The slogan evoked strong reactions: it was vigorously debated within the black community[11] and feared by many white Americans.

Many in the United States, both European- and African-Americans, attacked the notion of "Black Power" entirely in reaction to the more hostile proponents of a slogan that was used by both advocates of nonviolence and advocates of violence, both integrationists and separatists, and both capitalists and socialists. Roy Wilkins of the National Association for the Advancement of Colored People, for example, denounced Black Power as "a reverse Mississippi, a reverse Hitler, a reverse Ku Klux Klan."[12]

The intense hostility to the term was probably caused by a combination of factors, including the failure of the white press to communicate an adequately nuanced picture of the combination of black economic, political, and cultural development that the term often referred to, and the subsequent demonization by the white press of "Black Power" advocates like Stokely Carmichael. The negative reaction was also due to the adolescent posturing of activists such as Carmichael who failed to make effective use of the press to articulate the legitimate goals the term encompassed and instead succumbed to the temptation of delivering fiery, cathartic rhetoric for the press and the television cameras.[13] Regardless of the meanings of and the reactions to "Black Power," and regardless of the actual success or failure of using the term, the slogan had a forceful and significant cultural presence that registered in the *Apes* series, especially in *Battle*.

The anxiety inspired by the very concept of "Black Power" was in no small degree a combination of the above factors and guilt amongst many whites. As James Baldwin pointed out, we tend to imagine power taking the same form in which we have previously known it. And as Dr. Nathan Wright, the chairman of the 1967 "Black Power Summit," observed, "white people are afraid of the term [Black Power] because they see in it a mirror of *white* power. And that spells abuse" (emphasis in original).[14] As mentioned in Chapter One, fear comes not only from the recognition of difference but also from the recognition that the "other" may in very significant ways be the same.[15]

Joyce Corrington believed that up to that point in the series the audience "was rooting for the apes to win, and if we had thought that [the audience] had ever thoroughly identified the apes with the blacks I don't think [the audience] would have been rooting for the blacks to take over and dominate the whites." Corrington's comments suggest that, consciously or not, she and her husband and co-writer John were appealing to *specifically* white sensibilities or at least to viewers who feared "black militancy." And whereas *Conquest* allowed the catharsis of seeing non-white protagonists decisively defeat white racists, *Battle*'s adamantly antigorilla stance denies audiences this pleasure.

The attempt to respond to white fears of reverse racism led the Corringtons to endow Aldo with a less nuanced characterization than was the case with the series' previous antagonists. Unlike Zaius in *Planet*, or Hasslein in *Escape*, Aldo is depicted as a totally unsympathetic antagonist. While Zaius' fears are presented as somewhat justified and Hasslein debates the morality of his actions, Aldo is a one-dimensional villain. Even Breck and Kolp are granted the opportunity by the writers to express the rationale for their malevolence. But Aldo is denied this opportunity, and, unlike the situation with almost all the other *Apes* antagonists, the audience is denied a glimpse into Aldo's psychology. By presenting the symbolic "reverse racist" as an unambiguous villain, the filmmakers missed an opportunity to explore more rigorously the complex and painful racial politics that inspired *Battle*.

With none of the complexity of previous *Apes* antagonists, Aldo is motivated only by hatred and the desire for personal power. He grunts in admiration when military dictators are mentioned. He imprisons the humans in the horse corral, creating a human concentration camp. "[Aldo] still remembers the old days," Caesar says in the *Battle* shooting script. "I think he'd like to bring them back," MacDonald warns.[16] He is not entirely correct, however. Aldo wants to do more than enslave the humans; he wants to exterminate them.

Aldo's ideology is explicitly racist and genocidal. During a campfire gathering with his gorilla soldiers, he vows to "create a super-race" and to "smash . . . all humans." His fanaticism even leads him to kill Caesar's son, named Cornelius after Caesar's father. When Cornelius overhears Aldo's plans, Aldo chops down the tree branch on which he is perched, fatally wounding him and thus violating the apes' most sacred law.

A simple-minded militarism characterizes Aldo. He chants repeatedly, and somewhat mechanically and maniacally, "Guns! Guns! Guns are power! We shall get them and we shall keep them!" The audience already knows from *Beneath* that when racist militaristic gorillas attempt to increase their power, crisis is the result. The same is true in *Battle*.

Aldo seizes power, raids the armory, and has the humans rounded up and put in the corral. When MacDonald protests that he is acting against Caesar's orders, Aldo sits in Caesar's chair and regally declares, "Caesar is not here." In this shot he is framed with the camera tilted in the opposite direction from the tilted shots of the film's other villain, Kolp. The reversed visual echo reemphasizes that Aldo and Kolp are mirror images of each other.

As in *Conquest*, the tensions between white liberal supporters of the civil rights movement and more nationalist African-Americans emerge in *Battle*, this time coded as hostility between the predominantly white humans in the ape village and the gorillas. No doubt the gorilla's blood-thirsty fireside gathering matched the image many had of a Black Panther meeting. The ape village's political council, while composed of all three apes races, is devoid of humans. When Caesar invites a few humans to the council to help make plans to defend the village against the mutants, Aldo and the gorillas indignantly yell, "No humans in council!" and storm out in protest over the deviation of policy. Ironically, the gorilla unwillingness to work with humans recalls both White resistance to integration and the changing organization of civil rights groups, as some formerly integrated organizations implemented all Black membership policies. Thus the scene equates Black "separatists" with White segregationists.

Among the humans in the village, whom Aldo eventually herds into a concentration camp, most have long hippie-style hair and therefore physically resemble some of the same white liberals who felt betrayed and threatened by the changes in the black liberation struggle. The humans in the village probably would have felt similar hurt and resentment at being imprisoned by the apes with whom they were trying to live peacefully. Corrington remembers that the humans in the village were

> sort of your liberals . . . who were integrationists trying to make things work between the two groups. . . . [The African-American] community at that time was pretty militant, you had the Black Panthers and stuff like that. . . . That may have been what we were reflecting there, just because one group seems good . . . they're [still] just as capable of racism and discrimination on their side. [The gorillas] not being nice to even the people who were trying to work things out was perhaps a little bit of a reflection of that time.

Corrington's recollections exemplify the complicated, and sometimes contradictory, thoughts and intentions that artists can bring to their work. While pointing out that the film was not meant as a "racial treatise," she also remembers that "we were very conscious of race." While stating that she and John Corrington did not think of the apes as representing African-Americans, she notes that "reverse racists . . . [were] probably on our mind" when the gorilla characters were conceived. And even though she asserts that there was only "a little bit of a reflection of that time," her comments demonstrate that the *central* conflict between apes and humans in the ape village was in fact shaped by the conflicts between African-Americans and whites, specifically between black nationalists and white liberals — the same tension that shaped the ideological debate in *Conquest.*

Just as the earlier films registered a sense that U.S. politics had become morally questionable, *Battle,* and arguably *Conquest* to a lesser degree, registered white backlash.[17] That the riots and Black Power were two of the core issues of the last two films expresses the level of white anxiety, including, and perhaps especially, *liberal* white anxiety, over the direction of the black liberation struggle. White backlash is further manifested in the fact that, in marked contrast to *Escape* and *Conquest,* in *Battle* it is white humans who are now the primary victims of racial oppression. It is also a function of white backlash that the villains in the series went from the lightest apes, the orangutans, in *Planet,* to the darkest apes, the gorillas, in *Battle.* The dark apes have gone from a dominated underclass at the series' beginning to intimidating overseers at its end.

Conquest and *Battle* are not reactionary films. In *Conquest* the audience witnesses the brutality of enslavement from the point of view of the enslaved, and through most of the film the audience is meant to identify with Caesar. Similarly, *Battle* begins with a recounting of the cruelties inflicted upon apes by humans. This puts the gorillas' desire for revenge in historical context, while still depicting the apes' mistreatment of humans as unacceptable reverse racism.

And while white backlash registered in the depiction of the dark apes

White backlash had its impact as the dark apes' rise against the lighter apes' authority became *Battle*'s central problem. The concentration camp in the background signals the underlying anxiety that the racial underclass could become the racial overseers and leave no satisfaction on which to rest.

as racists, in *Battle*, as in each of the last three *Apes* pictures, the apes are predominately the sympathetic characters. In the later *Apes* films, while there are a few sympathetic humans (Lewis Dixon, Stephanie Branton, and Armando in *Escape*, the MacDonald brothers in *Conquest* and *Battle*), most of the human authority figures, those who are empowered to represent and act in humanity's behalf, are white antagonists (Hasslein in *Escape*, Breck and Kolp in *Conquest*, and Kolp in *Battle*). Even the gorillas, the bad apes in *Battle*, are shown as straying from the path and eventually returning to it, in contrast to the human villains, who show no capacity for repentance.

Nevertheless, for the fifth *Apes* film, more practical problems than the specter of reverse slavery might have been the struggles of apes and humans to get along with each other and the difficulty of overcoming the vestiges of institutional and cultural racism as the apes strive for dignity and equality. This approach would have addressed itself more usefully to the realities of U.S. race relations at the time. While in the imaginary world of cautionary science fiction, the victimized and the victimizers might have traded places with relative ease or speed, this was not the case in U.S. society. *Battle* is not a self-consciously reasoned assessment of racial realities, however, but rather an expression of the depth of whites' racial anxieties and, to a certain degree, as the hint of racial harmony at the film's end suggests, of their racial hopes.

Aldo's human double is Kolp, Breck's security inspector from *Conquest*. Kolp has replaced Breck as governor. (Breck died in the war the Lawgiver mentioned.) Driven insane by nuclear radiation, Kolp now rules over the bombed-out remains of the capital city from *Conquest*, now called the "Forbidden City" by the apes. The scenes in the human city are filmed at a tilt, giving the city a disconcerting feel and visually emphasizing the unbalanced mentality of its inhabitants (who are the forerunners of the mutants in *Beneath*).

Like his predecessor Breck, Kolp possesses a deep hatred of apes. Fittingly, therefore, his seat of power is the battle-damaged former control center of Ape Management. And like Aldo, Kolp is resentful and dreams of exterminating his racial enemies. His racism ("He's an animal, he's only an animal!" he says of Caesar) matches Aldo's, as do his plans for racial domination: "Caesar. Your people weakened our city by rebelling against your human masters. But we who survived will create a new race. And you and yours will be brought low. And you shall learn again what it is to have a master."

Unlike MacDonald, Aldo and Kolp do not learn from the past—they are stuck in it, and neither one is willing to let go of his resentment and anger in order to create a more just present. These two figures, a racist ape and a racist human, while enemies, are in fact mirrors of each other. After a certain point, the film seems to suggest, it is difficult, perhaps even irrelevant, to say who is aping whom.

Positioned in between these two ideological counterparts is the interracial trio of friends: Caesar, orangutan Virgil, and MacDonald (because Hari Rhodes was unavailable to reprise the role of MacDonald from *Conquest*, Austin Stoker was cast as MacDonald's brother). They form the model of interracial understanding and cooperation that the film advocates and that the film's ape society has yet to create.

Battle shows us the early stages of the racially hierarchical ape society of *Planet* and *Beneath*. There has been some role reversal since the first two films, however. Chimpanzees have switched places with the orangutans and are now the political elite, while orangutans have become the intellectuals. The gorillas are still the military, but the burden of menial work has been taken over by the humans. While the seeds of ape racial differentiation and possibly animosity exist, racial stratification amongst the apes is not stressed. As in *Conquest*, this shifts attention away from the racial divisions amongst the apes and focuses attention onto the species division and hostility between apes and humans.

As mentioned, human beings are in a subordinate status and are now forced to do the servant labor the apes had to do in *Conquest*. (In his *Battle* treatment, Paul Dehn envisioned a credit sequence in which the humans were doing exactly the same jobs as the apes in *Conquest*.) As David Gerrold wrote in his *Battle* novelization, "the apes were proud that they had thrown off the yoke, but they failed to realize that they had not thrown it away. They put men into it and made them live in shame."[18]

Human subservience is indicated in the first scene after the credits. At the completion of the credits, Aldo rides into the ape village to find a man struggling to lift a supply cart. He pushes him out of the way, saying, "I'll show you how." Aldo lifts the cart, allowing the humans to repair it. When the human says, "Thanks, Aldo," the gorilla roughly grabs him and orders, "You will call me by my proper rank—General!" Here Aldo has underscored both his superior physical strength and emphasized his higher position in the new power relation between former slave and former master. The man, having been successfully intimidated, meekly answers back, "Yes, General."

Aldo proceeds immediately to the only place where humans beings have any remaining authority over apes, a place that is apparently the only site of contested power in the village: the schoolroom. The schoolroom is the setting of an important power struggle between Aldo and the white human teacher.

The teacher is called simply "Teacher." When Cornelius' writing assignment reads "Ape shall never kill Abe" instead of "Ape shall never kill ape," the teacher corrects a presumed misspelling. Cornelius has to remind him that "Abe" is his real name. Abe replies somewhat forlornly, "Everyone has always called me Teacher [so] I had forgotten." Abe had forgotten his own name because his identity had been subsumed in his role as servant to the apes. He is not the only human in this position: a woman in the village is simply referred to as "Doctor." This is emblematic of the state to which humanity has fallen in the film, one not of total subjugation but at least of subordination: humanity's own identity is now second to and defined by humanity's service to the apes.

As Aldo enters the makeshift school, a raised outdoor platform with benches and a blackboard in which the three ape races all sit separately, the students are obediently reciting the apes' golden rule: "Ape shall never kill ape." "Shall ape," Aldo interrupts, "ever kill man?" The teacher chastises Aldo for being late and later humiliates him for his poor writing skills. By humiliating Aldo in front of the other gorillas in the class—and probably worse, in front of the chimpanzees and orangutans—Abe steps out of his place and challenges Aldo's superiority.

In retaliation for Teacher's humiliation, Aldo tears up Cornelius' writing assignment. "No, Aldo, no!" Abe instinctively yells, at which point all the apes are aghast. Aldo is even physically repelled. A shocked Virgil reminds Abe that because the humans had electrically conditioned apes to fear the word *no*, Caesar has forbidden humans to ever speak the word to apes, although apes can say it to humans.

Born out of resentment for past wrongs, this was the first law made by the apes, a law that established the unbalanced power dynamics that were to prevail in the new society. We see here the first explicit evidence of inequality: apes determine what humans can and cannot do, and the privileges accorded each group are different. In saying the forbidden word, Abe had been "uppity," an intolerable violation of U.S. racial protocol. Aldo leads the gorillas in a rebellion against human authority and against Caesar's authority by tearing up the schoolroom. Abe barely escapes.

The choice of the schoolroom as the problematic site of human authority over ape and of the film's first power struggle between ape and human is significant in that it recalled the contemporary struggle between blacks and whites over community control of schools. That blacks were not in control of the curriculum and administration of schools in black communities was a source of resentment for many African-Americans. And the efforts of blacks to gain community control was a source of resentment for many whites.

The struggle in *Battle* is in some regards simplified but similar. As in real life, in *Battle* the schoolroom is the site of white authority over non-white, an authority that Aldo both resents and challenges. The teacher's name, "Abe," recalls Abraham Lincoln, who is perhaps for some the ultimate image of "benevolent" paternalistic white authority over blacks, the very type of authority that whites were accused of wielding in the community control debates. Thus early in the movie, the filmmakers set the tone by plugging not only into the general theme of racial oppression but into a specific and very contentious racial power struggle.

We later see more evidence of the power imbalance between human and ape. Apes even dictate human eating habits. Eating meat is against the law. When MacDonald jokes that he is hungry enough to eat a horse, Caesar disapprovingly reminds Lisa that humans used to eat dead animals. MacDonald replies, "Now we live and chew nuts—at our masters' command." Picking up on the resentment, but not too concerned about it, Caesar casually says, "We are not your masters." MacDonald looks back and quietly but firmly responds, "We're not your equals."

It is important to unpackage this statement. A member of a subordinate group, specifically a black man, protests to a member of a dominant group that he is denied equality. On the textual level, it is a fairly straightforward criticism of the fact that the apes have replaced one system of inequality with another. On the subtextual level, it is more complex. It may be a reminder to the audience that black Americans are still not equal.

Or it may say that, even after the tables have been turned, the former slaves, as MacDonald subtextually remains, still suffer. The suggestion therefore is that revenge holds no solace—the black man is still not free.

Thus *Battle* has an African-American who might in the real world seem to have the most to gain by reversing racial oppression express the film's position that asymmetrical distributions of power, no matter who is on top, are always wrong. Having MacDonald stress this point is a strategy to bring greater attention and authority to the position and to send out a signal to those who might be attracted to such a reversal. "One slavery does not avenge another," MacDonald insists in the novelization.[19] Without questioning the validity of that point, it bears mentioning that more than just philosophical conviction, but also white fear of retaliation and of losing a privileged position, was likely wrapped up in sending this message.

As with his brother in *Conquest*, MacDonald's advocacy adds authority to the film's message. In *Battle*, MacDonald states that he used to supervise the archives section of the old city. That is, MacDonald is a historian in a series which privileges knowledge of history. As the voice of history, his is the voice of authority and therefore the voice to be heeded. As a historian, he possesses historical knowledge on a textual level just as he, like his brother, is linked to the history of racial oppression and liberation on a subtextual level. Thus identified textually as an expert on history and linked subtextually to racial struggle, MacDonald carries a dual qualification to advise Caesar on racial matters.

Even though the direction of racial domination has changed in *Battle*, and even though the MacDonald in *Battle* is supposed to be the brother of the MacDonald in *Conquest*, structurally MacDonald's role has stayed stationary as the outside insider. Instead of his role in *Conquest* as the non-white adviser to the white governor who oppresses non-whites, MacDonald in *Battle* is the human adviser to the nonhuman king who oppresses humans. MacDonald is still positioned between the dominated and the dominating and still advocates for the oppressed.

Either MacDonald or his brother must have prevailed upon Caesar to avoid violence, for when attacked by the mutant humans in the Forbidden City, Caesar does not fire back and later orders his apes to stop killing once the ape village has been successfully defended. This contrasts Caesar with Kolp, who, surveying the ape city prior to his attack, declares, "When we leave, I don't want to see one tree left standing, two pieces of wood nailed together, or anything left alive. I want it to look like—that city we came from." Caesar's ability to be merciful also contrasts him with Aldo, who ambushes the retreating humans with a call of "No prisoners! No prisoners!"

The naive Caesar does not understand the threat Aldo poses. Caesar does not act when MacDonald warns that "Aldo's hatred is [not] confined to humans." And when Caesar's dying son warns him that there are those who would hurt him, Caesar immediately suspects the threat comes from humans, not fathoming that the gorillas' disloyalty could be the danger.

Likewise, Caesar is oblivious to the dangers inherent in creating another system of racial domination. Caesar begins to understand the danger arising from racial discord only after MacDonald takes him across the desert to the old city's archives section to view tapes of Zira describing the Earth's destruction. Here again the *Apes* characters look to the past to shape the future: MacDonald, aware that enmity between ape and human will destroy the Earth, as Zira and Cornelius witnessed, unless the course of events is changed, stresses the danger to spur Caesar towards ensuring equality.

This scene suggests the actualization of the possibilities inherent in the audience's viewing of the film: it is after Caesar views footage of his parents' description of Earth's future destruction—basically after he watches movies—that he is convinced that he must take action to change the future. MacDonald's taking Caesar to view films of predictions of the future has a similar purpose to making films that act as social commentary: to encourage audiences to internalize the film's message and act accordingly. Thus a parallel is established in which the characters in *Battle* do what *Battle*'s audience was supposed to do: watch filmed prophecies and then act to prevent their becoming realities. By stressing the power of knowing the future in order to change it and by showing the efficacy of watching films as a spur to political action and social change, the *Apes* series here self-referentially validates itself as political film. At the same time *Battle* does not overstate that value, for it demonstrates that movies alone are not enough to effect fundamental change.

Despite the knowledge gained by the trip to the archives, Caesar initially fails to heed the advice of MacDonald, the film's peacemaker, a peacemaker who relies on an understanding of history as a basis for his authority. Early in the film, when Caesar is first concerned about Aldo, MacDonald tries to advise him, "You know Caesar, history shows . . .," but Caesar cuts him off, saying, "That is human history—not ape history." Caesar's ahistoricism is a metaphor of U.S. ahistoricism and similarly leads to political and moral negligence.

Caesar fails to replace old models of racial domination with new models of racial equality. And the price for refusal to heed history's lessons is escalation of racial hostilities and an attack from without and from within against Caesar's fantasy of a harmonious community. The threat of internal racism, represented by Aldo, is doubled by the threat of external racism, represented by Kolp, and Caesar's failure leads to race wars on two fronts.

Again biblical resonances are crucial: the forces of hell (the Forbidden City is twice compared to hell) lead an attack on the paradisal community Caesar thinks he has created. Again we have a cautionary tale: the crisis of race relations is so overwhelming and builds to such an internal and external pressure that it cannot be contained—it escalates and eventually explodes.

In both *Conquest* and *Battle*, the film's violence is proportional to the pressure of racial conflict as a central theme. These are the films most concerned with race, and they are the ones that are the most violent. The *Apes* series in general, and these two films especially, maintain that violence is the primary language of cross-racial contact.

Like *Conquest*, *Battle* visually references real-world incidents of racial violence. At the same time Aldo imprisons the humans, Kolp attacks the village, using school buses as troop carriers. The images of the ape huts exploding are not unlike the similar scenes of destruction the audience would have seen on television from the Vietnam War, another war in which race played a major role. Thus the situation of the apes resembled that of the United States, which was also embroiled in race wars on two fronts: Bob Moses, a prominent civil rights leader, had observed in 1964 that "the guerilla war in Mississippi is not that much different from that in Vietnam."[20]

Aldo's imprisonment of the human beings in the corral "for security," despite the fact that the humans showed no disloyalty, recalls the U.S. government's forcing Japanese-Americans into concentration camps under the same pretense and with a similar lack of good cause, during World War II. The prominent visibility of an Asian man in the corral—in a series in which Asians had almost never appeared—emphasizes this connection. The corral, its fences barbed with wooden spikes, also resembles both the Nazi-created ghettoes in Europe and the Nazi murder camps. The screenplay specifically indicated that the corral shot "should in some vague way, make one think of a concentration camp."[21] This resemblance links Aldo's Nazi-sounding rhetoric of creating a "superrace" to the Nazi methods of destroying the "inferior races."

After the battle with Kolp and his forces, Caesar orders Aldo to release the humans. Aldo refuses and shouts to his soldiers, "Kill them! Kill them all!" Set in a village resembling those of Vietnam, the scene brings back chilling memories of the My Lai massacre, images of which may have been fresh in the audience's mind as the gorillas were about to "replay" that tragic scene.

A key reference to real-world racial conflict was the school bus—it is also one of the most complicated references in the *Apes* series. On the most straightforward level, Kolp's use of the buses is emblematic of his attempt to reinstate human authority, the very authority challenged and rejected by the gorillas' destruction of the schoolroom. As the school bus is retreating, the gorillas attack, kill all the humans inside, and surround the bus, cheering as Aldo triumphantly walks on the roof, shouting, "Now we go back to *our* city" (emphasis in original).[22] Thus the rebellion against human authority in the schoolroom at the film's beginning is duplicated and projected onto a larger scale towards the film's end.

But the scene is more complicated than that because by the time of *Battle*'s release, the image of the bus had become closely linked to real-world episodes of racial conflict. Rosa Parks' refusal to give up her bus seat to a white man in 1955 was one of the defining moments for the civil rights movement. The "Freedom Rides" challenging segregation in interstate bus travel were also some of the earliest events of the movement to gain national attention. The Freedom Riders were frequently harassed by law enforcement officers and were attacked, sometimes with police cooperation, by unorganized groups and by organized groups of whites like the Ku Klux Klan.

School buses in particular gained more symbolic importance as the debate over busing as a means to ensure racial integration in schools raged into one of the most divisive issues of the late sixties and early seventies. In the case of school integration and busing, blacks again faced fierce, sometimes violent, opposition from white communities that attracted national attention. In South Boston, for instance, white opponents of busing taunted African-American children being bused by waving bananas at them to suggest that the children were apes. Thus, at the time of *Battle*'s release, buses had been connected to racial conflict in the public's consciousness for two decades.

In *Battle*, from the apes' perspective, the unwanted racial "other" dwells in a dangerous decrepit city (the mutants' bombed-out Forbidden City) and uses a school bus to encroach on the peaceful "suburban" ape community. This interpretation likens Kolp and his followers to inner-city African-Americans. This view also frames the apes' resistance as similar to the reactions of suburban whites who opposed busing inner-city black children into white neighborhoods. While a reading equating the apes in general with white segregationists is hard to sustain, the above reading is consistent with the construction of Aldo and his gorilla followers as "reverse" racists and segregationists.

But the scene cannot be convincingly read as a simple inversion in which the gorillas attacking the mutants metaphorically become the white residents of South Boston taunting African-American children. While the humans in the ape village are depicted as racially oppressed, nothing in the film suggests that Kolp and the mutant humans from the Forbidden City can be seen as surrogates for economically deprived black children.

The interpretation of the gorillas as surrogates for anti-busing whites would be consistent with the film's point that the formerly oppressed can take on the brutal behavior of the oppressor. The point seems irrelevant to the scene, however, because the humans from the Forbidden City are not the oppressed riding to combat racism, but rather are oppressors riding to reimpose enslavement.

The scene could be read as an expression of white backlash: picturing a symbolic revenge for busing by inverting the symbol of "forced integration" and showing unwanted whites forcing themselves upon a community of non-whites (i.e., giving non-whites a taste of their own medicine). However, since the invading humans are all killed, the scene cannot function effectively as a white revenge fantasy (though it might serve as a validation of white paranoia).

In some regards the scene is a reversal of the real-life struggles because in the film whites use the school bus to move into the non-white space. The scene is consistent with the real-world busing controversy, however, in that the bus remains the vehicle in which the unwanted racial "other" seeks to assert power and is violently resisted.

Having the white racists drive the bus inverts the school bus symbol and complicates the scene. Does the use of the bus suggest that the means used to achieve liberation, in this case busing, may be turned against that liberation? The scene could be seen as raising the question about the true nature of busing: Is busing a legitimate means to achieve integration or a hostile racial intrusion? If we take the former position, are we aligned with Kolp? If we take the latter, are we equated with Aldo?

The scene is so very complicated in large measure because of the construction of Aldo and the gorillas as both currently oppressing and formerly oppressed. In relation to the humans of the village, they are oppressors who are trying to deny the freedom of others. In relation to the humans of the Forbidden City, they are the formerly oppressed fighting to maintain their freedom. Yet in this scene they act both like formerly oppressed trying to prevent reenslavement and like the white racists who oppressed blacks and attacked them on buses.

The gorillas are constructed in such a way that they do double or even triple duty: it is difficult to know if in this scene they are standing in for African-American racists or white racists or a combination of both. In the film, and particularly in this scene, do they represent white brutality, legitimate black self-defense or, because they slaughtered the humans as they retreated, black revenge?

Thus the scene confuses the referents and renders a coherent, consistent interpretation nearly impossible. But it is perhaps the case that a tidy reading is not necessary, even if one were possible. For even if the scene does not resolve these issues in a clear way and allows many different interpretations, it may be enough for the scene just to raise these questions and, in so doing, connect the film's events at some level to the real-world conflicts which helped shape the movie. Even unclear allegory may be evocative.

Battle's action is bracketed by the schoolroom incident near the film's beginning and the school bus attack near the film's end—both conflicts between white humans and the darkest apes—that recalled community control and busing, two of the most emotionally explosive racial power struggles of the time. This bracketing served to set the film's tone and weave real-world racial battles into the fictional *Battle*.

Throughout the series, racial conflict was the most salient manifestation of the human paradox. *Battle* similarly connects racial conflict to fundamental questions of human behavior. Having shown the apes as racially oppressive, the film uses Aldo's murder of Caesar's son and the reaction it provokes to show the apes susceptible to the self-destructive nature of humans.

When Aldo gives the order to massacre the humans in the corral, Caesar runs in front of the soldiers to stop them. "Move, Caesar," Aldo orders, "or we shall kill you!" For the apes this is unthinkable; even some of Aldo's soldiers are shocked. Virgil, framed with Lisa and a gorilla, declares, "Ape has never killed ape—let alone an ape child. Aldo has killed an ape child. The branch did not break. It was cut, with a sword." This shot has a striking dissonance: the words, of ape murder, are words of disharmony, but the picture, all three ape races together, is one of togetherness. The juxtaposition of the image and the dialogue points out the disparity between the ideal of racial harmony and the reality of racial hostility.

The reaction shots that follow underscore the sense of horror and ape unity evoked by the revelation that Aldo is now the simian Cain and that his hatred of humans led him to hurt an ape. The gorillas who were aiming their guns at Caesar lower them in shame. "Aldo. You killed," accuses a pointing gorilla. "Aldo killed," repeats an aghast orangutan. "Aldo has broken our most sacred law," a chimpanzee says gravely. The apes start grumbling in disapproval. "What's the matter with them?" a human asks MacDonald. "I guess you might say they just joined the human race" is his response. And indeed the all-important distinction between ape and human, that "man destroys man, apes do not destroy apes," has been obliterated.

Planet used the ape to critique humans: if the "savage" animal can in fact become "civilized," then humans are not necessarily superior to apes. *Battle* goes in a different direction and suggests that if "civilized" apes can act like "savage" humans, then apes are not necessarily superior to humans. This point was important enough for the Corringtons to emphasize by writing in their first draft screenplay that "one of the chief moral advantages apes have always claimed above humanity is now gone. . . . The end of ape innocence has come: all that talk of Dr. Zaius in *Beneath* and *Planet* has now come to naught. . . . Ape and man are on a similar moral level."[23] The human paradox has become the ape paradox.

Throughout the series, the apes define humanity in solely negative terms ("alone among God's primates he kills for sport, or lust or greed"), and they are determined to assert their difference from humans ("man destroys man, apes do not destroy apes") and maintain that difference ("ape shall never kill ape"). At the end of the series, the apes symbolically "join the human race," but their method of entry is murder. The ability to, as Taylor says, "make war against [one's] brother," is the mark of being human. Thus *Battle* does not totally escape the series' essentialism, an essentialism which presents a rather grim view of human "nature," even if that nature is learned rather than given. Considering this view of "human nature," it is not surprising that the filmmakers had such a hard time envisioning reconciliation, let alone redemption.

Following Virgil's revelation, the outraged apes start chanting "Ape has killed ape" as Aldo, apparently reverting to his primitive instincts, tries to escape by climbing a tree. An infuriated Caesar follows him. When Aldo takes out his sword and tries to strike Caesar with it, Caesar throws him to his death, just as, earlier, Aldo had sent Caesar's son spiraling out of a tree to the ground. Both instances of the ape fall are at once metaphoric and literal: the apes' moral fall causes and is symbolized by the physical fall. That both falls are connected to trees in the apes' would-be Garden of Eden is significant because the association of the tree with the apes' moral pollution is a visual and thematic link to the story of the fall from grace in *Genesis*.

As noted, *Battle* has a religious tone. There is a struggle between paradise and hell; hell must be fought back and paradise must be purged so God's will can be fulfilled. At first glance Aldo appears to function as a scapegoat onto whom the community's sins are projected and then vicariously cleansed through his death. The film undercuts this notion, however.

During the battle scenes, Caesar is merciful and orders the apes to stop killing once it is clear that Kolp has lost, whereas Aldo is merciless and orders his soldiers to slaughter the retreating humans.[24] Thus it appears that, unlike Aldo, Caesar is by nature unable to kill unless attacked.

Up until Caesar's confrontation with Aldo, it seems that the chimpanzee and the gorilla have fundamentally different natures, just as apes were assumed to have a fundamentally different nature from humans. But just as the distinction between ape and human unravels, the distinction between chimpanzee and gorilla is undone when Caesar takes vengeance by slaying Aldo. In killing the killer, Caesar himself becomes the killer. He takes on Aldo's sin, and there is no symbolic redemption. Society cannot be vicariously cleansed, it must be actually transformed. Thus the film in fact disavows scapegoating and thereby critiques one of the most common aspects of racism. *Battle* is consistent with the ideological position of the *Apes* series that, on the personal and the collective level, projection, revenge, and violence fail to redeem.

Caesar, the hero of the film, therefore embodies the problem of ape society, which is emblematic of the problem the film addresses: Caesar's revenge for his son's death echoes the apes' revenge for the racial domination practiced by humans. This point is made in the scene directly following Aldo's death. Worried about the implications of his actions, Caesar asks Virgil, "Should one murder be avenged by another?" the corollary question being "should one slavery be avenged by another?" Virgil's answer: "Only the future can tell. So let us start building it."

The next shot shows the chains on the corral being cut. But much to the apes' surprise, the humans do not rush forth in appreciation of their liberation.

> MACDONALD: If we appear to be lacking in gratitude, Caesar — what have we to be grateful for? If you mean to set us free then free us completely.
>
> CAESAR: What do you mean?
>
> MACDONALD: We are not your children, Caesar. We have a destiny, too. As equals. Respecting each other. Living together, with love.
>
> CAESAR: Love? The human way is violence and death.
>
> VIRGIL: Aldo wasn't human. Was he, Caesar?

As MacDonald makes this demand to be completely freed, he is foregrounded in the shot and a white man, slightly blurred, is in the background. The shot textually foregrounds ape-human antagonism, but visually reminds us that black-white conflict is always looming, undergirding and giving meaning to the story. Furthermore, MacDonald's lines may be directed to the audience as much as to Caesar. Another subtextual plea is thus made for racial justice and black-white equality.

The importance of MacDonald's spoken plea is consistent with the series' attribution of extraordinary power to the ability to speak. *Battle* is the only film in which there is a real possibility of the parties working out their differences because it is the first time in the series when each species can talk to the "other."[25] In *Battle*, direct communication by other than violent means is finally possible.

Consistent with the other films in the series, however, MacDonald's plea does not succeed. It is the counsel of Virgil, a fellow ape, that is decisive. The scene replicates the climax of *Conquest*, in which Lisa, not MacDonald, convinces Caesar to spare the humans. The scene thus emphasizes that, while mediators may help, those with the power to control and distort the lives of others must through acts of courage and a leap of faith relinquish that power, for they also have the greatest ability and responsibility to create a just society.

Ironically, while in the last three films the apes were surrogates for blacks, by ceasing to scapegoat humans as the repository of evil and by resolving to confront the evil within themselves, the apes were in fact following the advice that Winthrop Jordan had given whites:

Conceivably there was a way out . . . from the vicious cycle of degradation, an opening of better hope demanding an unprecedented and
perhaps impossible measure of courage, honesty and sheer nerve. If the
white man turned to stare at the animal within him. . . . If he once fully
acknowledged the powerful forces which drove his being, the necessity
of imputing them to others would drastically diminish. . . . If he were willing to call the beast no more the Negro's than his own, then conceivably
he might set foot on a better road.[26]

The exchange between Caesar, MacDonald, and Virgil underscores
that the apes and human beings are not so dissimilar after all. And the film
argues that racial heritage, even the heritage of victimization, does not protect one from becoming a victimizer. As Baldwin emphasized, "there *is* no
animal level beneath which 'we' cannot fall" (emphasis in original).[27]

The obliteration of the distinction between human and ape and the
exercise of political choice hold the key to the *Apes* series' second theory
of racial oppression. As we have seen, in *Planet* and *Beneath*, there is no
explanation of the apes' history and the most likely explanation for their
tendency to oppress the humans is biological determinism. Not so by the
end of the series. Beginning with *Escape* and then continuing in *Conquest*
and *Battle*, the series provides the missing history of the planet of the apes
and critiques the racial theory of the first film.

By creating a story in which the apes, in essence, become human,
Battle is suggesting that racial characteristics are more the product of
history and culture than of a biological "nature." This point — that identity
is created rather than just given — is a critique of another racist notion
which appeals to biology and the mystique of blood to bolster the belief that
there are inherent bodily differences that serve both as stable markers of
"race" and as reliable determinants of action and character. (If environmental and cultural factors are taken into account in racist ideologies, they
are often interpreted in a Lamarckian "acquired characteristics" framework in which environmentally induced characteristics may be inherited,
thus rendering them practically the same as genetic traits.)

Battle challenges the biological mystique of these assumptions by
demonstrating that physical appearance and genes are not reliable guides
to character. Contrary to the expectations established in the earlier films,
in *Battle* ape *does* kill ape; chimpanzees *can* be vengeful and murderous;
orangutans *can* want peace with humans and may search for truth rather
than suppress it; humans *can* choose peace, even if they have superior
weapons; and even gorillas, whose portrayal as villains *is* consistent with
the rest of the series, are not irredeemably villainous.[28]

Thus *Battle* emerges as a discourse about the mutability of racial identity, and, as Joyce Corrington's earlier comments suggested, about both the

possibility and the need to change one's "nature," to adapt, to evolve, in order to survive. This theme also resonates with Baldwin's insights:

> Identity would seem to be the garment with which one covers the naked-ness of the self: in which case it is best that the garment be loose, a little like the robes of the desert, through which robes one's nakedness can always be felt, and, sometimes, discerned. The trust in one's nakedness is all that gives one the power to change ones robes.[29]

Battle makes the same suggestion as Baldwin: if identity is not a biological given, not the body, but merely a garment, it can be taken off and adjusted. We can even discard it and choose a different one.

By showing apes acting contrary to "ape nature," that is, acting the way humans are supposed to act due to "human nature," *Battle* deemphasizes "nature's" role in determining the course of human events. Reversing *Planet*'s theory, *Battle* locates an explanation for racial conflict in the realm of culture and politics rather than biology. *Conquest* and *Battle* state that political decisions, not biological determinants, created the planet of the apes. This statement implies not only that a victim may become a victim-izer but also that both the roles of victim and victimizer may be renounced. Oppression and victimization emerge as the results of *choices*, not of biological, or even historical, "inevitability."[30]

The implications of this theory are precisely the opposite of the im-plications of *Planet*'s theory of racial conflict and oppression. Rather than scapegoating a genetically predetermined, and therefore unalterable, "human nature," assigning responsibility to *and accepting responsibility* in the historical/political realm means that one can meaningfully affect the problem. This move suggests that we can and — if we wish to survive — *must* change our "nature" and consciously shape our reality. In *Battle* the human paradox is a problem, not a prison. *Battle* thus participates in what Haraway identifies as primatology's ongoing discourse about "the reform and recon-struction of human nature." As Corrington noted, the script "was a state-ment that . . . by acts of will you can change what seems predestined . . . . Through consciousness . . . by trying to rid themselves of this sin of vio-lence [it was possible for the characters] . . . to change their future."

Through the device of the historical time loop, we see that humans have created apes in their own image, or, more precisely, that the *apes* created *themselves* in humanity's image. Thus the species difference, quite sharp in *Planet*, *Beneath*, and *Escape*, is blurred by *Battle*. By eliminating this fundamental distinction between ape and human, by depicting the apes and the humans as increasingly similar and by portraying the oppressed as oppressors, *Battle* tightens the likeness of apes and humans. This tighten-ing of the likeness accompanied the transformation of the series toward a more direct allegory of black-white relations and corresponded to the tightening of the likeness between blacks and whites in the minds of many. For example, Corrington, who is white, commented that she did not see blacks as "innocent" or as analogues to noble savages because "they're just as bad as" whites.

In the *Apes* series, apes and humans cannot begin the process of truly living together until the apes experience and acknowledge their fall. The possibility of peace is envisioned as existing only after the antagonistic parties realize the ways in which they are the same. Racial difference is thus identified as a source of racial conflict, and only after difference is no longer recognized may peace have a chance.

The *Apes* series' assumptions of the essentially troublesome nature of difference and of the preferability of likeness resonate with the assumptions of scientific primatology. Discussing the "scientific" conclusion that "because the genetic interests of individuals are not identical ... conflicts of interest perpetually endanger the survival of cooperative relationships," Haraway notes that "evolutionary biology's bottom line on difference ... [is that] in the end, non-identity is antagonistic; it always threatens 'the survival of cooperative relationships.' In the end, only the sign of the Same, of the replication of the one identical to itself, seems to promise peace." Haraway asks: "Can patriarchal monotheistic cultures ever allow another primal story?"[31]

Battle both asserts the age-old bottom line that racial difference necessarily is a problem leading to racial violence and argues that the realization that there *is* no difference is the solution to that problem. But this is neither a real departure from the formulation of difference as "dilemma" nor a solution to the "dilemma": the insistence on eliminating difference *reinforces* the notion that difference is inherently a problem. There is no need to deny what does not matter.

If nondifference is the key to peace, then the presence of difference is by definition intolerable and must always lead to conflict and war. The notion that we should treat each other well because we are "all the same under the skin" implies that we should brutalize anyone who is truly unlike us, anyone we deem not the "same under the skin."[32] Note, for example, that in the *Apes* series, the mutants in *Beneath* have the closest thing to a racially egalitarian society and are all literally the same under the skin. But they are also hostile to the apes, who do not pass the test of sameness.

If the apes must become "human" in order for peace to prevail, is it then the case that, for example, African-Americans must become "white"? Obliteration of particularity and imposition of hyper-assimilation are high prices to pay for acceptance. My question here is: Will U.S. racial mythology—or our racial reality—ever allow another story of cross-racial, cross-ethnic interaction? Difference should be neither an idol nor a devil. We must *accept* difference—and neither worship it nor fear it, neither mystify it nor deny it — if we are to resolve the conflicts surrounding dissimilarity.[33]

Battle's message of sameness lurking under the illusion of difference is implicit even in the *Apes* series' production techniques. The film contends that difference is a mask, much like the makeup used to disguise humans as apes. Under the elaborate ape appliances used to differentiate the actors from humans are in fact human faces. *Battle* argues that difference is an illusion caused by layers of misrepresentation and interpretation (like layers of makeup) that mask essential sameness.[34]

Perhaps more than any film in the *Apes* series, *Battle* displays considerable ambivalence about the issues it raises. For example, the film's assumption that difference is intolerable and must necessarily lead to violence is a central belief of racism, and is all too often a self-fulfilling prophecy. However, *Battle*'s interracial trio of Caesar, Virgil, and Mac-Donald, like the mediating characters throughout the *Apes* series — chimpanzees that help humans and humans of various races that help apes — undermines the assumption that difference threatens "cooperative relationships." These characters all choose to cross racial boundaries to fulfill mutual needs and desires. Therefore the series' heroes demonstrate that difference need not preclude cooperation.

The free will issue resonates with the biblical themes the Corringtons wove throughout *Battle*. From the series' beginning, knowledge is contained in the "Forbidden Zone" — like the forbidden tree of knowledge in Garden of Eden. The apes declare the zone of knowledge forbidden to ensure that their "innocence" does not become "contaminated," as Dr. Zaius fears. But unlike Zaius in *Planet* and *Beneath*, in *Battle* the ape leadership has the courage to go into the Forbidden City and eat the fruits of its knowledge. As in *Genesis*, the apes thereby forfeit their innocence. Yet, also as in *Genesis*, the knowledge of good and evil which they gain is necessary for them to realize that they have free will and can make meaningful choices.

The series had been moving towards the highlighting of political choice since *Escape*. All the later films suggest that the problem of racial conflict is one of political, historical choices rather than simply an inherent tendency to oppression and violence. This is implicit in *Escape*, where, as we have seen, the humans could have chosen not to enslave the apes and thereby prevented the entire enslavement-revenge cycle. But the point is more explicit in *Conquest*, when Caesar chooses to go through with the revolution after debating its merits with MacDonald and later chooses to change his tactics and act with compassion after Lisa protests. Neither of Caesar's actions is caused by a predetermined nature. And in *Battle*, effects are demonstrated to have political rather than biological causes when war, peace, slavery, and justice are shown as deliberate decisions, not uncontrollable urges. Patterns of power and violence are no longer naturalized as in *Planet*, but are now historicized—shown as the results of intentional choices.

This shift makes a place for will. Caesar, realizing the options and the consequences, chooses to change his path, Aldo chooses to remain on his. Even in Kolp's case, the question arises whether he is in fact driven by radiation-induced insanity or simply by a desire for vengeance. Kolp's actions cannot be explained away by radiation-induced "madness," for his assistant Mendez appears to have been exposed to the same radiation and nevertheless chooses peace.

While the change to a focus on the importance of will and choice was implicit in Paul Dehn's scripts for *Escape* and *Conquest*, the change was nowhere apparent in his treatment for *Battle*, which depicted a total inversion of slavery and a continuation of a brutal cycle of race wars that the apes seem compelled to perpetuate. Thus Dehn was unable or unwilling to follow through on the implications of his own earlier work. The Corringtons, however, continued the movement Dehn had begun towards emphasizing will and choice as central to power and politics.

This is by far the most significant difference between the Corringtons' concept for *Battle* and Paul Dehn's. Dehn's *Battle* treatment culminated his vision of the *Apes* series, a vision that pictured life as an unending cycle of tit-for-tat hostility and brutality from which no one can escape. In this worldview, the flow of history resembles the effect created when two mirrors face each other: a fixed system of repetition, endless, monotonous, and enclosed. Neither knowledge of the past nor foreknowledge of the future makes any difference. This renders people much like passive mirrors who have no choice but to reflect back what is put in front of them, unable to amend it.

But by having the apes commit to changing the future by rejecting past behavior and changing current behavior, the Corringtons' *Battle* screenplay empowers the victim to *choose* not to become a victimizer. Thus *Battle* rejects the idea of a victim as, to use Joel Kovel's phrase, "the clay on whom social inscriptions are written." For, as Kovel points out, "where there is no responsibility, there is no creativity either. History simply recycles itself."[35]

While some might argue that Dehn's vision is a more "realistic" view of history, the fact remains that the *Apes* series was about the *future* and that there is no compelling reason that a fictional—or the actual—future must stay locked into a repetition of what has traditionally been. Why not have the courage to envision the future breaking out of the destructive cycles of the past? While we cannot escape the facts of history and we must confront its consequences, we need not condemn ourselves to imprisonment in them. Especially in science fiction, where we are able to go "where no one has gone before," why not challenge the assumption that what *has* been *must* be? This imaginative leap might seem difficult during a time when U.S. society had been so battered, but it is not impossible. Indeed, it is out of such painful times that we might expect the emergence of fantasies of transcendence that, while not denying the reality of present crises, imagine successful problem resolution. While *Battle* is not a naive denial of the real difficulties, conflicts, and dangers of life, the filmmakers here at least tried to do what Judith Shatnoff had criticized the makers of *Planet* for not doing — imagine "life in other terms developing other values" and suggest that history is not necessarily destiny.[36]

The latter part of the *Apes* series argues that knowledge of the future is crucial for controlling it. And in a sense, "knowledge" of the "future" is what the *Apes* series had been giving audiences all along in an attempt to encourage them to make good choices. Although the specifics of that future — an ape-controlled world — were fictional, the characteristics of that future — an endless cycle of racial oppression and resentment, worship of violence, cataclysmic destruction — were factual and part of the audience's past, current, and likely future experience. In contrast to *Planet* and *Beneath*, the later films' message is that, depending on what we do, the future may — *but need not* — look like the past. Only in the context of a world in which political realities are based on controllable choices, rather than on biological programming, would such a message hold any relevance. Shifting focus from the biological to the historical and political realm was necessary for the films to have any positive effect. The filmmakers needed to present ethical actions as potentially fruitful rather than ultimately futile.

It is only in *Conquest* and *Battle* that the activity of the peacemakers has a chance of being successful. But even here the prospects for reconciliation are in doubt. Both MacDonald brothers initially fail to persuade Caesar. The persuasion comes only after the intercedence of Caesar's fellow apes and after much violence. Ironically, the final two films are the most positive about the possibility for political solutions, and yet are also the most anxious about what must be endured to get there. A slim possibility for peace seems to be the best the filmmakers could envision.

Assigning historical relevance to political activity, however, was an attempt to make manifest the possibilities inherent in the *Apes* series' various mediating figures: effective political action in the cause of racial justice. In the first three films, resistance is futile against oppressive authorities: in *Planet*, Zaius suppresses the facts of ape history, in *Beneath*, Ursus gets his imperialist war, and in *Escape*, Hasslein murders Zira. In *Conquest* and *Battle*, however, those who challenge oppressive authority ultimately prevail: Caesar defeats Breck; Kolp and Aldo are killed; and Caesar and MacDonald make a commitment to begin again.

In the Corringtons' screenplay, the commitment to "begin again" is juxtaposed with the dire consequences of failing to achieve racial peace. In the script, before Kolp begins the attack on the apes, he tells his assistant Alma that they must cage the beast or "destroy the whole zoo" and orders that should the humans lose the battle, she should fire their nuclear missile at the apes. When Alma learns that Kolp has been killed, she prepares to launch the Alpha and Omega bomb.

Alma is stopped by another of Kolp's assistants, Mendez, who earlier in the film had counseled Kolp against going to war. He is the ancestor of the Mendez who led the mutant population in *Beneath*. And it is here in the fifth film where the perplexing worship of the Alpha and Omega bomb is finally explained. As Mendez stops her, he exclaims:

> This is the Alpha and Omega Bomb! It can destroy not only Ape City, but the entire Earth! Activate it and we become nothing. Leave it, and its very presence will ensure that at least we remain *something* — and may become something better. It must never be exploded. It must be respected — even venerated. For one of its ancestors made us what we are. And what we are, shall from this day forward, be called beautiful [emphasis in original].[37]

Finally, three films after *Beneath*, the mutant religion practiced in that film is put into context: We see here how the bomb became a Christ figure for the mutants as the descendant of their maker. The linkage with *Beneath* cleared up some of that film's most confusing elements. However, although the scenes were filmed, all references to the bomb were eventually edited out of the film's final cut.

This was a point of much debate between the Corringtons and producer Arthur P. Jacobs. Joyce Corrington recalls that she and John Corrington saw the bomb scenes as central to the film. They wanted the bomb scenes to establish the threat that the sin of violence could end with the destruction of the Earth and to underscore the necessity of preventing that destruction by changing behavior. As she puts it:

> Structurally the bomb was very important to us because . . . we thought we had to keep the consequences of the fall alive and major. . . . What we wanted was a statement that . . . possibly by acts of will you can change what seems predestined. Because if you have predestination, they're gonna blow up the Earth again and you're just in this endless loop of blowing up the earth and escaping and coming back in time again over and over again. . . . [The point was] bringing the bomb up where you could see it . . . bringing it out of . . . [the] subconscious into . . . consciousness . . . [to say] this is our destiny, if we don't work things out this is going to destroy us.

The time loop could be used either to suggest an unending cycle of predetermined violence or, as the Corringtons preferred, to give the characters an opportunity to break that cycle through deliberate present-day action. The Corringtons saw the bomb scenes as crucial for moving the *Apes* series' resolution towards the latter possibility and for framing the characters' choice as reversing the sins of racial hate and violence or facing total annihilation. Only after Caesar is shown the threat of global destruction which racism brings does he begin to move toward real cooperation and peace. Joyce Corrington's impression is that either Jacobs had a more pessimistic view and did not understand how the characters could change the future depicted in *Planet* and *Beneath*, or that he just did not want to deal with the bomb issue any more.

The Corringtons were correct in their belief that the bomb scenes add a heightened sense of urgency. If Joyce Corrington's assessment of Jacobs' concerns is correct, however, Jacobs was right in that the mention of the bomb could be interpreted as a prediction of eventual nuclear doom, given the dubious prospects for peace that the *Apes* series depicts. It is plausible that the references to the bomb were taken out due to concern that they might have sabotaged whatever positive message *Battle* may have offered. Even with the bomb scenes taken out, the film suggests only a slim possibility for racial peace between ape and ape, ape and human, and, we may assume, between human and human.

The scenes of the Alpha and Omega bomb and of the mutant's developing bomb-worship likely would have keyed the audience's memory of *Beneath* and its cataclysmic ending. The memory of that ending might have made more difficult, though not necessarily prevented, the audience's imaginative consideration of alternate futures in which calamity might be averted. Not picturing the bomb at all renders Earth's possible destruction less an issue.

Even without the bomb scenes, the nuclear destruction theme established in *Planet* and maintained throughout the series remains present and is specifically referred to when Caesar views the tape of Zira describing Earth's destruction. And one critic noted that *Battle* "ends appropriately on a note of reconciliation between man and ape. But we can't help remembering that in *Beneath the Planet of the Apes*, the second picture in the series and obviously set much further into the future, they eventually destroyed the world."[38] Thus, even with the bomb scenes gone, the nuclear threat remained, and was as likely to justify Jacobs' fears by tempering *Battle*'s hopeful elements as it was to fulfill the Corringtons' hopes by underscoring the film's warning.

Although edited out of the theatrical and video versions, the bomb scenes, and a few other edited scenes, are sometimes included in television broadcasts of *Battle*. Consequently, both versions of the film have entered into the culture and, given that much of the *Apes* audience grew up seeing, or currently sees, the films on television, many viewers may be more familiar with, and respond to, the version with the bomb. In any case, neither version offers an especially good prospect for peace.

The *Apes* series appeals to a desire for racial reconciliation, but that reconciliation never fully comes within the films' narratives. The films create suspense by continually encouraging the audience to wonder if racial peace will be achieved, then answering "no," only to offer that possibility again. *Planet* and *Beneath* end with entirely depressing scenes which leave no room for hope. But, as the producers became aware of the viability of continuing the series, the films' endings changed. The narratives of the last three films end with scenes of violence and destruction followed by a scene of hope: the surviving chimpanzee baby in *Escape*, Caesar's message of reconciliation in *Conquest*, and the apparent beginning of peaceful coexistence in *Battle*.

The motivation for this pattern may have been primarily to keep open the possibility for another sequel by never quite concluding the story. This pattern's effect, however, is continually to offer the audience hope of reconciliation and then dash that hope in the opening moments of the next film. In a move that worked against the traditional narrative closure of Hollywood film, the *Apes* series never allows for a definite resolution. The series repeatedly makes overtures towards racial peace, moves toward it, approaches it, but never actually reaches it.

The refusal, or failure, to create a state of just and peaceful racial coexistence mirrors that of the society out of which the films came: racial peace remains a goal ostensibly aspired to but never actually achieved. By depicting a repetitive race war continuing throughout the centuries, without any real victory for any side, the *Apes* saga analogized the American war over the color-line that had raged on for four centuries — also with no winners.

Battle's final scene comes after Caesar, believing that the threat of war from the humans may not be over, says that the apes "must be patient and wait." Caesar's face fades out and in its place appears the face of the Lawgiver introduced in the film's prologue. We see that the Lawgiver has been speaking to a group of ape and human children. The move from a segregated schoolroom at the film's start to a racially mixed class indicates that there has been some racial progress. He looks at the crowd of human and ape children (only chimpanzee children for some reason) to whom he has been telling the story and says: "We still wait, my children. But as I look at ape and humans living in friendship, in harmony and at peace, now some six hundred years after Caesar's death, at least we wait with hope for the future." A little African-American girl then says, "Lawgiver, who knows about the future?" At that point a chimpanzee pulls her ponytail and she pushes the chimpanzee down. The Lawgiver's response is the series' final line: "Perhaps," he tells her, "only the dead." The camera then pans to a statue of Caesar, and as the shot tracks in close on its face, we see that the statue is crying.

Since this scene takes place six hundred years after Caesar's commitment to peaceful coexistence, the children's interactions should be seen as a signal of the state and the direction of ape-human relations. The scene was intended by Director J. Lee Thompson to be ambiguous, and a variety of interpretations can be sustained. The girl was deliberately written as black, but Thompson does not recall if there was a conscious reason. While we cannot ascertain the intention of this choice, we can assess its effect. The pulling of her hair, and the subsequent pushing, could be mere childhood roughhousing and a symbol of the playful coexistence of ape and human. Or it could be a sign that there is subtle hostility between the apes and human beings that is manifested in violent play.

If it is a symbol that relations between ape and humans are good, it could have implications for human racial relationships, the very relationships that were the primary, if unstated, concern of the series. It might suggest that if African-Americans feel comfortable enough to playfully push members of the former master race, the relations between them and the other former master race, whites, may have likewise improved. That a black child feels comfortable playfully pushing an ape child could also be a sign that African-Americans have better relations with the apes than do whites and have a privileged position relative to whites, as MacDonald did throughout *Battle*. This might imply that relations between apes and whites and between African-Americans and whites are still strained.[39]

Likewise, the series' last image, that of the crying statue of Caesar, may be variously decoded. We know that Caesar is dead and the Lawgiver declares that only the dead know the future. Therefore Caesar might be crying tears of joy because he knows that racial peace has at last been achieved. He may, however, be crying in sadness because racial hostility has not abated. Corrington thinks that the latter interpretation is more correct, given her understanding of Jacobs' views about changing the future. She argues that Jacobs "couldn't imagine getting out of the time track [in which Earth was destroyed]. I think that's what the tears were for . . . [that there] was no hope of getting out of destroying the Earth again. . . . With the crying statue you're saying you're locked into the destruction.[40]

Thus Caesar may be crying because his efforts to avoid cataclysm were in vain. He may be crying because his son was sacrificed, be it in vain or not. Or perhaps he cries in saddened bewilderment, wondering, as should we, why—in the film as in reality—so much fear, hatred, and violence was generated and endured by so many just to create an integrated classroom.

By the series' end, the filmmakers were including references to the other films that they knew could only have been picked up by *Apes* "buffs."

Battle makes an interesting play with time, which would have been noticed only by those with a detailed memory of the first film. The Lawgiver begins his story in 2670. When Taylor begins his speech in the opening of *Planet*, the ship's "Earth Time" clock reads 2673. Thus the series takes us almost full circle in terms of time — we are right back where we started. As we see the statue of Caesar crying, out in space Taylor is about to start his soliloquy on the human paradox. But in terms of racial conflict, does the series really return where it started? Have we moved forward? Indeed, can we, move forward? These are questions that the films invite us to ponder. Like the Lawgiver, we may wonder what Taylor may find when he lands.

After the final battle, Caesar declares his intention to "rebuild what's ruined and begin again." He asks MacDonald, "can we make the future what we wish?" MacDonald, the voice of history, can answer only with a hopeful, but not positive, "I've heard that it's possible, Caesar." Thus what the future holds is an open question which we must try to answer, but not a question which the films can answer.

FIVE

Conclusion: Television, Comics, Toys and Comebacks

As we have noted, the *Apes* series is dystopian. The filmmakers took the conflicts of the time, intensified and escalated them, and refused to imagine their successful resolution. This is a distinction from many other popular culture treatments of conflict, which often derive their appeal from the symbolic resolution — or suppression — of societal anxieties and tensions. Examples of this technique in the treatment of racial conflict can be seen in two recent movie examples, the *Rocky* series and *Edward Scissorhands*.

In the *Rocky* series, success and self-respect for working-class white men are achieved through the continual abuse and battering of the bodies of, predominantly, African-American men. The *Rocky* films owe their privileged place in U.S. culture not only to their "rags to riches" appeal, but also to the enduring myth of white victimization by "reverse racism." In this series, most of which coincided with the Reagan and Bush administration's assault on the victories of the civil rights movement, the threat posed by independent assertive black men competing with the white hero is neutralized by their physical defeat (Apollo in *Rocky II*, Clubber in *Rocky III*) or by their subordination to serving the goals and needs of Rocky (Apollo and his trainer in *Rocky III* and *Rocky IV*).

In *Rocky* film after *Rocky* film, racial regeneration is achieved through racial violence. Released during a time when many had concluded that efforts on behalf of black Americans had "gone too far," the films, intentionally or not, symbolically managed this "crisis" by depicting both the successful containment — through brutal violence — of African-American aspirations and the repositioning of blacks back to "their proper place." The *Rocky* series attempted a cultural curtailment of the possibilities for non-whites, limiting them to servant or enemy.

In *Edward Scissorhands*, a white woman ventures into a dark and mysterious castle and finds the film's hero. Edward is brought back to the

146

predominantly white community, and on the basis of physical difference is sequentially feared; fetishized; exploited; suspected and unjustly persecuted for a variety of crimes, most importantly the false charge of sexually assaulting a white woman; chased out of the neighborhood; and almost killed for daring to love a white teenage girl. His life endangered, Edward escapes back to his original home, with the aid of an African-American police officer who sympathizes with him and presumably identifies with his plight.

The connection with the African-American officer is crucial, for the film recapitulates much of the experience of African-Americans in the United States and of the United States' history of racial conflict, even down to the belief that the demise of the community's most rabid racist can right the wrongs in which the whole community participated and from which the whole community profited.

The film functions as fantasy in that, even in exile, Edward still is in a position of service to the white community. Worshipping the beauty of the white girl, Edward sculpts ice statues of her. The ice chippings are carried on the wind and provide snow for the town. With a blanket of cold whiteness covering the town and hiding the culpability of its citizens, the town enjoys the fruits of Edward's labor without confronting his existence or their shameful treatment of him. The fantasy goes even deeper, for once he is removed from their presence, the remaining members of the community pay no price for their inhumane actions, their sins having been vicariously "atoned for" by the death of the town bully.

Like much of U.S. politics and culture, *Scissorhands* assumes that the presence of a racial "other" necessarily constitutes a conflict — often irreconcilable — that must "inevitably" lead to violence. Difference being unmanageable, the film concludes that the only solution to the problem of Edward's presence is his banishment, a proposal advocated by some to this day as a solution to the "problem" of the black presence in the United States.

Both the *Rocky* films and *Edward Scissorhands* present symbolic solutions to the United States' problem of racial conflict, albeit negative ones: the *Rocky* films locate the solution in the subordination of black to white Americans and *Scissorhands* suggests the solution lies in a back-to–Africa, or back-to-the-ghetto, style separation of the races.

No such easy solutions, positive or negative, are offered in the *Apes* films. Ape and human are depicted as being in a state of continual mutual animosity which nothing seems to resolve. The characters who advocate racial reconciliation fail and sometimes die for their efforts. In all the *Apes* films, save for *Battle*, despite the best hopes of those who are committed to racial peace, violent racial oppression cannot be stopped. That the advocates for racial peace are consistently valorized in the films, and yet consistently fail, expresses frustration over the slow progress towards racial harmony. This mixture of hope and doubt is perhaps the most pertinent expression of the anxiety of the times. The characters themselves understand the "inevitability" of racial violence. In *Escape*, when Cornelius asks Louis whether he and Zira will be killed if they are found, the human's grim answer is "Ultimately." And Armando assures Caesar in *Conquest* that Caesar must stay hidden, for "the mere fact of your existence would be regarded as a great threat to mankind."

That the films present a struggle for racial dominance, rather than, for instance, a competition between economic ideologies, as the cause of the Earth's destruction indicates the tremendous weight the *Apes* movies place on solving this seemingly unsolvable problem. Each of the *Apes* films advocates racial peace with conviction and also forcefully—indeed violently— rules out that possibility at the same time. *Battle* holds out the possibility in the end, but even here it is tenuous. The audience is told that "the greatest danger of all is that the danger never ends." Peace is possible, but the threat of renewed hostility is always looming. Permanent harmony cannot be assured, and a tense truce may be the most we can accomplish. Vigilance is required, and the chances for reconciliation are presented as, at best, questionable.

The *Apes* films, to use anthropologist Clifford Geertz's terms, are both models *of* and models *for* race relations. They are models *of* race relations in that they observe and depict that different races exist in a state of contention and that this state continually produces asymmetrical relations of power and domination resulting in violence. Even the racially oppressed, once in power, give in to division and oppression. Apes and humans, of various races, are shown as capable of being victimizers and bigots. No one gets off the hook (except, arguably, chimpanzees, with whom the audience is supposed to be aligned throughout the five films. This lapse, however, is corrected in the television show, where we see some dishonorable and even psychopathic chimpanzees.)

The films are also models *for* race relations and act as myth, "provid[ing] a scenario or prescription for action,"[1] in that they advocate racial cooperation and peace and also present examples of race relations that break out of the hostile pattern. The *Apes* series depicts members of hostile species (apes and humans) banding together; it shows members of different races (chimpanzees, orangutans, and gorillas; Latinos and whites; blacks and whites) uniting when faced with a common threat; and it shows opposition to racial oppression as the coalescing factor between racial constituencies.

The series' distribution throughout the five films of components of the civil rights coalition—African-Americans, Jews, Latinos, women, liberal whites—presents a model of and a model for transracial politics. And the interracial cooperation and compassion of key characters (e.g., Zira and

Cornelius' relationship with Taylor, Armando's relationship with Caesar, the relationship among MacDonald, Virgil, and Caesar) are models of and models for transracial friendship and political alliance within a multiracial society. Indeed, the integrity of the characters who are dedicated to racial respect and equality somewhat mitigates the series' otherwise misanthropic and pessimistic propensities.

The *Apes* series shows racism as resulting in part from individual attitudes and choices and lauds individual acts of resistance against racist oppression. Indeed, the positive presentation of the mediating characters like Drs. Zira and Cornelius in *Planet* and *Beneath*, Drs. Branton and Dixon in *Escape*, Armando in *Escape* and *Conquest*, and the MacDonald brothers in *Conquest* and *Battle* extols individual acts of love, compassion, and courage in the face of racial oppression, and it promotes doing the right thing despite the appearance of political futility or personal risk.

But the *Apes* movies do not present idealized fantasies of simple problem resolution. The filmmakers understood the truth of Frederick Douglas' observation that there is no progress without struggle, and the *Apes* characters must face the difficulties implied by that observation.

Unlike other liberal "problem films" dealing with race, the *Apes* films do not depoliticize racism by excessively personalizing it as solely attitudinal and therefore remediable by tolerance or solely due to ignorance remediable by education. Racism is not depicted as only a matter of individuals not getting along. The *Apes* movies show racism as also the assigning of negative meaning to physical difference and the ascribing of essential characteristics to groups separated by physical difference. The series further shows racism as the use of those differences and essentialist assumptions as rationalizations for inequalities in social position, privilege, and power and as rationalizations for systemic exploitation, abuse, and violence.

Since racist attitudes are not the only problem, reforming attitudes is not the only solution. In *Battle*, for example, Caesar, unlike Aldo, does not appear to harbor hatred for humans; nonetheless Caesar dominates and exploits humans. And in *Conquest*, the apes are not passive objects waiting to be emancipated by enlightened humans who finally realize that apes also have feelings. Rather, the apes are active subjects who take the power needed to leverage their freedom. The *Apes* movies show racism, not as an absolute dictated by DNA or as a whim of opinion, but as a political and an interpersonal reality, as part of the messy world of material reality and historical contingency.

The series can be praised for its progressive view towards race relations and racial equality and for the positive images it provides of non-white characters. The films' heroes are the racially oppressed and the racially marginalized. The characterizations of racial minorities are quite sympathetic: the professionalism and calm temperament of Dodge, the African-

American astronaut in *Planet*, are countered to the vanity of Landon and the misanthropy of Taylor (Dodge is often framed separately in the film to set him apart from their childish bickering); the chimpanzees, the "Jewish apes" in *Planet* and *Beneath*, are intelligent, virtuous, and admirable; Armando is compassionate and self-sacrificing; and the brothers MacDonald are wise, courageous, and have a great amount of integrity. These characterizations are significant in a culture rife with thoughtless, negative, ethnic stereotypes.

The *Apes* movies contain a number of progressive impulses and quite critical insights. The series itself, however, is evidence for one of its main points — that one may "ape" the mistakes of others. In this regard the human makers of the *Apes* films resemble their apes. We have already noted the racial assumptions bound up with the use of a white man as the icon of "civilized" humanity. Additionally, at the same time the series critiques a racially hierarchical ape society, its characterizations of the different ape races make that hierarchy seem appropriate.

The gorillas, for instance, are depicted as inherently stupid, physically powerful, and belligerent — stereotypes often associated with African-Americans. For example, in the opening scenes of *Battle*, Aldo is established first as physically strong when he lifts the cart the humans were unable to lift and in the next scene is established as stupid when he is unable to write well in school. Thus the gorillas, through Aldo, are stereotyped as physical and anti-intellectual. And just as "society's dregs" are dominated by the "primitive animality" of Stoddard's "Under-Man," it is the gorillas who, when threatened, revert to "savage" instinct (for example, the gorillas' panicked yelps and grunts when faced with the mutants' illusions in *Beneath* and Aldo's climbing into the tree to escape Caesar).

In addition to these being dangerous and insulting images of African-Americans, this is also a rather inaccurate and unflattering portrait of real gorillas, who are in fact considered quite gentle. Therefore the gorilla's image in the films seem derived not from actual observations of the dark apes, but rather from stereotyped expectations of dark humans.

Other stereotypes and negative images are present in the *Apes* films. Negro's function in *Beneath* is to aid in interrogation by psychically inflicting pain — thus the black man is again associated with violence. In *Battle*, peace and divine will are predicated on the subordination of dark (bad) apes to light (good) apes. And, regardless of intention, in *Conquest* and *Battle*, African-Americans are still being compared to apes. The very sense of the aptness of comparing black humans to apes, to "monsters" of a sort, speaks to the degree of white alienation from blacks and to the fear that whites had in fact created, or brought, monsters into their midst.

We have discussed how the films establish deniability for themselves and the audiences. Deniability, unfortunately, may be a cover for denial.

A case can be made that the *Apes* series is complicitous in the United States' racism because, rather than insisting that viewers confront and combat racial oppression and commit themselves to humane racial interaction, the films enable the audiences to escape from the painful task of critical introspection and change. Despite the filmmakers' intentions and Schaffner's suggestion that watching the films is like looking into a mirror and requires self-examination, the *Apes* films do not insist that people look at themselves: they can always look away, that is, look at the apes. Thus the failures and fears of white America are again projected onto a racialized other.

But this may be less a particular shortcoming of the *Apes* series than an inherent problem in using allegory. Addressing a problem through allegory may potentially allow the audiences to focus on the story without paying attention to the underlying conflicts and themes. This is perhaps what Serling was referring to when, speaking about his difficulty getting television networks to confront racial problems, he bemoaned that "you don't conquer intolerance by disguising it, by clothing it in different trappings, by slapping at it with a wispy parable."[2] This is not to invalidate allegory as an artistic or political means of expression, only to point out its limitations. Alternatively, we can argue that allegory may allow one to deal with difficult issues or to get unpopular viewpoints past the audiences' defenses in a subtle way. Despite his frustration with the constraints of allegory, Serling himself recognized the freedom it allowed and pointed out that on "The Twilight Zone," he learned that "things which couldn't be said by a Republican or Democrat could be said by a Martian."[3]

In addition to expressing elements of racist ideologies, the series did not challenge gender assumptions. The female characters in the films became less and less integral as the series continued. Conflicts regarding values, politics, and power were handled almost exclusively by males. Especially in *Conquest* and *Battle*, it is in the absence or relative silence of women that men come together to decide issues of war, peace, and society's, indeed Earth's, direction.[4] Public space and the terrain of social conflict are repeatedly gendered as male space.

The difficulty, perhaps the impossibility, of the films totally extricating themselves from the racism and sexism of U.S. society, even as they struggle to do just that, speaks to the ways that culture is simultaneously both constraining and enabling. Cultural producers base the form and content of their work, in part, on other cultural products. This is one of the processes of cultural continuity, and one of the reasons for the conservative element present even in some cultural expressions that aspire to being politically progressive or countercultural.

The *Apes* saga is an excellent example of one of its own insights regarding the difficult dynamics of change: like the apes in the films, we internalize the values, terms, and tendencies of our culture and often replicate them even as we may struggle to change them. The *Apes* series, and its various missteps despite good intentions, demonstrate that our ability to formulate solutions to problems and the very vocabulary needed to conceptualize those problems and solutions are determined in part by our culture. Even as we seek to change our culture, we must confront the limitations of our ability to do so, limitations arising from our internalization of our culture's values, assumptions, and norms. Culture may thus in certain ways function as an ideological tar baby: the harder we struggle against it, the more entangled in it we may become. Therefore, even in the act of rebelling against the sins of the past, we may replicate them. Even in the midst of radical gestures, there may be reactionary counterstrokes. There is no cultural production without cultural reproduction. It is also the case that reproduction may be production. Culture is not a simple process of rote repetition. Even in traditional forms, shifts in meaning, values, and political ideology, while sometimes slight, are possible. Changes in the cultural field may not always manifest themselves in great leaps in one direction or another. Rather, they may develop in subtle twists and turns over time.

And it must be remembered that the cultural field is not monolithic. Culture is always in a state of contestation between competing parties, interests, and "sub-cultures." Like political actors, cultural actors may vie for position and the ability to promote their own models "of" and "for." Ground may be gained, only to be lost and refought over in a continual cultural game of king of the mountain.[5]

In the *Apes* series, relations between various ape and human races shift from film to film, all the while remaining within a stable, overarching construct of ape-human conflict. This fluidity is itself an example of the possibility of both change and continuity in cultural expressions. And the question of change and continuity in society, of whether we are merely prone to or actually doomed to replicate the sins of the past, is one of the *Apes* series' central questions.

The *Apes* movies were popular with a variety of audiences of different ages and interests. The films were seen as Swiftian satire, thought-provoking science fiction, action adventure, political commentary, and "simple" entertainment. After their theatrical release, the five films earned tremendous ratings in their initial television broadcasts. Following this success, on September 13, 1974, CBS premiered the *Planet of the Apes* television series. Jacobs had planned to do an *Apes* television show as far back as 1971, while he was still planning *Conquest* as the final *Apes* film, but the success of the films on the big screen caused him to delay his television plans and go on to make *Battle*. A sixth *Apes* film was even considered prior to *Battle*'s completion. Jacobs died in 1973, however, and Stan Hough, who had originally suggested to Mort Abrahams that APJAC do a sequel to *Planet*, produced the television show.

Developed by Anthony Wilson, the hour-long television show concerned the adventures of white astronauts Alan Virdon (Ron Harper) and Pete Burke (James Naughton), who leave Earth in 1980 and crash-land on the ape-dominated Earth in 3085, nearly 900 years prior to the events of *Planet*.

The apes wish to stay in a state of innocence, free from the death and destruction that brought down human society. Knowing that humans used to rule the world, the ape political elite fears the two twentieth century astronauts and worries that Virdon's and Burke's radical idea that humans are equal to apes might infect domesticated humans. Virdon and Burke, who hope to return to their own time eventually, join up with a sympathetic chimpanzee named Galen (Roddy McDowall), and the three are relentlessly pursued by the gorilla security chief, General Urko (Mark Lenard).

Instead of following through on the possibility for peace introduced in *Battle*, the television show depicts apes and humans as having failed to change the course of history and build a just society together. Set some 400 years after the Lawgiver's pronouncement of hope for the future of ape-human relations at the conclusion of *Battle*, the *Apes* television series frustrated those expectations by showing the victory of "reverse racism" over equality, as the formerly oppressed apes lord it over the degraded humans, who are now the apes' servants, and, in some cases, slaves. (In this aspect, the *Apes* show may have anticipated the rise of the white cry of "reverse racism" that would later gain currency.)

Although the show dealt little with the ape culture, there is some evidence of ape racial hierarchy: the orangutans are on top, having regained their status as the political elite (the political council, for example, is composed of one chimpanzee, one gorilla, and three orangutans, with orangutan Zaius [Booth Coleman] apparently the most powerful).[6] The gorilla military is in the middle. And the chimpanzees, again scientists, doctors, and minor bureaucrats, are at the bottom. While there is no reference to outright discrimination amongst the ape races, there is the suggestion that, as in the films, each race has its prescribed place. For example, in an episode entitled "The Tyrant," Galen learns that his cousin is to be replaced as a village prefect by a gorilla and indignantly protests "our kind always fills administrative spots, not gorillas." He later discovers why the traditional racial pecking order was violated: the gorilla got the job only through theft and bribery.

The fourth episode, "The Good Seeds," established class differences amongst the apes: only rich apes have bonded humans, only rich apes with friends in the government own farms, and only landed apes and the police are allowed to ride horses.

Since the television show did not often address the divisions amongst the apes, the main racial split was between the apes and the predominantly white humans (the only people of color are extras). In a nearly direct reversal of *Escape* and *Conquest*, but continuing some of the ideas in *Battle*, the responsibility for racial oppression is almost entirely shifted away from the white humans and onto the non-white apes, who, from their "central city" (read "inner city"?), impose their will upon the white humans living in the outlying rural areas (read "suburbs"?). While not speechless, as in *Planet* and *Beneath*, the humans are distinctly subordinate to the apes. Humans are unable to own land, are without political power, education, technology, literature, medicine, and any kind of autonomy. They serve as laborers, servants, tenant farmers, and in some cases slaves, and are almost uniformly deferential and passive.

Like real-life racists, the arrogant apes see the racial other as inferior, stupid, and childlike, and they rationalize the denial of rights to humans as being for the humans' own protection. Wishing to maintain their own superiority, the apes generally prevent the humans from using any talents they might have.

Galen's position, stated in the first episode, "Escape from Tomorrow," that "maybe it would be better if no creature ruled another, if all worked together as equals," is in direct opposition to the dominant ape ethos. His joining up with the two humans marks him as a racial apostate, and his status as a somewhat privileged young liberal ape running with humans likens him to young white liberals, or "hippies," hanging out with blacks.

Other than the offhand remark about human inferiority or a human's occasional resentment of oppressive apes, the *Apes* television show did not often deal with the issue of ape-human racial animosity. Two notable exceptions were the third episode, "The Trap," and the thirteenth episode, "The Liberator." Written by Edward J. Lasko, "The Trap" is sort of a "Defiant Ones on the Planet of the Apes," but is in fact more straightforward and less outlandish than *The Defiant Ones*. In "The Trap," Urko has tracked Galen, Virdon, and Burke to the ruins of an earthquake-prone northern California city. He has a rope around Burke and is struggling to subdue him when a temblor hits, opening up a hole in the ground into which the two adversaries fall. The opening is then covered by falling debris, and Urko and Burke are trapped underground in the remains of a subway station.

Burke convinces Urko that they must work together to get out of the trap before the air runs out. As they are working, Urko comes across a twentieth century zoo advertisement depicting a caged gorilla entertaining humans. The infuriated Urko cuts the poster down, folds it up, and hides it under his uniform. Meanwhile, Virdon and Galen convince the reluctant gorilla Zako, one of Urko's soldiers, that he and the other gorillas must work with Virdon and Galen from the outside to save Urko and Burke. They also extract a promise from Zako that the three fugitives will be released if they successfully rescue Burke and Urko.

Just as the opening is cleared and Burke and Urko are about to be hauled up by their comrades, Urko confronts Burke with the poster and tries to kill him. In the attack Urko receives an electrical shock, passes out, and is then hoisted out of the hole. He wakes long enough to order Zako to shoot the fugitives. Zako does not understand why Urko is so insistent that they be shot, as it is against ape policy to kill prisoners. Urko responds, "You don't understand. Trust me. Kill them, kill them, kill them!" and passes out again. Zako has Urko sent away to receive medical help and then releases the fugitives, explaining, "You are enemies of the state, but I gave my word." As they leave, he finds the poster Urko dropped, looks at it, and, realizing its import, tears it up in slow, burning anger.

"The Trap" is the *Apes* television show's most heartfelt symbolic address of American race relations. Urko and Burke are metaphorically and literally tied together in their conflict. They fall into a trap, the ancient subway station, which is metaphorically the trap of their own history. In the trap are the remnants of both that history's achievement (the station's technical marvels) and its oppression (the treatment of the apes). Ape and human are both literally (physically) and metaphorically (historically) caught up in this trap. In order to work their way out and satisfy their mutual need to survive, they must each overcome their bitterness and hatred. Urko's and Burke's struggle to work together is doubled by the apes and humans outside, who must also work together to save the pair. Both Urko and Burke are wounded by the experience, which nonetheless offers necessary lessons. It is, however, unclear if they learned the lessons offered by their crisis.

"The Trap" makes the point that the races are bound together in conflict, bound together in a painful history, and bound together in the need to learn from that history and cooperate if they are to free themselves from it. The episode's setting is also telling: Burke and Urko must pass through the subway station to freedom just as enslaved Africans in the United States also used an "underground railroad" to liberate themselves.

The interracial cooperation needed to escape from the trap is more in evidence here than in the films, but the episode presents the cooperation as fragile and threatened by the memory and legacy of past abuses, which are symbolized by the poster. The poster destroys the trust Burke and Urko had been building. And it is not only in anger but also in pain that Zako tears the poster up, leaving the audience to wonder if given another opportunity, knowing what he now knows, Zako would kill the fugitives.

"The Trap" ends by making the point that not just the apes but also the humans must amend their racial attitudes. When Burke wonders why Zako let them go, Galen asks Burke whether Burke would obey an order he knew was wrong. Burke answers, "I guess not," and Galen playfully, yet chidingly, responds, "You don't think you are any better than a gorilla, do you?" Although he said it in good humor, Galen makes the point that, rather than assume that gorillas are without conscience, Burke should examine his own racial prejudices.

It would have been unlikely that a chimpanzee in the *Apes* movies would imply that a gorilla was trustworthy. In the television show, however, the gorillas, while still the villains and often as boorish as those in the films, were occasionally portrayed with somewhat more depth and sensitivity. The gorillas are not just mindless brutes and bigots as in the movies: Urko is far more intelligent than Ursus and Aldo; in "The Deception," Perdix, a gorilla police chief, fights against "The Dragoons," an ape Ku Klux Klan that terrorizes humans and sympathetic apes; and a gorilla with Zako's integrity was nowhere to be found in the films.

In addition to "The Trap," racial oppression was also a central issue in "The Liberator," in which Virdon, Burke, and Galen attempt to break up a slave ring. In this episode by Howard Dimsdale, the three fugitives come across a village that twice each summer month must give the gorillas five humans as slaves. The humans are chosen by lot, but the village may also fill its quota by capturing humans from a nearby village or by capturing any humans in its territory. One villager chosen by the lottery refuses to go and captures Virdon and Burke to go in his place. Virdon and Burke try to convince the humans that they must resist the gorillas, and they offer to help the villagers fight. Brun, the village leader and high priest, and his son Miro maintain that apes rule over humans by divine will and refuse to disobey the law.

When Talia, Miro's fiancée, is chosen by lot to be part of the next group of humans to be enslaved, Miro strikes a deal with Virdon, Burke, and Galen: their freedom in exchange for taking Talia with them to safety. After the villagers give chase, the fugitives hide in the village temple, knowing the humans will not follow them because it means death for anyone but the village leader to enter. The astronauts soon discover why: a natural source of poisonous gas is located under the temple, gas from which Brun was protected by a secret gas mask hidden in his ceremonial uniform. They discover that, while pretending to be obedient, Brun is really storing the gas and making bombs to use against the apes. Virdon and Burke try to convince him that this will only start an arms race because the apes will then develop their own gas bombs and retaliate. "You can't win freedom by destroying the world. . . . Fight against slavery, all slavery, but not this way," they tell him. Brun is unconvinced. Galen is outraged and, unwilling to let Brun try to exterminate his species, attacks Brun and sets the bomb cache afire. When Brun runs back inside, the bombs explode and he is killed. Miro decides he will form a truce with the next village and fight against the apes. Declining the fugitives' offer to help, Miro says that men must fight where they have roots, and Galen, Virdon, and Burke go on their way.

Of all the television episodes, "The Liberator" is one of the most densely packed with social issues. The clash between tradition and change, the tension between duty and desire, resistance to the draft, chemical warfare, the arms race, and the conflict between science and religion (which science wins when the astronauts find the gas: a "rational" scientific explanation for religious phenomena) are all wrapped up in the story. The Vietnam War's influence is noticeable when the astronauts try to inspire the village to fight rather than "just roll over." Miro's refusal of Virdon and Burke's help and his statement that "men must fight where they have their roots, so this isn't your fight" seem a critique of getting involved in foreign wars. And it is significant that once the astronauts get the "natives" to fight, they do not do the fighting themselves. Instead they leave, much like advisers or green berets who have successfully trained the locals to fight the war without themselves getting mired in it.

Racial oppression and resistance are also very much at issue in "The Liberator." As in *Conquest*, the racial concerns are signaled by the presence of a number of African-Americans. African-Americans almost never appeared on the show, and when they did they were relegated to the background in crowd scenes. Although the African-Americans in "The Liberator" do not have speaking parts, they are prominent and quite often in the foreground. As in *Conquest*, the increased African-American presence in a story dealing with slavery and resistance adds visual resonance to the tale.

Like *Conquest*, "The Liberator" argues in favor of a degree of violent resistance to oppression as long as it does not go "too far." After the astronauts try to convince the passive humans to fight, they then argue against the genocidal extremes of Brun's plan. Brun is a human composite of Caesar the liberator and Aldo the murderer. Virdon's counsel to "fight against slavery, all slavery, but not this way" recalls both *Conquest*'s insistence that the chains of captivity be cast off and *Battle*'s warning that the enslaved of the past must not become the enslavers of the future. Miro's determination to resist the apes, coupled with his rejection of his father's methods ("I am not my father, I make my own way"), suggests he has achieved a balance between passivity and vengeance. Unfortunately, "The Liberator" does not indicate what that elusive balance looks like.

As mentioned, save for the above two stories, racial conflict was not often an explicit component of the *Apes* television episodes. The episodes usually involved Galen, Burke, and Virdon coming across a human village and helping the less-advanced inhabitants out of some predicament.[7] They are usually able to do this because of Virdon and Burke's greater scientific, technological, and medical skills which the show continually privileges over and against "backward" human and ape religions, traditions, and "superstitions."[8]

Typical of this pattern is "The Good Seeds," in which the astronauts show crop cultivation techniques and other farming skills to a family of ape farmers. In the sixth episode, "Tomorrow's Tide," the astronauts teach the humans in a forced-labor fishing detail how to make nets to catch fish rather than spearing them. The twelfth episode, "The Cure," features the astronauts helping a malaria-stricken human village drain its stagnant swamps and teaching the chimpanzee chief medical officer to make an antidote from the bark of a nearby tree. Virdon and Burke's know-how is also presented as superior to ape ignorance in "The Trap" when the astronauts alone have the technical skill to get Burke and Urko out of the subway station and in "The Liberator," when a wounded Miro is saved not by Brun's prayers but by Virdon's tourniquet.[9]

This positioning of the astronauts as superior to the apes and to the humans of the thirty-first century even affects Virdon and Burke's relationship with Galen. Despite his vision of all creatures working as equals, Galen's relationship with the two astronauts is not one of equality. Galen is often awed by their technological skills, characteristically mistaking them for magic. And while he has a certain ape pride, as evidenced by his defense of gorillas' character in "The Trap" and his violent reaction to Brun's extermination plans in "The Liberator," Galen is generally deferential and usually follows whatever plan of action his human companions devise.

Most of the humans and many of the apes whom Galen, Virdon, and Burke encounter are poor and uneducated, wear simple clothes, and live in modest shacks or huts. Therefore, the image that was repeated week after week was one of white Western men going to "native" villages and using their superior knowledge, technology, and talents to solve the locals' problems. The heroes of the "Planet of the Apes" television series consequently emerge as a type of roving peace corps working in a future that is iconographically and metaphorically "third world." The show perhaps anticipated a post–Vietnam War view of the world in which the non-whites have won the war but the "inherently superior" whites are winning the battles. Thus, while in some regards less political than the movies, by showing the victory of "civilization" over "primitivism," the "Planet of the Apes" television series presented, in a fictional world, the successful use of the nonviolent "nation building" strain of U.S. counterinsurgency policy at precisely the time that, in Vietnam, America's real-world counterinsurgency strategies were failing. As defeat in Vietnam became more certain, the need for compensatory fantasies grew. Consequently, whereas the United States may have lost the hearts and minds of the peasants of Vietnam, it at least won the hearts and minds of the peasants on the planet of the apes. The hearts and minds of the television audiences were not so easily swayed, however, and "Planet of the Apes" was taken off the air after only fourteen episodes.[10]

The following year, on September 6, 1975, the apes' saga returned to Vietnam in "Return to the Planet of the Apes," NBC's Saturday morning animated *Apes* series. The return to the Vietnam War as a source for the themes and conflicts of the *Apes* material was probably due to the influence of Doug Wildey. Most famous for his work on the animated action adventure series "Jonny Quest," Wildey served as a storyboard director, associate producer, and supervising director for "Return to the Planet of the Apes." Wildey, who developed the animated series' concept and general storylines, had only seen *Planet* and *Beneath* prior to working on the show. Consequently he was not aware of the degree to which the *Apes* parable had begun to address domestic racial conflict. Wildey therefore brought the animated *Apes* show back to the Vietnam War themes which had pervaded the first two films.

Produced by David H. DePatie and Friz Freleng, the half-hour animated series focused on three U.S. astronauts: the white mission commander Bill Hudson (the voice of Tom Williams), a black astronaut named Jeff Allen (the voice of Austin Stoker, who had portrayed MacDonald in *Battle*), and another white astronaut named Judy Franklin (Claudette Nievens), who crashed on Earth in the year 3979 C.E.[11] The inclusion of a black man and a white woman in the crew under a white male commander serves the same function as the similar demographic among *Planet*'s astronauts: it is a nod to affirmative action and the progressive movements of the sixties and seventies but also preserves fundamental power privileges by leaving the white man in control.[12]

The three find Earth's population divided into three groups: a band of mute white human beings living in caves in the desert; a city of human "Underdwellers" modeled on the mutants in *Beneath*, but without the bomb worship; and a city of apes who dominate the planet. Throughout the animated series season-long run, the astronauts attempt to evade capture by the apes, while protecting the defenseless humans from the aggressive gorilla army.

The ape's racial hierarchy closely resembles that of *Beneath*: the orangutans, led by Dr. Zaius (Richard Blackburn), have the most authority as the political elite; next in power are the gorillas, led by General Urko (Henry Cordin), who are the police and the military; and least in influence are the chimpanzees, represented by Zira (Phillipa Harris) and Cornelius (Edwin Mills), who serve as academicians and scientists. The simian senate is composed of all three ape races, but the high council, which seems to make the most important decisions, is entirely orangutan. Urko has ambitions of leading a military takeover, and Zaius, aware of this, plays the gorilla military and the chimpanzee intelligentsia off against each other to protect his position.

The mute humans are used as menial laborers, pets, game for hunting, objects of scientific study, and war game targets. In a storyline that recalls the conflicts in *Planet* and *Beneath*, Urko sees the humans as a threat and advocates their extermination, while Cornelius argues that even though they are animals, the humans have the right to live and should be studied for insights into simian origins. As in *Planet*, *Beneath*, and the television series, the orangutans on the high council are the only ones who know that humans once ruled the Earth but through "greed, folly [and] lust for power, destroyed [their] world." Any sign that the humans were regaining higher intelligence and the power to speak would lead the orangutans to authorize Urko's extermination plans.

As in the films and the live-action television series, racial fear and resentment are an issue in the animated show. Zira and Cornelius are among the few apes who are not afraid of humans regaining intelligence. In the eleventh episode, "Terror on Ice Mountain," by Bruce Shelly, the two chimpanzees find a human book entitled *A Day at the Zoo*, which, like the zoo poster in "The Trap," proves that humans once ruled the Earth. Zira and Cornelius know that this proof of human intelligence and civilization might help convince the apes to grant rights to the humans.

But the opposition is still too strong, so Cornelius and Bill hide the book among the Ice Apes, an order of religious orangutans whom Wildey compared to "Tibetan Monks."[13] Their presence recalls the Buddhists whose self-immolation to protest the Vietnam War remains one of the most powerful memories of the war. The Ice Apes worship a gorilla god named Kygor and believe that "all creatures with loving hearts are equal." That orangutans would worship a gorilla god and have such egalitarian sentiments demonstrates much more liberal views toward racial difference than those of the other orangutans in the animated series or in the films and live-action show. Significantly, this monastic order dedicated to equality is located on a snow-covered mountain top and is therefore as physically far removed from the other apes as it is ideologically distant from them.

But the ape society's domestic conflicts over equal rights for the humans only come up in two episodes, while the bulk of the episodes concern the apes' war on the desert humans. While it merits stressing that the animated series, like *Planet* and *Beneath*, was by no means an exact parallel to the Vietnam War, the resemblances to the war which began to take shape in the early episodes are crucial.

In the second episode, "Escape from Ape City," written by Larry Spiegel, Bill decides that the astronauts must teach the unarmed humans, who are subject to attack by the heavily armed apes, to make better use of the terrain. Jeff suggests that they move the humans to a different location less vulnerable to ape attack, and the two start planning the building of fortifications and a defensive perimeter.

In the eighth episode, "Trail to the Unknown," also by Spiegel, with some help from Zira and Cornelius, Bill, Jeff, and Judy transfer the humans to "New Valley," help them carve pueblos in a mountain, and use a laser drill salvaged from their ship to build a defensive wall.

Thus early on in the "Apes" animated series, the U.S. forces decide to interpose themselves by acting as advisers in what could be seen as a "foreign civil war" and by relocating the "natives" to more secure positions, just as the United States moved many South Vietnamese into strategic hamlets. From that point on, the astronauts get involved more and more deeply. Paralleling the increase in U.S. involvement in Vietnam, the battle becomes more and more "Americanized" as the astronauts go far beyond simply teaching the humans to make better use of the terrain. They eventually make forays into the ape city to get weapons and supplies for the humans and later defend the humans from ape attack.

The U.S. commitment is solidified in the fourth episode, "Lagoon of Peril," by J. C. Strong. The sighting of the astronauts' spaceship causes panic among the apes, who fear intelligent humans have landed and will incite the other humans to revolt. The apes send an expedition to verify if the ship is real or a rumor. Realizing that the apes will launch an extermination offensive if the ship is discovered, the astronauts destroy the ship and thereby forgo their only chance of escape in order to protect the native humans.

Consequently, in the "Return to the Planet of the Apes" show, as in Vietnam, the U.S. forces are past the point of no return, having stumbled into the middle of an escalating war they can neither leave nor win, even with their superior weapon, the laser. Mired in a "wilderness" setting, the U.S. forces are outnumbered and, while their stated intent was to help train the natives to protect themselves, they increasingly take on the brunt of the war effort.

The issue of air power, so important during the Vietnam War, comes up repeatedly in the animated series. In "Screaming Wings," by John Barrett and Jack Kaplan, Urko has refurbished a World War II fighter plane and is building a fleet of duplicates which he plans to use to bomb the humans into submission. Judy steals the plane, which the astronauts then use to fend off attacks against the humans. The issue of air superiority comes up again in "Terror on Ice Mountain," by Bruce Shelly, in which the astronauts build a hot-air balloon that the apes fear the humans will use as a weapon, and in "Attack from the Clouds," by Spiegel, and "Battle of the Titans," by Shelly, in which both the apes and the humans are threatened by a giant flying reptile.

Not only did the war front resemble Vietnam, but the apes' homefront resembled the United States during the war. The press is suspicious of both the politicians and the military. A series of setbacks makes the gorilla army look incapable of victory. Confidence in the army is eroding, and Urko is continually in search of a new offensive that will, in the words of one of his soldiers, "bring the [humans] to their knees" and "end the [human] problem forever," thereby restoring faith in the military. The apes' fear that if the humans are not stopped they will "infest our cities and threaten our children" echoes the "domino theory" and the arguments in favor of "containing" Communism. However, since the cave-dwelling humans neither take aggressive action against the apes, nor pose a credible threat, the apes' consuming fear seems entirely out of proportion and nonproductive—like the United States' obsession with Vietnam.

Much of the critique of U.S. involvement in Vietnam comes through in the characterization of General Urko. Typical of this critique is the twelfth episode, "Invasion of the Underdwellers," by J. C. Strong. In an effort to frame the human underdwellers and foment support for attacking them, Urko disguises himself and other gorillas as underdwellers and commits a series of break-ins throughout the apes' city. Eventually his plot is exposed, and Urko, already suffering compromised credibility because of his continual defeats, is temporarily relieved of command.

Since Urko is both a military and political figure, the episode critiques the corruption of, and expresses disconfidence in, both the military and the political elite. The use of falsification to secure support for war recalls military misinformation scandals like the Tonkien Gulf incident, while the use of break-ins and illegality for personal political gain links Urko to the Watergate break-ins and President Richard Nixon.

The animated "Apes" series equates Urko with Nixon through the continual portrayal of Urko as corrupt and constantly paranoid that everyone is out to get him. The show also links Urko to Nixon through a number of visual likenings to the disgraced president. In "Trail to the Unknown," by Spiegel, Urko, previously drawn without eyebrows, yells, "is there a conspiracy against me?" At that point he is drawn with bushy eyebrows and exaggerated jowls reminiscent of common caricatures of Nixon. A number of times in other episodes when he is acting particularly paranoid or corrupt, he is likewise drawn with either bushy eyebrows, exaggerated jowls, or both.[14]

When *Planet* was released in 1968, the Vietnam War was unpopular. By 1975, when the animated series premiered, the war had been lost. Subsequently, the war's meaning had changed, and the cultural needs and cultural response regarding the war now included not only critique, but also recuperation. The animated television show was not just a critique of the war, but an inverted reenactment in which the U.S. forces back the winning side.

This reworking begins in the third episode, "Tunnel of Fear," by Spiegel, when Jeff compares the humans to the Native Americans of Arizona and New Mexico and suggests the astronauts help them protect themselves by building American Indian–style pueblos in the side of a mountain. In Vietnam War parlance, "Indians" was a common metaphor for the North Vietnamese, while the U.S. troops were seen as the traditional "cowboys."[15] While not necessarily supporting the North Vietnamese, the animated show reverses the traditional valence of the "cowboys and Indians" metaphor and suggests that Indians, rather than cowboys, would have been the appropriate role for the U.S. to play in the war.

To that end, the show reverses the actual tactics of the war and allows the fictional U.S. forces, with their insurgent evade-and-ambush tactics, to appropriate the winning strategy while switching the failed U.S. offensive strategies of "search and destroy" and the "big unit war" to a gorilla army commanded by a Nixon stand-in.[16] Thus we become the guerrillas and the gorillas become us.

By creating a Vietnam War allegory in which the enemy's side, the apes, takes on the negative attributes of U.S. society, the animated "Apes" series metaphorically purges the United States of the corruption and controversy that dogged the country during the war. The metaphor also purges the U.S. representatives of the hostility and racism that was in fact part of the war. Unlike in Vietnam, the humans' fight is purely defensive. The astronauts use no racial slurs equivalent to "gooks" to demean their adversaries and, unlike the racial supremacist apes, have no racial animus. And while the United States actually suffered profound racial and gender divisions during the war, the U.S. forces in the animated show, a white man, a black man, and a white woman, are painlessly integrated into an efficient team representing a microcosm of U.S. pluralism and meritocracy.[17]

The animated "Return to the Planet of the Apes" is a fantasy that simplifies the issues and displaces the corruption and cruelty of both sides onto the apes, while the U.S. representatives emerge as sanitized green berets, smoothly integrated along racial and gender lines, fighting a good fight unmarred by the real war's misinformation, mistakes, and massacres.

Wildey says he did not intentionally base the "Apes" animated series on Vietnam. But he need not have intended to make the series a forum for responding to the war in order for it to serve as such. Meaning depends on more than artists' individual intentions. As we have seen, a society's political and social conflicts, and the issues those conflicts raise, will naturally be absorbed into and influence that society's popular culture. For example, Wildey's sense that in Vietnam "nobody was quite sure what the hell they were doing and still people were dying and it seemed totally senseless" is reflected in the fact that week after week the astronauts get involved in another adventure without achieving any real progress.[18] While he did not deliberately base the animated show on U.S. politics, as Dehn and Thompson *had* done with *Conquest*, when asked about the Vietnam War parallels years later, Wildey's reply was similar to Joyce Hooper Corrington's: "I guess that was probably in the back of my mind someplace," and he acknowledged, "In retrospect, you know, strangely, I never thought of it that way but . . . for what it's worth, that's what it was all about and I guess that's why I had them destroy the rocket ship. . . . Once they're there, they're there."

In a way, the animated series brought the *Apes* saga full circle as regards the Vietnam War: whereas *Planet of the Apes* anticipated the United States' defeat, "Return to the Planet of the Apes" returned to the battlefield and reimagined the war in a way that allowed for a U.S. victory. By symbolically transferring corruption, cruelty, and controversy to the other side, showing Urko punished for trying to mislead the public into war, and appropriating for the U.S. forces the winning strategy, "Return to the Planet of the Apes" acted as a recuperative fantasy offering a fictional space in which the United States avoided the mistakes made in the actual war, retained its honor at home and on the battlefield, and came out the winner.

The animated series was not the end of *Apes* production. From 1968 to 1976 the *Planet of the Apes* saga could be observed in a multiplicity of ways throughout the United States *Planet*, one of biggest hits of 1968, received Oscar nominations for Jerry Goldsmith's score and Morton Haack's costume design and was presented with a special Academy Award for John Chambers' makeup effects. While *Planet* was the best-received critically, all of the films received positive attention from the press and the critics. During the production of *Battle*, songwriter Paul Williams, who portrayed Virgil, appeared on the "Tonight Show" with Johnny Carson, singing in full ape makeup, and talk show host Mike Douglas hosted an episode of his show also in full makeup. Licensed by Twentieth Century–Fox, actors Bill Blake and Paula Christ drew large crowds as Cornelius and Zira at their live *Apes* performances in shopping malls and car shows. And, in the seventies, the Los Angeles Zoo named its newborn gorilla "Caesar."

There was also Marvel Comics' *Planet of the Apes* magazine, the covers of which monthly depicted vivid scenes of usually violent ape-human conflict, primarily with gorillas as the aggressors and white humans as the victims. From 1974 to 1977, the black and white magazine ran behind-the-scenes news features, interviews of those involved in the production of the films and the live-action television program, interpretive essays, a letters column, comic book–style adaptations of the films, and original *Apes* adventures written for the magazine by writer Doug Moench.

Read from the United States to France to Malaysia, the *Apes* magazine was one of the most popular Marvel had ever produced. When the magazine came out in 1974, Marvel was inundated with an average of three to four hundred letters per week about the magazine, a figure which was "unheard of."[19] In fact, the response was so overwhelming that after a few months the editors announced that due to the large volume they would no longer

Between 1963 and 1973, *Planet of the Apes* **went from a small science fiction novel to an international popular culture phenomenon.**

Sixty companies were licensed to turn out 200 items in one of the largest movie merchandising campaigns in history (photo courtesy of Fashion Studio).

be able to send personal replies to the letters. From 1975 to 1976, Marvel
Comics reprinted the magazine's serialized adaptations of *Planet* and
Beneath in a full-color monthly comic book series entitled *Adventures on
the Planet of the Apes.*

There were also multiple printings of the novelizations of the films,
live-action shows, and animated shows written by accomplished writers
like Jerry Pournelle, John Jakes, and David Gerrold.[20] That such well-
respected writers were hired to adapt the films and Oscar-winning screen-
writers wrote four of the five screenplays indicates that *Apes* was seen as
serious science fiction not to be tinkered with by amateurs.

Concurrent with the live-action and the animated *Apes* television
shows in the mid-seventies was an explosion of *Apes*-related merchandising. Some sixty companies were licensed to turn out two hundred items,
including plastic model kits of the ape characters, puzzles, kites, soap,
wind-up toys, dart gun and archery sets, coloring books, coin banks, trash
cans, trading cards, 45 rpm record/comic sets, mugs, cereal bowls, and
lunch boxes.

Today, when such mass merchandising and multimedia blitzes are so
common — promoting everything from movies to rock groups to wars — this
Apes saturation may seem unremarkable. But at the time, few television

A performer in *Apes* garb poses with young admirer Joey Waxman at a Los Angeles street fair in the mid-seventies (photo courtesy Dina Waxman).

shows or films—"Star Trek" and the James Bond and Disney pictures were among the few exceptions—enjoyed such massive production of consumer goods. For its time, the *Apes* phenomenon was rather extraordinary and probably helped pave the way for the mega-merchandising campaigns that were to follow for other films and shows.

Some of the *Apes* toys even encouraged a more involved relationship to the world of the *Apes* phenomenon than just watching the films and television shows. Children could enact their own ape-human adventures by purchasing action figures; various playsets, including a toy treehouse and a "Forbidden Zone Trap"; masks; a board game; hand puppets; Halloween costumes; and toy rifle sets.

As with toy soldiers, many of the *Apes* toys and playsets were designed to involve children in the violent aspects of the ape-human encounters. The gorilla dolls all were sold with guns or clubs, and a number of the playsets, for example, the "Prison Cage" set, simulated sites of violent ape-human conflict. These toys invited children to enter the mythic space of the planet of the apes and to role-play, to participate in the conflicts embodied in the *Apes* films and television programs much as they would in a game of "cowboys and Indians."

The game "cowboys and Indians" displaces history into myth and ritualizes U.S. racial oppression and racial violence as "play." This allows children symbolically to enter the mythicized world of U.S. racial conflict, in which the roles of racial hero and racial villain are, with the simplicity of a child's game, distributed respectively to cowboys and Indians. Similarly, on playgrounds and streets from New York to Indiana to California, the saga's conflict was recreated as play and children played "planet of the apes" in much the same way, though not in the same numbers, as they played "cowboys and Indians." In these games the apes, especially the gorillas, were typically the racial aggressor.

Even after their initial popularity had died down, the *Apes* films and television shows were still in the public eye. Fox decided that there was enough of an ape audience in the early eighties to reedit ten episodes of the live-action television show and sell them to network and independent syndication as five "TV movies" with what were the most outlandish titles of the *Apes* corpus: *Back to the Planet of the Apes*; *Forgotten City of the Planet of the Apes*; *Treachery and Greed on the Planet of the Apes*; *Life, Liberty, and Pursuit on the Planet of the Apes*; and *Farewell to the Planet of the Apes*. In some markets the TV movies were accompanied by newly filmed segments in which Roddy McDowall returned as a grey-haired Galen who hosted the broadcast with introductory and concluding comments.

The *Apes* series stayed in the culture as well through its influence on other popular culture projects. In 1972, DC Comics pushed the animals-ruling-the-world motif of the *Apes'* series even further when they released the *Apes*-influenced *Kamandi: The Last Boy on Earth*, a comic about a human on a future Earth ruled by intelligent rats, dogs, grasshoppers, snakes, tigers, and, of course, apes. Mixing elements from the various films, the tigers have a leader named Caesar who has a nuclear weapon that is revered like a god, and the cover of the first issue even had Kamandi passing the fallen Statue of Liberty.

The resemblance between the apes and the Wookie Chewbacca was reportedly helpful in getting the *Star Wars* concept sold to Twentieth Century–Fox in the mid-seventies. Resonances of *Apes* could also be seen in the many science fiction films and television shows during the eighties which used alien creatures and alien worlds to consciously consider racial relations. These efforts include *Enemy Mine*, *Alien Nation*, and the television miniseries and weekly series *V*.

Apes' influence even spread to Japan, where in 1987 Tsuburaya Productions released the film *Time of the Apes*, in which two children and their aunt are cryogenically frozen and are revived thousands of years later to find Earth under ape domination.

We are far from past the *Planet of the Apes*. Significantly, today, in a time of rising awareness of and concern regarding race relations and racism, *Apes*' cultural presence is being reasserted. Pierre Boulle's original novel was rereleased in 1989. Jerry Goldsmith's *Planet* soundtrack was rereleased in the early nineties with the addition of the previously unreleased music that accompanied the hunt sequence. A new book entitled *Planet of the Apes Revisited* has chronicled the making of the *Apes* films.

In the early nineties, the live-action and animated "Apes" television shows returned on the cable Sci Fi Channel. Cable and "free" television stations still run all five theatrical or TV films in day, week, or month-long festivals. (A recent day-long *Apes* marathon on the cable USA Network featured clips of Roddy McDowall talking about making the films. In contrast to Jacobs and Abrahams' confusion upon meeting Sammy Davis, Jr., McDowall highlighted racial conflict as one of the political issues addressed by *Apes*.) In 1991, a *Planet of the Apes* marathon was even an event at the countercultural "International Pop Underground Convention" in Washington state.

The past few years have also seen a significant rise in the referencing of *Apes* by artists across the nation working in a variety of popular culture media. A pop-punk band from Anchorage, Alaska, calls itself "Dr. Zaius." Redd Kross, a Los Angeles pop-trio, formed originally as a punk group in 1978 by two brothers aged 11 and 14, recently recorded the song "Zira (Call Out My Name)." Redd Kross' guitarist Jeffrey McDonald said of the song, which appears on their "Third Eye" album, "We didn't want to say 'ape.' . . . . We wanted it to seem like a regular love song, but the people that were cool enough would figure it out."[21] And Gone Native, a Rockabilly trio from Connecticut, performs a tune entitled "Beneath the Planet of the Apes."

Comedians Dennis Miller, who specializes in referencing pop culture, Fred Klett, and Paul Mooney have all done bits about *Apes*. Mooney, an African-American who often plays upon racial resentment in his act, picks up on the racial apocalypse element of *Planet of the Apes*. He says it is his favorite movie because in it white people cannot speak but gorillas can, and he argues that because they have thin lips, straight hair and light skin, it is in fact whites who look like monkeys.

The 1993-94 season of the popular animated TV comedy "The Simpsons" included two spoofs of *Planet of the Apes*. That same season, an opening sketch on "Saturday Night Live" featured guest host Charlton Heston falling asleep in his dressing room and waking up in 3978 to find the NBC studio overtaken by apes. The sketch included regular cast members in full ape makeup and costume playing favorite "Saturday Night Live" characters. The joke even extended to the opening credits, wherein the names and pictures of the cast were replaced by those of *Apes* characters.

In the movies, Mel Brooks spoofed *Planet*'s Statue of Liberty scene in his 1987 science fiction farce *Spaceballs*. In *Mrs. Doubtfire* (1993), a puppet orangutan complained about humans getting all the good simian roles in *Planet*, and Ben Stiller's look at "Generation X" in *Reality Bites* (1994) contained a much talked-about appearance by a Dr. Zaius coin bank.

The political subtext of the *Apes* films has even been absorbed and redeployed in performance art. Scenes from *Escape* of Cornelius and Zira being interrogated were featured in Martha Rosler's "Global Taste: A Meal in Three Courses" (1986) in which video monitors showed "three interrelated videotapes simultaneously juxtaposing images of language production, product consumption and the development of consumers."[22] And in 1993 at New York's Whitney Museum, scenes of a caged Taylor from *Planet* were used in a performance art piece by Guillermo Gomez-Pena and Coco Fusco which "explor[ed] the ludicrous and tragic plight of populations caught between a tribal identity that the mainstream wants to romanticize and a problematic future."[23]

Aside from direct references and affectionate spoofs, *Apes* continues to influence popular culture. In 1994, Leonard Nimoy, Mr. Spock of "Star Trek," co-created the comic book *Leonard Nimoy's Primortals*. While researching the film *Star Trek IV: The Voyage Home*, Nimoy thought of the concept for this story, which concerns the return to Earth of prehistoric creatures who had been saved from extinction by an alien race who removed them from Earth. He later collaborated with author Isaac Asimov and developed the idea into a short story. Nimoy describes the *Primortals*, as "sort of [a] *Planet of the Apes* relationship between an advanced nonhuman society dealing with humans."[24] Like *Apes*, *Primortals* may eventually evolve into movies, television, and books. Even a new version of the comic *Kamandi*, entitled *Kamandi at Earth's End*, was released in the early nineties. The original *Apes*-influenced *Kamandi* comic was in turn an influence on *Teenage Mutant Ninja Turtles*.

Renewed interest in and reference to *Apes* is undoubtedly due in part to the prevalent fixation during the past fifteen years with recycling popular culture from the fifties and sixties, particularly science fiction and adventure. *Star Trek*, *Superman*, *The Untouchables*, and *Batman*, to name just a few, have all been remade or updated in new film and television versions. Movies based on fifties and sixties television shows like *The Addams Family*, *The Fugitive*, and *Maverick* have been enormously popular. Reunion shows and updated versions of old shows and movies abound. Books on fifties and sixties shows have proliferated, and episodes of the seventies sit-coms "The Jeffersons" and "The Brady Bunch," a show which has had at least five television incarnations over the past twenty years, have also been performed as stage plays. The year 1995 even saw the premiere of *The Brady Bunch* movie. Everything old is new again.

Beyond pop-culture nostalgia and baby-boomer economics, political ferment is also a likely factor in renewed interest in *Apes*. One *Apes* fan noted in 1991 that "there are similarities to today and the era when *Apes* was at its peak. There are environmental concerns, dissatisfaction with the government and confusion over ... [the Persian Gulf] war on the horizon."[25] In the midst of this ferment, *Planet of the Apes* has become the subject of renewed cultural production as artists attempt to revive and refit the *Apes* saga.

Between 1990 and 1993, Adventure Comics Company in California produced eight new comic book series and miniseries based on the *Apes* films, and they were among the company's most popular sellers. The first series, *Planet of the Apes*, ran for two years and chronicled the efforts of Caesar's grandson Alexander to lead ape society. Its first issue had three printings and, at over 40,000 sold, was the biggest selling debut issue ever for a noncolor comic.[26]

Simultaneously, Adventure Comics developed five four-issue miniseries: *Ape City*; *Planet of the Apes: Urchak's Folly* (written in Australia); *Ape Nation* (which brings together the worlds of *Apes* and *Alien Nation*); *Planet of the Apes: Blood of the Apes*; and *Planet of the Apes: The Forbidden Zone*. There were also two single-issue comics, *A Day on the Planet of the Apes* and *Planet of the Apes: Sins of the Fathers*, a prequel to *Planet*.

Apparently finding a receptive audience for *Apes* material, a year after the release of its first *Planet of the Apes* comic, Adventure Comics rereleased the first four issues of that series in a collection entitled *Monkey Planet*. Adventure also rereleased the first four issues of "Terror on the Planet of the Apes," an original Doug Moench story from the seventies' *Planet of the Apes* magazine, as well as rereleasing in comic novel format the original magazine's adaptations of the first three *Apes* movies.

These numerous comic series work within the framework of apehuman conflict established in the films, rather than focusing on racial stratification among the apes. But while the comics play upon ideas and motifs established in the films, a number of the comic series take these concepts in interestingly different directions.

Planet of the Apes: Urchak's Folly, written by Australian Gary Chaloner, is a kind of *Planet of the Apes* meets *Bridge Over the River Kwai* combined with elements of the pro–Native American Westerns. The story concerns the malevolent gorilla Colonel Urchak, who was ordered by ape leader Alexander to carve out a road to the unexplored western wilderness. In the western lands live the "Mud People," a self-named, interbred ape-human race which has been converted by a human priestess named Miranda to "Taylorism."

Taylorism is a religion that teaches ape-human equality and, expanding an idea from the ending of the Corringtons' original *Battle* script, the Taylorites await Taylor not just as a man who will bless them if they have achieved peace but as a man "who will hold our world in our hands . . . [and] offer us salvation."[27] With Taylor as their messiah, the sign of the Taylorites is a lowercase "t" resembling a cross. Their holy book is the personal journal of Dr. Louis Dixon, one of the animal psychologists who befriended Zira and Cornelius in *Escape*. Like the transformation of secular history into religious myth in *Battle*, Dixon's writings about the apes' future contact with Taylor are interpreted as prophecy and are the source for the Taylorite religion.

Contrary to Alexander's orders, Urchak plans to invade the western lands to destroy the "savage" Mud People, whom he sees as "an impure and repugnant race."[28] He has the orangutan architect Claudius build a bridge to the western lands, which he will use for the invasion. Claudius, however, is not willing to let his bridge be used to destroy the Mud People and so blows it up. The Mud People eventually attack, and armed only with spears, bows, arrows, and hatchets against the gorilla's guns, they free Miranda from Urchak's jail cell. With Urchak defeated and his army destroyed, Miranda heads east to continue her missionary activity.

Urchak's Folly is notable for the willingness to violate the miscegenation taboo that the producers of *Beneath* had been unwilling to challenge two decades earlier. Although the comic does not detail the history or culture of the Mud People, let alone address the tricky question of their biological viability, the very presence of a mixed ape-human race shows that Chaloner had a greater willingness to confront the possibility of interracial love. *Urchak's Folly* even touches upon prejudice against those deemed mentally ill.

A tale of racial resentment and reconciliation in the American South, *Planet of the Apes: Blood of the Apes* takes place in the remains of Memphis, Tennessee (referred to as "'Phis" in the comic), and focuses on a gorilla soldier named Tonus. Tonus' wife Deetera was a scientist who did research on humans and was devoted to integrating humans into ape society. After she was killed by a human, Tonus became bitter and dedicated himself to killing the members of an ape underground that was supplying books and weapons to a colony of human Taylorites, led by a black man named Luther, who are teaching other humans to read and talk.

Tonus finds himself falling in love with Valia, an ape who reminds him of Deetra, and, like her, is also an animal rights activist. Sensing something decent within Tonus, Valia tries to convince him that apes and humans can live together and learn from each other.

After the Taylorites capture Tonus as he is trying to murder two humans, Luther, whose name and nonviolent character link him to Martin Luther King, Jr., decides to release the infamous killer, reasoning that "letting *him* live, the hardest of all the apes, will show [the apes] that man is made of okay stock" (emphasis in original).[29] Luther's presence underscores

Blood of the Apes' theme of racial understanding, as does the peaceful protest march he leads on Memphis to seek racial equality.

Eventually Tonus changes his mind about humans. When a gorilla general named Stedal leads an army to wipe out the humans as they stage their march, Tonus tries to protect the humans. Both Tonus and Valia are mortally wounded in the massacre. A bewildered Valia asks why the apes attacked, and Tonus, believing that apes will never accept humans as equals, answers, "because it's the nature of ape."[30]

As Tonus crawls over to the dying Valia, she tells him that she is not who he thinks she is and peels off her ape mask, revealing that she is in fact a human woman named Myndith, a Taylorite leader. The shocked Tonus stammers, *"You're not an ape!* But . . . I . . . you . . . we. . . ." She answers, "I know what you're trying to say. I have fallen in *love* with *you* also. We're not as different as you thought . . . are we" (emphasis in original).[31]

This simian-human *Romeo and Juliet* story goes even further than *Battle* in challenging essentialist assumptions about racial identity and character. In the first issue of *Blood of the Apes*, Tonus is even more unrelenting than Ursus or Aldo in his hatred and murderousness, yet by the end he is reformed and achieves a change of heart never achieved by, or even suggested as possible for, a gorilla in the films. While Tonus states that it is "ape nature" to hate and kill humans, his own transformation undermines that assumption, as does the fact that a number of ape animal rights activists risk their lives on behalf of humans.

The whole notion of an essential ape or human "nature" is further debunked by the fact that Myndith is able to act enough like an ape that Tonus cannot tell the difference. And the fact that an ape and a human actually fall in love and are "not as different" as assumed also argues against the idea of a distinct ape or human "nature."

Yet *Blood of the Apes* is not a complete departure from earlier treatment of interracial love in the *Apes* films and television shows. Tonus and Myndith are in each other's arms as they die, but they *do* die. Thus, as in Pierre Boulle's original book, an ape and human may fall in love, but in the end "the separation is essential."

Planet of the Apes: The Forbidden Zone, by Lowell Cunningham, focuses on the city Primacy, an integrated community of apes and humans of various races who live on a foundation of equality for all primates. Children are taught in classrooms integrated along species, racial, and gender lines; interracial and interspecies friendship is the norm; and power is shared between ape and human. The political leader of the city, for example, is an orangutan male and the security chief is a white woman.

The peaceful city faces attack both from the Ape City's army, led by the hostile gorilla Colonel Arvo, and from the mutant humans in the Forbidden Zone. The enclave of racial peace is thus threatened on one side by racist apes and on the other side by racist mutants described as "xenophobic *Zealots!* [Who will] destroy anyone and anything the *least* bit different from themselves (emphasis in original)."[32] Pell Shea, the Primacy security chief, maneuvers the two invading armies so they meet each other on the battlefield and destroy each other in mutual hatred while Primacy survives relatively unscathed.

The Forbidden Zone does not paint a portrait of Primacy as a conflict-free utopia. There are tensions between apes and humans. For example, some gorillas resent Pell Shea serving as security chief instead of a gorilla. Nonetheless, there is still a fundamental commitment to a just society based on respect and the sharing of power and responsibilities. That commitment does not necessarily come easily. Cunningham makes the point that the apes who were formerly enslaved by the humans and the humans who were conquered by the apes have substantial reason not to trust each other, and yet they still make the leap of faith and take the actions necessary to build a viable community together.

But the peace they have created is vulnerable. When they are imperiled by the racist ideologies that threaten to crush them from both the ape and the human side, the tensions within Primacy are exacerbated and the citizens' commitment to respect and equality must withstand the challenge.

As mentioned, the Adventure comics do not focus on racial stratification among the apes. In fact, in Adventure's regular monthly *Planet of the Apes* comic it is often unclear which apes are members of which ape race, which suggests that racial differentiation among the apes was not particularly important in the author's story concept. Nor are character, temperament, and occupation strictly determined by race, as they were in the films and television shows. Gorillas may be scientists, and orangutans may be architects. There are good apes and bad apes, violent apes and loving apes, in each race. Although the gorillas are still the military and renegade gorillas are still the stock villains, chimpanzees, orangutans, mutants, humans, and aliens also are antagonists at times.[33]

The change is most significant in the greater diversity among the gorillas. The depiction of the gorillas is much more varied than in the films or in the live-action television series. The gorilla Sergeant Caspian plots to stop Urchak; Tonus' superior Colonel Noorev disapproves of his murderousness in *Blood of the Apes*; and, in *The Forbidden Zone*, not only is Colonel Arvo's son Julius an archeologist rather than a soldier, but General Brak, the head of the gorilla army, opposes Arvo's invasion of Primacy, arguing that "we have [nothing] to *fear* from this society. Tyranny travels *easy*, but I doubt anyone has yet succeeded in exporting *equality*" (emphasis in original).[34] Even the most honorable gorillas in the live-action show never renounced the doctrine of ape supremacy as did Tonus and Brak.

While exploring conflicts established in the movies, these comics all depict a greater level of ape-human cooperation than did the earlier *Apes* stories. The films and television shows pictured ape-human partnership only in isolated cases among apostates and fugitives. In these comics, however, factions and even entire societies based on interracial understanding are counterposed with factions or societies based on racial hostility. Urchak's genocidal scheme is resisted by an underground composed of all three ape races (instead of just chimpanzees, as we would expect from the films and television shows), as well as a mutant and a human. In *Blood of the Apes*, the animal rights activists publicly advocate rights for humans.

And, unlike the films, in which the advocates of racial peace fail, the comics at times depict the survival and flourishing of racial peace and justice. Perhaps exhibiting a post–civil rights movement sensibility, these comics go beyond advocating the *dream* of equality and depict the difficult struggle to create and sustain the *reality* of equality.

The continual exposure to the original films and shows, the increased referencing of *Apes* throughout popular culture, and the production of new *Apes* material not only remind older *Apes* fans of the series, but also introduce new fans to the saga as well. Terry Hoknes, for instance, first saw the films during the eighties as a teenager in Canada and was "drawn to *Apes* because the series provoked the viewers to use their imagination about the future effect on our society if there was a nuclear war . . . [and] because it uses apes and man to portray the struggle between races and classes in our modern society."[35]

Spurred in part by the new comic series, Hoknes is now the president of the "International *Planet of the Apes* Fan Club." Begun in 1991, the fan club, while small (there are currently around three dozen members), has members in five countries, with ages ranging from 17 to 35. The club publishes a bimonthly magazine called *Ape Chronicles*, which includes articles about the films, biographies of the actors, articles about primate studies, rare photos, original cartoon strips, unused story ideas from the films and television shows, and classified advertisements to buy, sell, and trade *Apes* merchandise.

In 1992 the fan club combined its efforts with those of two teenagers from California who had started publishing *Ape Crazy*, a newsletter focusing on reviews of the new *Apes* comics from Adventure Comics company. In January 1995 yet another *Apes* fan magazine, *The Sacred Scrolls*, premiered. *The Sacred Scrolls* is published quarterly by Zaki Hassan, a teenager from Hanover Park, Illinois, and features articles about the movies as well as original stories that tie in to *Planet*. *Apes'* appeal extends beyond the United States and Canada; Brazil, too, has an *Apes* fan club, which publishes a newsletter in Portuguese.

As we have seen, the *Apes* series referenced and built upon the cultural works that preceded it. In the three decades since the release of Pierre Boulle's novel, *Planet of the Apes* itself has become a part of cultural myth. Although not as pervasive as the myths of cowboys and Indians, the *Apes* saga similarly provides imagery and a frame of reference regarding racial conflict and political cataclysm that have been used in both U.S. popular and political culture.

This was evident in Spike Lee's 1989 look at race relations, *Do the Right Thing.* Centering on the tensions between the residents of an African-American neighborhood and a white family running the neighborhood pizzeria, the film features a scene in which the pizzeria owner's racist son complains to his father, "I'm sick of niggers. It's like I come into work, it's planet of the apes. I don't like being around them, they're animals." Using the phrase "planet of the apes" is more than just an ethnic slur likening African-Americans to apes. It is a statement expressing a sense of white powerlessness in a situation where the "natural" order has been reversed and the despised racial "other" now dominates—precisely the anxiety that *Planet* evoked.

That anxiety can be used in very different ways. Gangsta rap trio Da Lench Mob exploited this same sense of black domination and white powerlessness in their 1994 album "Planet of da Apes." A follow-up to their 1992 album "Guerrillas in tha Mist," "Planet of da Apes" is billed in the album's press release as "a virtual cinemascape" that can be "best described as the soundtrack to Armageddon." The press release quotes one group member as declaring that "Armageddon is here" and that the "1992 L.A. uprising [was] a mere warm-up act." The album was co-produced by rapper Ice Cube, who himself mentioned *Planet of the Apes* in his recent song "You Know How We Do It." The cover features one band member holding a bandolier and another holding a gas mask in anticipation, or perpetration, of racial warfare. Although the original *Planet of the Apes* was shown at the album's premiere party, the album does not specifically deal with the movies, but rather plays off of white fears of racial apocalypse by presenting a series of black revenge fantasies.

The use of the phrase "planet of the apes" to convey this sense of racial dis-ease has also entered U.S. political culture. Photo-journalist Rex Perry recalls that "planet of the apes" has come up as a term of contempt at every Ku Klux Klan rally he has covered, and ironically *Planet of the Apes* has become a favorite "cult" film among skinheads.[36] Just months before the release of *Do the Right Thing*, at a white supremacist rally in Pulaski, Tennessee, on January 14, 1989, a man performing a "heil Hitler" salute brandished a sign reading "NAACP Planet of the Apes." Thus the far-right white here links African-American advancement to a fictional world in which racial "inferiors" have taken over. This manipulates precisely the same fear verbalized by the character in *Do the Right Thing*, fear similar to the fears

Apes' imagery has entered the debate over the very issues that the filmmakers created that imagery to address: white supremacists commonly use "planet of the apes" as a shorthand for racial apocalypse and the loss of white dominance. Photo reprinted with permission of Rex Perry.

manipulated by Da Lench Mob on "Planet of da Apes"—fear of a power reversal resulting in the loss of white dominance.

But the *Apes* series' message is inverted by the Klan and Da Lench Mob. The antiracist *Apes* parables argued that the United States must eliminate racial oppression to prevent a racial apocalypse. White nationalists have appropriated and transformed *Apes'* imagery to assert that oppression must be increased to prevent racial apocalypse, while Black Nationalists have appropriated and transformed *Apes'* imagery to celebrate and catalyze that apocalypse. Thus, moving from the movie and television screens, "planet of the apes" has entered reactionary racist discourse as a shorthand for racial apocalypse. We see here yet again that intentions do not control results.

The iconography of *Planet of the Apes* has also become part of our national cultural and political language in less pathological contexts. Scenes from *Planet* have been featured in a number of documentaries about political and cultural turmoil in the sixties, about fears of nuclear war, and

Politics flows into popular culture, which then flows back into politics. Greenpeace used *Planet's* imagery as a shorthand for nuclear cataclysm. Photo ©1988 Greenpeace; art by Lilian Gerring. Reproduced by permission of Greenpeace and Kurnit Communications.

about the Statue of Liberty. *Planet's* closing shot has become one of the most remembered and powerful scenes from sixties cinema. In the late eighties, needing a potent image to convey the threat posed by nuclear testing, Greenpeace used *Planet's* final vision on a poster warning, "Do nothing, and nuclear testing will eventually come to an end." *Apes'* imagery and its themes of loss of order have been invoked to describe and debate issues ranging from urban decay to the Bosnian civil war to international trade to gun control. ("This isn't the *Planet of the Apes*," Governor Jim Florio once admonished gun-lobby advocate Charlton Heston. "This is New Jersey."[37])

The political use of *Apes'* imagery by reactionary nationalists such as the Da Lench Mob or Neo-Nazis, and by progressives such as Greenpeace activists, illustrates that the language, images, and structures of a myth are available to serve varied political agendas. The referencing of *Apes* in debates specifically regarding racial conflict and war demonstrates that *Apes'* imagery has entered the debate about the very issues that the imagery was created to address. *Apes'* movement from politically influenced fiction to fiction used to influence politics exemplifies the continual exchange in which politics flows into popular culture, which then flows back into politics.[38]

The reawakened concern for the political issues *Apes* addressed, the cannibalizing of baby boomer popular culture, the increased interest in and references to *Apes*, and *Apes'* growing presence in popular and political culture all paved the way for a major new *Planet of the Apes* project. In 1988 Twentieth Century–Fox announced that 21-year-old writer-director Adam Rifkin was to write a sixth *Apes* film. Rifkin disregarded the other four sequels and wrote a direct sequel to *Planet.*

Entitled *Return to the Planet of the Apes*, Rifkin's script bore some resemblance to Pierre Boulle's *Planet of the Men.* In this story, set some years after Taylor escaped to the Forbidden Zone at the conclusion of *Planet*, ape society is torn by a civil war between the peace-loving chimpanzees and the war-mongering gorillas. (There are only three orangutans left on the planet, for reasons which are never explained.) Humans are used as slaves. Zira has died, but Cornelius lives and is a member of a group of "Simiantarians" advocating both peace between apes and human emancipation. Needing convincing proof that the apes' warring ways will destroy them, just as war destroyed the humans, Cornelius takes his three-year-old son Pax with him into the Forbidden Zone to ask Taylor to return with him and reveal the truth of the planet's history to the apes.

Cornelius convinces Taylor, who also has a three-year old son, named Duke after John Wayne, to come back to the ape city with him and warn the apes. When they address the ape leadership, gorilla general Izan orders Taylor killed and seizes Pax, vowing to raise him as a gorilla. The general banishes Cornelius, threatening to kill Pax if Cornelius ever returns. Just before Taylor dies, he asks Cornelius to raise his son Duke, and Cornelius returns to the Forbidden Zone to live out his exile among the humans.

Twenty years later, when Duke learns how his father died, he goes to the ape city to assassinate Izan and is captured. Duke reveals the truth about Pax's true father to him, but Pax is loyal to Izan and refuses to believe Duke's story. When Cornelius and some humans come to rescue Duke, Izan prepares to kill Pax. Cornelius begs Izan to kill him instead and spare Pax. Izan agrees but orders Pax to pull the trigger and kill Cornelius as a sign of loyalty. Realizing that Duke has told him the truth, Pax turns on Izan, takes power, and promises to end the civil war and the oppression of the humans.

The *Return* script is consistent with the films and television shows in a number of regards. Again knowledge of the past is presented as the key to controlling the future. And again the gorillas are the villains: Izan is in fact described as "the blackest of the black gorillas." Thus, as in *Planet* and *Beneath*, the script assumes that race determines character.[39]

In fact, the script revisits the nature-nurture debate. The issue is framed by Pax, who, when three years old, asks Cornelius, "why are some apes good and some apes mean?"[40] The answer the script gives is that goodness and meanness are both genetic. The device for answering Pax's question is Izan's abduction and raising of Pax. Pax appears to have taken on Izan's mannerisms and ideology but eventually cannot go against his "natural grain" by killing Cornelius.[41] "Once a chimp, always a chimp" is Izan's accusation and, apparently, the script's message.[42] Just as Izan cannot ultimately turn the genetically peaceful chimpanzee into a bloodthirsty gorilla, Cornelius similarly fails to impart his peaceful "nature" to the "naturally" belligerent Duke.

In a move that counters *Battle*'s conclusions regarding the nonexistence of a biologically based "racial character," the script posits a basic chimpanzee "nature" and reverts back to the biological determinism of *Planet* and *Beneath*. While criticizing Izan's racial oppression, the script makes the racist claim that we are our origins, that environment does not matter because it's all in the blood. Consequently, the *Return* script simultaneously criticizes racist practice and endorses racist principles.

Of all the *Apes* stories, *Return*'s political symbolism is at once the most labored and the most confused, never achieving meaningful consistency. For example, the ape empire, under gorilla domination, is described as a decadent duplicate of ancient Rome, complete with gorilla prostitutes sitting on Izan's lap feeding him grapes and bananas. But it is also written as an analogue to the Soviet Union. In a draft dated July 6, 1989, the humans implausibly attack the apes using restored two thousand–year-old cars. Thus, in a scene that might have pleased Ronald Reagan, using the resurrected symbols of U.S. consumerism and individualism, John Wayne leads an army which triumphs over an evil empire and makes possible Pax's reign. Embodying a Reagan slogan, peace ("Pax" is the Latin word for "peace") is achieved through strength.

The cold war imagery is interspersed with references to conflict in the Middle East. In the beginning, gorilla chief Tafara (Arafat spelled backwards) and chimpanzee chief Nebb Gurio (whose name is a nearly exact anagram of the name of the former Israeli prime minister Ben-Gurion, and whose eye-patch recalls the former Israeli defense minister Moshe Dayan) have signed a peace treaty. At this point Izan (Nazi backwards) assassinates Tafara and wounds Gurio, whom he later kills. Unless Rifkin intended to make a general statement about hatred destroying cooperation, it is rather anachronistic to have the Nazis preventing peace between the Israelis and the Palestinians.

This relationship between these three characters as symbols of real-world politics might make more sense if, because of the name similarities, Izan is interpreted as a stand-in for Iran. But even if this were the case, the symbolism is superficial and significantly related neither to the story nor to the political conflicts associated with the names. Likewise, Pax's Kennedyesque declaration that "the torch has been passed to a new generation of primates" seems placed in the script for its own sake.[43]

This lack of symbolic coherence might be one of the reasons that Fox passed on the script. The proposed screenplay was not well received by the studio, especially by studio head Joe Roth, who took over after Rifkin began to write the script and is said to have been adamantly opposed to doing any *Apes* project. As Arthur P. Jacobs learned, however, in Hollywood, the winds of fortune are ever-changing.

On November 8, 1993, *Time* magazine ran the following news item: "A vicious war between hostile races! Caged humans and imperialist beasts! Conspiracy rampant! Sound like a perfect Oliver Stone subject? Well it is. The director of *Platoon* and *JFK* is ready to produce a new *Planet of the Apes*."[44]

Time was perceptive in that, in many ways, Oliver Stone would seem perfect to spearhead a new *Apes* film. Aside from his persistent exploration of the sixties, out of which *Apes* emerged, Stone, more than most mainstream filmmakers, understands the connections between political ideology and cultural myth and is unapologetic about using film as a political art form. In fact, an article in *Sci-Fi Universe* magazine states that it was "the . . . spiritual and cultural elements of Stone's [films] that interested 20th Century–Fox in the first place."[45] The article points out, however, that the "spiritual and cultural" dimensions are "unspecified."

The proposed film, *The Return of the Apes*, originally written by Terry Hayes (*The Road Warrior*), is scheduled for release in 1996; it concerns a mysterious epidemic causing the world's babies to be stillborn. A scientist theorizes that the disease is built into human DNA, and he travels back in time to find the first modern *homo sapiens* and prevent the mutation that causes the disease. Upon arriving, he finds ancient Earth ruled by a species of advanced apes.

The previous work of Hayes and the potential casting of Arnold Schwarzenegger as the scientist suggest that the focus will be more on violence than on the progressive political critiques provided by the first *Apes* films. The pairing of the liberal Stone with Schwarzenegger, whose political conservatism correlates with the conservatism of his films, at first glance seems odd. But it is perhaps no more so than the pairing of the formerly black-listed Michael Wilson with the very conservative Charlton Heston. Just as Jacobs and company explored different possibilities with Heston's persona, so too could Stone and company approach Schwarzenegger's image with equal subtlety. Director Chris Colombus (*Home Alone*) and writer Sam Hamm (*Batman*) have apparently taken over the directing and writing duties. Fox plans to follow the new movie with an animated *Apes* television miniseries, an interactive CD-Rom video game, and perhaps sequels. The toy rights have already been sold.

Sci-Fi Universe reports that the new *Apes* picture "isn't just a marketing strategy or vehicle, but a real analysis of today." Of course, the nature of that "analysis" is still unclear. The threat of a seemingly unstoppable disease obviously has poignant implications in the age of AIDS, while the story's setting in the ancient past might present an interesting potential for exploring the genesis of struggles for racial dominance. Regardless of the tone and direction of the "analysis" offered by the new film, Columbus is inheriting an established mythological framework which, if used intelligently, provides an open field within which he may play with a variety of artistic and political possibilities. How well he plays with them remains to be seen.

The confluence of the political and cultural trends of the last several years have made the time right for a new *Apes* film. Our public mythologies, no less than our personal ones, are developed to address deep problems and concerns. When attention returns to persistent problems—like racial conflict—we can expect that the culture will return to, and reimagine, the mythic formulations formerly used to explore these issues. *Dances with Wolves* and *Unforgiven* returned to the myths of the West to reask and reanswer unresolved questions about racial difference and reconciliation and about the role of violence in American life. Like the original, the three successor "Star Trek" television series use the "Prime Directive" to debate the merits of a major power intervening in the affairs of others, an issue no less vexing when we look at Bosnia and Haiti today than when Gene Roddenberry and the nation looked at Vietnam in the sixties.

Similarly, an *Apes* story geared to the challenges and struggles of the nineties and the early twenty-first century will look both like and unlike the *Apes* stories used to address the sixties and seventies. As we saw in the case of the *Apes* comic books, both consistency and innovation will be required for the *Apes* mythology to register and respond to the way things have changed and the way they have stayed the same. This is the way any mythology stays fresh and relevant.

In the introduction, we noted Donna Haraway's characterization of primatology as a "survival literature" concerned with war, technology, power, and community. As we have seen, these themes pervade the *Apes* saga. These concerns are embedded in the notes Ted Post, the director of *Beneath*, wrote to himself during production in order to focus his thoughts about the film. His notes aptly crystallize the *Apes* saga's message:

> The world seems ready to destroy itself and *Beneath the Planet of the Apes* asks you not to contribute to that destruction. Our days on this planet at this moment are numbered and the reason for our finite, unrosy future is that we are corrupting ourselves out of existence — with our double standards, hypocrisy, injustice, anarchy, shortsightedness, very shallow forms of self delusion, profound national disarray, sickness, a cold war that does not end, a hot war that does not end, a draft that does not end, and a poisonous race conflict that does not end.
>
> What this film is attempting to say satirically is that it is possible we as a society have been playing the wrong game in the wrong ball park. The score board doesn't tell us whether our side is winning or losing. We are probably cheering (or booing) at the wrong times. The Establishment's home runs may really be foul balls, their balls, strikes, and we as a people, a society, had better do something about all this — fast.
>
> If excellence in the Establishment's effort ultimately leads to strengthening the military apparatus, then we have facilitated worldwide disaster rather than furthering the cause of truth and peace.
>
> Successful searches for truth in the services of evil lead to more evil rather than good.
>
> Conclusion: we are existing in a crisis of disbelief. Atom bombs for peace is a lethal contradiction.
>
> We must forge new links between the spiritual values of human self-fulfillment and the material society in which we live. We have to choose a life which affirms the infinite worth of every human being. The idea that lurks behind the film transcends the adventurous misfortunes of the hero.[46]

By projecting the cataclysmic results of U.S. politics, the *Apes* movies act as prophetic fiction warning of racial revolution, ecological devastation, and nuclear annihilation should the United States not change its path. "Survival literature" indeed.

"Can a planet long endure half human and half ape?" *Beneath* answers this question with an emphatic "no." The *Apes* series as a whole is slightly —

but only slightly—less definite in response. It does hold out the possibility of racial peace (a possibility effectively destroyed by the television shows), but that possibility is precarious and is envisioned only after racial hunts, mutilations, murders, attempted genocides, enslavements, wars, and the annihilation of the planet. Thus, in the *Apes* saga, racial peace is possible only after a great many of what James Baldwin might have called painful choices painfully arrived at.

While hope for the future is left open, the series says the same thing that so much of American racial mythology, from "cowboys and Indians" to *Birth of a Nation*, says: different races will meet and come together only in the context of fear, mistrust, hatred, persecution, and violence. Perhaps this is what Sammy Davis, Jr., was talking about.

Afterword: Beyond
the Planet of the Apes

The language of the racial "other" as "ape" is old, adaptable, and show-ing no sign of disappearing. In 1992 journalist Sam Roberts quoted pros-ecutors' description of a murder suspect from East New York as a vivid example of such stereotyping:

> He had a round face, thick lips, a flat nose and small ears, stuck close to his kinky hair. His arms had not waited for the rest of him. They dangled to his knees, completing a generally gorilla-like figure ... [he was] an animal in human guise.[1]

The man described was indeed a killer. But he was not, as we might expect from the pejorative description, an African-American arrested in 1992 for the shooting deaths of two African-American students at East New York's Thomas Jefferson High School, the crime that precipitated Roberts' column. In fact, he was a white Jewish man arrested during the 1940s. In the 1990s, however, it is no less likely for an African-American man to be arrested and described in such stereotypical terms than for a white Jewish man to be arrested and so described during the 1940s. In the midst of East New York's contemporary crisis, Roberts quoted the decades-old descrip-tion to point out that "The thrills are the same. Only the scapegoats change."

In this observation Roberts was, sadly, correct. Minutes after Los Angeles police officer Laurence Powell brutalized Rodney King, whom he later likened to a "monster," Powell described having gone to a domestic dispute in an African-American neighborhood by saying, "It was right out of *Gorillas in the Mist*." And in 1992 President George Bush's highest men-tal health official linked violence in inner cities to the aggressive instincts of male rhesus monkeys.[2] As these examples together demonstrate, we apply this same language to tell the same stories about racial difference with depressing regularity.

Just as *Apes*' first appearance on the U.S. cultural landscape was

185

preceded by and coincided with increased awareness of racial conflict and a need for cultural responses to make sense out of it, public discussion of race and of current and historical racism in the United States has substantially increased in the 1990s. Racial violence continues to be a staple ingredient of life in U.S. domestic and foreign affairs. More dramatically than most events, the vicious beating of Rodney King, the dehumanizing of King in the trial of the police officers who beat him, their acquittal, and the tremendous violence that erupted following that acquittal all speak to the persistence of racial bigotry, oppression, and violence which still dehumanize and deform our society.

In this time of economic dislocation, confusion, and pain, the old standby of scapegoating has been reinvigorated as white fears of being "overrun" by foreigners and minorities are continually fanned, while the powerful, wealthy, and white hands that manipulate the economy remain largely invisible. Bias-motivated crimes against cultural outsiders like African-Americans, Jews, and homosexuals are on the rise. From the Senate floor and school campuses to the movie houses and television screens to the radios and the book stores, the United States' racial problems, and the fact that race *is* a problem, have demanded increased public attention.

By answering "no" to the possibility of a planet long enduring half human and half ape, the *Apes* films suggest that those problems cannot be resolved. Thomas Jefferson, who "trembled" when he thought of the nation's racial problems two centuries ago, warned,

> Deep rooted prejudices entertained by the whites, ten thousand recollections, by the blacks, of the injuries they have sustained ... and many other circumstances, will divide us into parties, and produce convulsions, which will probably never end but in the extermination of one or the other race.[3]

While we might be disposed to recoil from the implications of Jefferson's pronouncement, the stories this country has told throughout its history—no less than the actions we have taken—regarding race demonstrate how hard it is for us to believe, even imagine, otherwise.

The fictional stories we write in books, in movies, on television, and the real-life stories we write in the streets, the courtrooms, and the voting booths are part of a limiting mythology and a history that maintain that racial difference cannot be accepted and must lead to "the extermination of one or the other race."

Nevertheless, we do not have to passively accept as final the answer given to us by Jefferson or, despite their best intentions, by the *Apes* movies. Like all fictions and mythologies, *Apes* provides an opportunity to rethink our history and experience, to consider different possibilities, to reimagine ourselves, and, yes, even to transform our realities. Fiction helps us develop a sense of the possible. If we can make the implicit meanings and values explicit, if we can recognize as choices what we take for granted, if we can identify in our fictional and real-life stories their hidden political assumptions, we have a better chance of rejecting these assumptions and embracing others. We must in our political realities and in our popular fictions reject the bottom line of Jefferson and the *Apes* series. We can consciously write our realities as well as our fictions, and we must choose to write stories in books, movies, television, the streets, the courtrooms and the voting booths that have a different bottom line, that provide a more humane sense of possibility.

Given that the language of the *Apes* saga has not been exhausted and given that there is both an increased recognition of racial problems and a need for cultural responses to them, it should come as no surprise if *Apes* continues to be a fertile mythological space in which stories and questions about racial conflict are explored. This time, however, we cannot settle for the same negative answer. We must tell the stories—both of our fictions and our lives—differently, and credibly, in a way that allows for a less "terrifying" answer to that "ultimate question."

Notes

Preface

1. Quoted in Michael Wines, "Views on Single Motherhood Are Multiple at White House," *New York Times*, May 21, 1992, p. B16.
2. Bush quoted in "Sitcom Politics," *Time*, September 21, 1992, p. 44.
3. Lance Morrow, "Folklore in a Box," *Time*, September 21, 1992, p. 50.
4. Michael Ryan and Douglas Kellner, *Camera Politica: The Politics and Ideology of Contemporary Hollywood Film* (Bloomington: Indiana University Press, 1990), p. 13.

Introduction

1. Frederick S. Clarke, review of *Escape from the Planet of the Apes*, *Cinéfantastique* (Fall 1971): 28.
2. Donald Willis, ed., June 14, 1972, review of *Conquest of the Planet of the Apes* reprinted in *Variety's Complete Science Fiction Reviews* (New York: Garland, 1985), p. 279.
3. Donna Haraway, *Primate Visions: Gender, Race and Nature in the World of Modern Science* (New York: Routledge, Chapman, and Hall, 1989), p. 1.
4. Haraway, *Primate Visions*, p. 11.
5. Given this relationship, it is not surprising that when candidates for political office attempt self-promotion by attacking their rivals, they describe the process as "defining" the opponent.
6. Haraway, *Primate Visions*, p. 122.
7. Quoted in David Johnson, "Michael Wilson: The Other 'APES' Writer," *Planet of the Apes* 2 (October 1974): 50.
8. Haraway, *Primate Visions*, p. 180.
9. Haraway, *Primate Visions*, p. 11.
10. Richard Slotkin notes that during World War Two, "Poster images of Japanese as ape-like monsters raping and murdering White women [drew] . . . heavily on the iconography of Black stereotypes." Richard Slotkin, *Gunfighter Nation: The Myth of the Frontier in Twentieth Century America* (New York: Atheneum, 1992), p. 319.
11. On the image of black men and women as being closer than whites to the hyper-sensuality of animals, see Haraway, *Primate Visions*, p. 354–55.

12. Topsell, Edward, *Historie of Foure-Footed Beasts*, 1607, cited in Winthrop D. Jordon, *The White Man's Burden* (New York: Oxford University Press, 1974), p. 15.

13. Johann Pezzl, quoted in Sander Gilman, *The Jew's Body* (New York: Routledge, 1991), p. 172. Thanks to Richard Slotkin for suggesting this book.

14. Jordan, *The White Man's Burden*, p. 18. Of course this kind of hostility can be sent in more than one direction. The August 27, 1965, issue of *Time* magazine, p. 11, claimed that "the Black Muslims promise to get this white, blue-eyed gorilla off your back."

15. While the names of other animals such as snakes and barracudas are used as descriptions of or insults for people, their use is not quite the same because other animals do not share apes' particular combination of likeness and difference. While phrases such as "strong as an ox" and "stubborn as a mule" both transfer a particular quality believed to be characteristic of an animal to a person, calling someone an ape or monkey, in addition to being a physical insult, speaks to a more general discomfort over the blurred distinction between "self" and "other" and between "higher" and "lower."

16. Cited in Allan Chase, *The Legacy of Malthus: The Social Costs of the New Scientific Racism* (Urbana: University of Illinois Press, 1980), p. 371. For a discussion of arguments about the "apishness" of "inferior" races and criminals, see Stephan Jay Gould, *The Mismeasure of Man*, (New York: Norton, 1981), Chapter 4, especially pp. 124–25.

17. Jordon, *The White Man's Burden* p. 16–17. Some Europeans seemed to quite enjoy fantasizing about sex with animals. Jordon, for instance, cites French political theorist Jean Bodini's assertion that "promiscuous coition of men and animals took place, wherefore the regions of Africa produce for us so many monsters," p. 16. On the association of Africans with apes in the Western imagination, see Jordan pp. 15–18, 103–4, and 198–99.

18. Haraway, *Primate Visions*, p. 369.

19. The meanings of the terms *text* and *culture* are vigorously debated within and between academic disciplines. While I have no desire to enter those debates here, I do want to clarify the way I use these terms in this discussion. I use *text* broadly to refer to anything which can be interpreted — from a cloud formation to a historical document to a verbal exchange. By *culture* I mean the nexus of the customs, concerns, values, and interpretations — the meanings — that a people derive from and ascribe to their collective experiences. For a useful discussion of *culture* and related terms in cultural history, see Richard Slotkin, *The Fatal Environment: The Myth of the Frontier in the Age of Industrialization 1800–1890* (Middletown, Conn.: Wesleyan University Press, 1986), Chapter 2, especially p. 21.

20. See Ryan and Kellner, *Camera Politica*, pp. 2–7.

21. From "A Testament of Hope," *A Testament of Hope: The Essential Writings and Speeches of Martin Luther King, Jr.*, ed., James Melvin Washington (San Francisco: HarperCollins, 1986), p. 315.

22. These were tag lines on the *Wild Bunch* advertisements.

23. Pauline Kael, Commencement Address, Smith College, May 27, 1973, cited in "Teaching Apes: A Review of *Planet of the Apes*" by Susan Rice in *Media and Methods Magazine*, October 1973 (Philadelphia: North American Publishing Co.), p. 46.

24. Michael Denning, *Mechanic Accents: Dime Novels and Working Class Culture in America* (New York: Verso, 1987), p. 77.

25. See Stuart Hall, "The Whites of Their Eyes: Racist Ideologies and the Media," in *Silver Linings: Some Strategies for the Eighties*, ed. George Bridges and Rosalind Brunt, p. 33 (London: Lawrence and Wishart, 1981).

26. Kael, Commencement Address, May 27, 1973, cited in "Teaching Apes: A Review of *Planet of the Apes*" by Susan Rice in *Media and Methods Magazine*, October 1973 (Philadelphia: North American Publishing Co.), pp. 45–46.

27. Joseph W. Reed, *American Scenarios: The Uses of Film Genre* (Middletown: Wesleyan University Press, 1989), pp. 5–6.

28. If this is the case, it is appropriate to ask how this process works. Michael Ryan and Douglas Kellner offer a model of this process when they suggest that "films transcode the discourses (the forms, figures and representations) of social life into cinematic narratives." Movies themselves "become a part of that broader cultural system of representations that construct social reality." They argue:

> Representations are ... taken from the culture and internalized. ...
> When internalized they mold the self in such a way that it becomes accommodated to the values inherent in those cultural representations. *Consequently, the sort of representations which prevail in a culture is a crucial political issue.* Cultural representations not only give shape to psychological dispositions, they also play an important role in determining how social reality will be constructed, that is, what figures and boundaries will prevail in the shaping of social life and social institutions. ... *Control over the production of cultural representation is therefore crucial to the maintenance of social power, but it is also essential to progressive movements for social change* [*Camera Politica*, pp. 12–13, emphasis added].

29. Haraway, *Primate Visions*, p. 5

30. Tony Bennett and Janet Wollacott, *Bond and Beyond: The Political Career of a Popular Hero* (New York: Methuen, 1987), p. 280.

31. Ibid., pp. 281–82.

32. James Baldwin, *The Devil Finds Work*, reprinted in James Baldwin, *The Price of the Ticket: Collected Nonfiction, 1948–1985* (New York: St. Martin's/Marek, 1985), p. 606.

33. Stuart Hall, "The Whites of Their Eyes," pp. 37–38.

34. Denning, *Mechanic Accents*, p. 75.

35. Cited in Richard A. Maynard, *The Black Man on Film: Racial Stereotyping* (Rochelle Park, N.J.: Hayden, 1974), p. 92.

36. Hall, "The Whites of Their Eyes," p. 35.

37. In "Onward and Apeward," *Time*, June 5, 1972, p. 62.

38. Victor Turner, *Dramas, Fields, and Metaphors* (Ithaca: Cornell University Press, 1974), pp. 29–30.

39. Oliver Stone's *JFK* is perhaps the most recent example of such an effect.

40. The latter strategy may in fact prove more profitable for the filmmakers by expanding the range of ideological opinion, and thus the number of viewers to whom the film may appeal.

41. See Slotkin, *Gunfighter Nation*, p. 351.

42. Obviously, other factors such as class, religion, and gender can substantially influence one's "reading" of a symbol or text. It would be exceedingly difficult for me to speculate, however, on how those factors influence our interpretations

of particular texts without falling into dubious essentialist generalizations and assumptions.

43. "From Book—Film—T.V." in *Planet of the Apes Posterbook* (London: Top Sellers, 1974), p. 1.

44. I want to make clear that I am stating interpretative claims for which I think I make a strong case. Though I might at times write with the language of certainty, I remain aware, and so should the reader, that interpretations are by definition uncertain and that other interpretations are possible.

45. "Onward and Apeward," *Time*, June 5, 1972, p. 62.

46. Alan R. Howard, review of *Battle for the Planet of the Apes*, *The Hollywood Reporter*, May 18, 1973.

47. Mark Phillips, letter to the editor, *Planet of the Apes* 11 (April 1991): 27.

48. This tactic was common during the "Red Scare" when campaigns against leftists in the film industry forced many filmmakers to allegorize their social and political concerns in the mythic language of the Western as well as in science fiction. See Slotkin, *Gunfighter Nation*, pp. 366–67. Nor was this method of dealing with race the invention of the producers of the *Apes* movies. For just one example, Delmar Daves, the director of *Broken Arrow*, released in 1950, "said that his pro-Indian Western, and others like it, offered a safe vehicle for unacceptably liberal ideas on racial and political coexistence." Slotkin, *Gunfighter Nation*, p. 726, n. 36.

49. Quoted in Dale Winogura, "Dialogues on Apes, Apes, and More Apes," *Cinéfantastique* (Summer 1972): p. 22.

50. Quoted in Rowland Barber, "How Much Milk Can You Get from an Ape?" *TV Guide*, December 7, 1974, pp. 9–10.

51. Clifford Geertz, *The Interpretation of Cultures* (New York: Basic Books, 1973), p. 93.

Chapter 1

1. This is not unlike the way racial difference had been described before, but there is a crucial difference in the *Apes* series: the *Apes* films *allegorize* race as species, they do not *mistake* one for the other.

Determining precisely what constitutes a "race" is a notoriously difficult problem (see, for example, James Shreeve, "Terms of Estrangement," and Jared Diamond, "Race Without Color" in *Discover: The World of Science*, 15, no. 11, special issue *"The Science of Race"* [November 1994]). Nevertheless, today most of us acknowledge that various races, however one may demarcate them, are all of the same species, that is, all human beings. But, historically, some have asserted that people of different races were in fact of different species. Theories of polygenesis, the belief that human beings of different races were different species produced by distinct creations, were asserted to explain racial difference, thus the claim for instance that Africans were of a different and inferior species than Europeans and so could be enslaved. While perhaps no longer explicitly in the mainstream, assertions of a species-based cause of racial difference have not totally disappeared today.

Indeed, this ideology seems like a variant of the underlying "logic" of comparing "inferior" people and groups to apes: it serves to explain the physical resemblance of different races while denying any fundamental relationship or consanguinity by emphasizing inherent biological "otherness" arising from separate origins. Difference thus constructed becomes a basis of hierarchy, discrimination, and enslavement. This also demands that bloodlines remain unmixed and "pure" to prevent racial "degeneration" — thus the obsession over miscegenation. Of course the very fact that people can mate and reproduce with those of another race belies the claim that different races are actually different species.

This construction of difference also seems to demand the "inevitability" of race wars. Thus Theodore Roosevelt, for example, could maintain that "on the border between civilization and barbarism war is generally normal, because it must be under the conditions of barbarism" (quoted in Richard Slotkin, *Gunfighter Nation: The Myth of the Frontier in Twentieth Century America* [New York: Atheneum, 1992], p. 52). This process of demarcation makes manifest the irreducible and irreconcilable difference between "self" and "other" which must be acted upon. And the ultimate denial of sameness and assertion of difference becomes murder. Since, so the "logic" goes, the presence of different — inferior — blood can always pose a threat, eugenics at best and genocide at worst emerge as the "rational" responses to difference.

2. Thomas Jefferson, quoted in Winthrop Jordan, *The White Man's Burden* (New York: Oxford University Press, 1974), p. 169.

3. See Allan Chase, *The Legacy of Malthus: The Social Costs of the New Scientific Racism* (Urbana: University of Illinois Press), 1980, especially chapters 7 and 12.

4. Ironically, in one of Serling's television plays, *The Velvet Alley*, directed by *Planet* director Franklin Schaffner, a kid tells an author struggling to finish a love story that it will not sell unless it has gorillas.

5. Rod Serling interview in *Show Business Illustrated*, November 28, 1961.

6. Quoted in "The Weary Young Man," *Newsweek*, September 28, 1959.

7. Ibid.

8. "Rod Serling Clarifies Comments on His Attitude Toward Contemporary TV," *Daily Variety*, January 19, 1968, p. 21.

9. Rod Serling, "Bitter Sadness, Special Irony Seen in the Passing of Dr. King," letter to the editor, *Los Angeles Times*, April 8, 1968.

10. Ellen Cameron May, "Serling in Creative Mainstream," *Los Angeles Times*, June 25, 1967.

11. Rod Serling, *Planet of the Apes*, March 1, 1965, p. 78.

12. Carl Foreman, Wilson's co-writer on *Kwai*, was also blacklisted and received no credit. Foreman also wrote *The Guns of Navarone*, directed by J. Lee Thompson, the director of *Conquest of the Planet of the Apes* and *Battle for the Planet of the Apes*.

13. "Vote No Censure by SWG on Michael Wilson, But Leak Is Embarrassing," *Daily Variety*, September 16, 1953.

14. Quoted in Dale Winogura, "Dialogues on Apes, Apes, and More Apes," *Cinéfantastique* (Summer 1972): p. 21.

15. The convention of having a white man fall asleep and then wake up in a time when white men are no longer in ascendance is arguably a call for wakefulness and vigilance against "the rising tide of color." This might especially be the case for Burroughs, who was greatly influenced by the eugenicist who popularized that phrase. See Slotkin, *Gunfighter Nation*, pp. 195–211, p. 702, n. 500. Sleeping also makes people vulnerable to possession in the film *Invasion of the Body Snatchers*, the crew of the Nostromo is asleep in the beginning of *Alien*, perhaps foreshadowing their destruction at the hands of the non-white beast, and Ripley is invaded by an alien as she sleeps in *Alien*[3].

It is also possible, though quite unlikely, that using the falling asleep device was a way to introduce the possibility that Taylor's adventures are a dream. David Desser points out that early filmmakers like Georges Méliès, Charles Chaplin, and Buster Keaton "to justify patently unreal occurrences . . . motivated them by a common appeal to literary or life-derived altered states, most significantly, dreams." David Desser, "The Cinematic Melting Pot: Ethnicity, Jews, and Psychoanalysis," in *Unspeakable Images: Ethnicity and the American Cinema*, ed. Lester D. Friedman (Urbana: University of Illinois Press, 1991), p. 380.

16. Pierre Boulle, *Planet of the Apes*, trans. Xan Fielding (New York: Vanguard, 1963), pp. 94–95.

17. Telephone interview with author, December 1990.

18. Michael Wilson, *Planet of the Apes*, January 13, 1967, p. 30.

19. Ibid., p. 61.

20. Ibid., p. 62.

21. Mort Abrahams, telephone interview with author, December 1990.

22. I use the term "race" deliberately, although chimpanzees, orangutans, and gorillas are in fact different species. In the films, however, the differences between the ape groups and their interactions and conflicts resemble race-based differences rather than species differences. For instance, all the apes can speak to one another, serve as co-workers, have ideological disagreements, be political rivals, be prejudiced against each other, occupy different social positions in ape society, and commonly identify as apes while remaining aware of which particular group they are a part of. Thus, although the three ape groups are in actuality distinct species, the film depicts them *as if* they were different races. This is in keeping with Boulle's original book, which alternately refers to the different groups as "families" and "species" but also refers to past "racial" barriers between them. Pierre Boulle, *Planet of the Apes*, translated by Xan Fielding (New York: Vanguard, 1963), pp. 94–95.

23. Compare *Planet's* use of the chimpanzees to Alan Spiegel's analysis of Jewish liminality in the sixties popular culture in "The Vanishing Act: A Typology of the Jew in the Contemporary American Film," in *From Hester Street to Hollywood: The Jewish American Stage and Screen*, ed. Sarah Blacher Cohen (Bloomington: Indiana University Press, 1983), pp. 257–75.

24. Boulle, *Planet of the Apes*, pp. 110–11.

25. Ibid., p. 51.

26. Quoted in Winogura, "Dialogues," p. 26.

27. In fact different species, i.e., chimpanzees and orangutans, cannot mate and reproduce. *Planet's* producers may not have been aware of that, however, at the time of their discussions and may have based their decision on other considerations.

28. *Dred Scott vs. Sandford* 60 U.S. 393, 15 L. Ed 691, cited in Derrick A. Bell, *Race, Racism and American Law* (Boston: Little, Brown, 1973), p. 8.

29. James Baldwin, Introduction to *The Price of the Ticket: Collected Non-Fiction 1948–1985*, (New York: St. Martin's/Marek, 1985), p. xiv.

30. Joe Russo and Larry Landsman, with Edward Gross, "Planet of the Apes Revisited," *Starlog* (April 1986): p. 47.

31. Quoted in Winogura, "Dialogues," p. 21. Also see Schaffner's comments in Vivian Sobochak, *Screening Space: The American Science Fiction Film*, (New York: Ungar, 1987), p. 182.

32. Frederick S. Clarke, review of *Beneath the Planet of the Apes, Cinéfantastique* (Fall 1970): 26.

33. Quoted in Winogura, "Dialogues," p. 34.

34. Richard Schickel, "Second Thoughts on Ape-Men," *Life*, May 10, 1968.

35. Similarly, Patt Elmore of Tennessee wrote to *Planet of the Apes* magazine to point out that the absence of female gorillas and orangutans in the films and the magazine's stories raised for her precisely the question of the female apes' place in society. Letter in *Planet of the Apes* 8 (May 1975): 5.

36. In Wilson's script Zira and Cornelius were equally assertive. John T. Kelly, in his uncredited rewrite, differentiated the two characters by making Cornelius more hesitant and in need of Zira's prodding.

37. Thanks to Paula Rabinowitz for this point.

38. Some of the dialogue Wilson originally wrote for the scene, such as an ape accusation against Zira and Cornelius that "there is a conspiracy afoot to undermine the very cornerstone of our faith. Two of the conspirators sit *there*" (emphasis in original), recalls McCarthy's assertion that he had a list of Communist conspirators within the U.S. government. Michael Wilson, *Planet of the Apes*, January 17, 1967, p. 75. And lines Wilson wrote for astronaut John Thomas, "back on Earth, in my time, men in power ... prized intelligence less than they feared it. And when intelligence threatened to expose their cherished myths they were impelled to suppress it, or emasculate it, or kill it," p. 82, suggest that Wilson was expressing some justified personal resentment about how dissent had been suppressed in the United States just a few years earlier.

39. Quoted in Kevin Thomas, "Balancing Act Pays Off for Patton Director," *Los Angeles Times*, May 7, 1970, sec. IV, p. 24.

40. Erwin Kim, *Franklin J. Schaffner* (Metuchen, N.J.: Scarecrow Press, 1985), p. 206.

41. Mort Abrahams, telephone interview with author, December 1990.

42. Charlton Heston, telephone interview with author, December 1990.

43. Kim, *Schaffner*, p. 206.

44. Ibid., p. 239.

45. Ibid., p. 239.

46. Ibid., p. 239.

47. Slotkin, *Gunfighter Nation*, p. 505. Despite a less-active career and the general disappearance of the epic pictures that were his specialty, Heston did not leave this persona behind in the sixties. As recently as 1990, a review of a Heston television movie noted that Heston "reprise[d] his favorite role as the Last Man, that lone representative of angry, moral righteousness, imperiled from every side by degradation and immorality." David Klinghoffer, "'Kidnap' Captivates Strangely," *Washington Times*, August 17, 1990, p. E3.

48. Appropriately, Taylor is from Fort Wayne, Indiana. Dr. Zaius, doubting the truth of Taylor's claim of other worldly origin, charges he made the story up and that his choice of a fort as the name for his home is an unconscious betrayal of humanity's innate belligerence. It may, in fact, have been an unconscious, or even conscious, reference to Heston's other screen "homes," or to John Wayne, another icon of Heston's type of "heroism."

49. On screenwriter Robert Ardrey's allegorization of social Darwinism in *Khartoum*, see Slotkin, *Gunfighter Nation*, p. 511. Ardrey did not confine himself to promulgating racist themes in movies, however. Misinterpreting the U.S. Congress'

study *Equality of Educational Opportunity*, also known as the "Coleman Report," which observed the correlation between educational performance and environmental factors like income, Ardrey, in his 1970 book *The Social Contract*, ignorantly proclaimed that "in the United States the evidence for [Blacks'] inferior learning capacity is as inarguable as [their] superior performance on the baseball diamond." (Cited in Chase, *Legacy of Malthus*, p. 463). Thus once again the racial other is rendered as primarily physical rather than intellectual. Ardrey was also an admirer of Konrad Lorenz, whose comparison of "subpopulations" with "inborn defects" to cancers led him to the genocidal recommendation that "inferior elements" be "effectively eliminated." (Cited in Chase, *Legacy of Malthus*, p. 349.)

50. Heston would continue this metarole in the early seventies in *The Omega Man*, written by *Battle* coauthors Joyce and William Corrington, where he was pitted against hordes of pasty-skinned, radiation-scarred mutants.

51. For a fuller discussion of Heston's race-war epics, see Slotkin, *Gunfighter Nation*, pp. 504–12. Slotkin notes that Heston's hero is at times aided by friendly natives. While the chimpanzees differ from these characters in that they do not welcome Heston's domination or tutelage, the chimpanzees role does echo that of the friendlies in the other Heston films when he must protect them in the last stand against the hostile gorillas under the command of the "fanatic" Dr. Zaius.

52. Slotkin, *Gunfighter Nation*, p. 505. For a discussion of the epic genre as it relates to the political climate of the sixties, see Slotkin, *Gunfighter Nation*, Chapter 15.

53. Richard Slotkin, "The Continuity of Forms: Myth and Genre in Warner Brothers' *The Charge of the Light Brigade*," *Representations* 29 (Winter 1990): 19.

54. Gary Gerani, "Knowing Your Place on the Planet of the Apes," *Planet of the Apes* 8 (May 1975): 40.

55. Blanca Vasquez, interview with the author, June 1992.

56. When I interviewed Heston in 1990, prior to my seeing *The War Lord*, he mentioned that people had made comparisons between the film and the Vietnam War which he and, he said, Schaffner had dismissed.

57. Slotkin, *Gunfighter Nation*, p. 511.

58. See Michael Ryan and Douglas Kellner, *Camera Politica: The Politics and Ideology of Contemporary Hollywood Film* (Bloomington: Indiana University Press, 1990), p. 14.

59. Pauline Kael, "Apes Must Be Remembered, Charlie," *New Yorker*, February 17, 1968, p. 108.

60. See Slotkin's discussion of *55 Days at Peking*, in *Gunfighter Nation*, pp. 506–10.

61. Ryan and Kellner note that in late sixties films dealing with rebellion or alienation, "the camera is frequently in close up, or else the lone individual is isolated in the frame against overcoded shots of natural settings." *Camera Politica*, p. 25.

62. Review of *Planet of the Apes*, *Daily Variety*, February 7, 1968.

63. The hunt sequence is one of the film's most effective scenes, an interesting interpretation of which arises when considering the work of psychologist Richard Sterba. In his article "Some Psychological Factors in Negro Race Hatred and Anti-Negro Riots," *Psychoanalysis and the Social Sciences* 1 (1947): 411–27, Sterba argues that the race riots and the violence against blacks that occurred in Detroit in June 1943 resembled a hunt and represented white displacement of repressed father

hatred onto blacks. Sterba explains (p. 416) that a number of his white patients even before the riots had had dreams in which black males were stand-ins for their fathers and notes that "Many dreams of being threatened by a Negro were understood as the expression and repetition of the dreamer's infantile fears of his father."

Tracing the connection between patricide, totemistic rituals, and hunting, Sterba argues that hunting, "particularly hunting of big animals in groups (perforce) is an expression of . . . patricidal tendencies. The animals usually chosen for group hunting are the deer, a typical father symbol with its proud and showy antlers as his male characteristic, and the fox, whose penis significance is obviously derived from his slipping into the fox hole. Father murder and castration are then unconscious aims of group hunting" (p. 423).

Patient dreams, such as one in which the patient was on a hunt lying in wait for his prey which turns out not to be a moose but a black man with the same facial scar as the dreamer's father (p. 425), and eyewitnesses who said the riots reminded them of hunts in which an individual black man would be chased by different groups of rioters "until he was cornered like an animal and knocked down" (p. 425), and pictures of the riots from the July 5, 1943, issue of *Life*, which "showed very clearly the man-hunting character of the riots" (p. 426) led Sterba to conclude that "psychologically, [anti]–Negro race riots are violent outbreaks of infantile father hatred" (p. 419). He cites the fact that anti-black riots regularly follow the allegation that a black man has raped a white woman and that only black men are targeted in the riots (pp. 419, 426) as further proof that the riots arise from oedipal competition and patricidal desires. If for the sake of discussion, we accept Sterba's thesis, then it is fitting that the introduction of racial violence in *Planet* and the first evidence of racial apocalypse in the film take the form of a hunt that reverses the traditional violent power relations of human over animal and light-skinned over dark-skinned. The hunt can be interpreted in terms of an oedipal drama of sexual competition in which Taylor expresses his colonial ambitions to possess the land at the same time that his gaze at Nova links her to the planet and implies the desire to "possess" her sexually as well. He is thus competing with the big bad apes, in this scene represented by the darkest apes, gorillas, father figures who repel his advances towards the land by driving him off of it and repel his advances on Nova by capturing and taking possession of her. Nova is later returned to him by Zira, the mother figure, only to be taken away again by the gorillas.

If the land is symbolically linked to Nova by the proximity of Taylor's statement of intention to "run the planet" and his desirous look at her, then the apes' struggle to prevent human re-domination of the planet may be seen as an attempt to protect their "feminized" property. White lynch mobs typically justified themselves by alleging that their black victims had raped a white woman. In the film, the apes seek to destroy the humans in punishment for "ravaging" the apes' land. The use of the term "ravage" is significant in that it commonly refers to sexual violence. The punishment typically meted out by lynch mobs was castration, a ritual also observed at the successful completion of hunts. Similarly, like lynchings and hunts, the hunt scene in *Planet* culminates with a symbolic emasculation as a gorilla shoots Taylor in the throat, rendering him unable to speak. Castration anxiety is also mobilized when Zaius plans to geld Taylor and again when he later threatens to lobotomize him, which can be seen as a symbolic castration.

64. Joseph Morgernstern, "Monkey Lands," *Newsweek*, February 26, 1968, p. 84.

65. This practice was by no means unique to *Planet* or to other Heston films. To cite just one example, *2001: A Space Odyssey*, released within a month of *Planet*, had white actor Keir Dullea playing astronaut Dave Poole, who also stands in for the rest of humanity. White men were not only unquestioningly considered appropriate to embody humanity but were considered suitable to epitomize other species as well. In *The Day the Earth Stood Still*, for example, Klaatu, the lone representative of an alien culture, was played by white actor Michael Rennie.

66. Rod Serling, *Planet of the Apes*, March 1, 1965, p. 123.

67. Jordan, *White Man's Burden*, p. 18

68. James Baldwin, *The Devil Finds Work*, in *The Price of the Ticket*, p. 591.

69. Boulle, *Planet of the Apes*, pp. 184, 186.

70. *Planet* novelist Pierre Boulle vigorously resisted the Statue of Liberty idea when a version of it was first included in Serling's 1964 script. In a letter to Jacobs dated April 29, 1965, in which Boulle criticized some of Serling's ideas, including the statue scene, Boulle even went so far as to add a postscript in which he condemned the statue concept as "a *temptation from the devil* [that would] annoy . . . the man in the street" (emphasis in original). Ironically this scene is the most remembered and probably the most popular scene in the *Apes* series.

This use of the Statue of Liberty in science fiction iconography is not unique to *Planet*, however. Examples of artwork depicting similar scenes occur in Robert Holdstock, consultant editor, *Encyclopedia of Science Fiction* (London: Octopus Books, 1978), pp. 11, 14. Holdstock asks, "Where would [science fiction] be without the Statue of Liberty? For decades it has towered or crumbled above the wasteland of deserted [E]arth — giants have uprooted it, aliens have found it curious. . . . [T]he symbol of Liberty, of optimism, has become a symbol of science fiction's pessimistic view of the future" p. 14.

Many of the examples presented by Holdstock are from science fiction magazines and story collections which predate *Planet*. Therefore, since Rod Serling may have been well versed in popular science fiction literature, these earlier scenes may have inspired *Planet*'s ending. Nonetheless, *Planet*'s finale remains the most vivid and best-remembered use of this visual trope. *Planet*'s conclusion probably inspired the similar scene on the cover of the 1972 comic book *Kamandi: The Last Boy on Earth* and a 1980s Greenpeace poster against nuclear testing. (See Conclusion.)

Chapter 2

1. Richard Slotkin, *Gunfighter Nation: The Myth of the Frontier in Twentieth Century America*, (New York: Atheneum, 1992), p. 554.

2. Shatnoff, Judith, "A Gorilla to Remember," *Film Quarterly* (Fall 1968): 56, 58. That "the past is the future" is also suggested by the fact that the apes have ancient Roman names — Galen, Zaius, Cornelius, Maximus. Thus history moves backwards or, at best, does not progress; the connection with Rome would associate the apes with another hierarchical society.

3. See Donna Haraway, *Primate Visions: Gender, Race, and Nature in the World of Modern Science* (New York: Routledge, Chapman and Hall, 1989), p. 127. For a contemporary example of this debate among primatologists, see Eugene Linden, "A Curious Kinship: Apes and Humans," *National Geographic* (March 1992): 2–45.

4. *Planet* was one of the top ten money-making films of 1968. Within three years of its release, *Planet*, which had eventually cost $5.8 million, had grossed between three and four times Fox's investment. *Beneath* would go on to make $14 million, almost three times as much as its $4.7 million budget. Figures quoted from Bill Ornstein "Jacobs Plans Enter Television," *The Hollywood Reporter*, May 6, 1971, pp. 1, 4.

5. Heston would get the chance to play humanity's savior in *The Omega Man* a few years later.

6. Serling's story ideas for the second *Apes* film are discussed in the article "Planet of the Apes Revisited," *Starlog* (April 1986): 42–47.

7. Pierre Boulle, *Planet of the Men*, July 1968, p. 19.

8. Ibid., p. 23.

9. This was the title of Stoddard's most famous book.

10. Boulle, *Planet of the Men*, p. 98.

11. Pierre Boulle, *Planet of the Apes*, trans. Xan Fielding (New York: Vanguard, 1963), p. 157. The "savior" language recurs as Merou describes the scene of Nova with their newborn son "lying on the straw like a new Christ, nuzzling against his mother's breast" p. 177. On Merou's power for racial uplift, see pp. 138–39, 156–60, 177, 181, 187.

12. Author Paul Dehn would touch upon this theme with the Ursus character in *Beneath*.

13. Quoted in Dale Winogura, "Dialogues on Apes, Apes, and More Apes," *Cinéfantastique* (Summer 1972): 19.

14. *The Dark Side of the Earth*, story outline, p. 3. No author or date is listed on the *The Dark Side of the Earth* proposal. (The same title was used for a Serling television play about the 1956 anticommunist revolt in Hungary.) The similarities to Serling's earlier *Apes* sequel story, which also used the phrase "dark side of the earth," though not as the title, suggest that the proposal could have been written by someone familiar with Serling's earlier work or by Serling himself. One of Mort Abrahams' chief objections to Serling's original story was that it lacked a shock ending like *Planet*'s. *The Dark Side of the Earth* in some regards provides a shock ending to the basis of Serling's story and could be his attempt to modify it to Abrahams' liking, although the proposal does not appear to have been written on Serling's typewriter. My thanks to Joel Engel for this information.

15. Quoted in Winogura, "Dialogues," p. 26.

16. Clayborne Carson, ed., *A Readers Guide, Eyes on the Prize: America's Civil Rights Years* (New York, Penguin Books, 1987), p. 55.

17. Paul Dehn, *Beneath the Planet of the Apes*, April 10, 1969, pp. 14–19.

18. My thanks to Christopher Corey Smith for this point.

19. Compare Richard Slotkin's discussion of Theodore Roosevelt's argument that the interbreeding of Germanic tribes in the isolation of Britain had created a kind of super-race and in the United States "the most vigorous offspring of that British 'race of races' returned to an environment very like the one that originally produced them: a wilderness, isolated from civilization, in which the forces of nature and the hostility of primitive natives forced them to engage all of their latent military capacity in order to survive." Richard Slotkin, "Nostalgia and Progress: Theodore Roosevelt's Myth of the Frontier," *American Quarterly* 33, no. 5 (1981): 622. On Roosevelt's view of racial history and his attitudes towards imperialism, see also Slotkin, *Gunfighter Nation*, Chapter 1.

20. See Allan Chase, *The Legacy of Malthus: The Social Costs of the New Scientific Racism* (Urbana: University of Illinois Press, 1980).

21. The fear of immigrants who have contracted the HIV virus, in particular refugees from Haiti, is a strain of the fear of contamination of blood lines by "degenerate" racial stock.

22. Compare, for instance, Roosevelt's assertion that hunting "cultivates that vigorous manliness for the lack of which in a nation, as in an individual, the possession of no other qualities can possibly atone." Theodore Roosevelt, *The Wilderness Hunter*, cited in Richard Slotkin, "Nostalgia and Progress: Theodore Roosevelt's Myth of the Frontier," *American Quarterly* 33, no. 5 (1981): 631.

23. Slotkin, *Gunfighter Nation*, p. 51.

24. Although I stress the resemblance between Ursus' rhetoric and U.S. ideologies of racial violence, other comparisons can usefully be made. In his story treatment for the film dated September 13, 1968, entitled *Planet of the Apes Revisited*, Dehn describes Ursus "yelling like Hitler in the Sportspalast on the eve of the Second World War. The tenor of his speech is Hitlerian too. He is yelling for 'living space'" (p. 11). In that same treatment, debating what is essentially "the human question" with Zaius, Dehn had Ursus arguing that "the wise thing would have been to exterminate the entire human species instead of herding thousands of them into camps so that your useless experiments can continue." At the mention of "camps," Dehn included a footnote stating that "the concentration camp parallel should be discernible"(p. 13).

25. For a discussion of other films that functioned as cold war allegories, see Richard Slotkin, *Gunfighter Nation*, Chapters 11 and 12. On films that functioned as allegories of the Vietnam War, see Chapters 13–17 and the Conclusion.

26. James Gregory had played another political demagogue with an enemy-is-us twist in *The Manchurian Candidate* several years prior to playing Ursus.

27. A script continuity flaw resulted in 3955 being given as the year in which *Beneath* takes place. Since the film takes place after *Planet*, however, the correct year should have been 3978 or later.

28. Paul Dehn, *Planet of the Apes Revisited*, treatment, September 1968, p. 7.

29. It is also possible that the choice of mask color is arbitrary or based on aesthetic preferences and is unrelated to genetic ancestry. This would further de-emphasize racial difference as a significant factor in the mutant society.

30. See Slotkin, *Gunfighter Nation*, p. 621. This fear had been the basis of the plot for the film *The Manchurian Candidate* several years earlier. Similar fears of mental manipulation would surface in *Escape from the Planet of the Apes* and *Conquest of the Planet of the Apes*.

31. Pauline Kael, Smith College Commencement Address, May 27, 1973.

32. Vivian Sobchack writes of the bomb worship in *Beneath*: "Total annihilation is finally unknowable, unimaginable—and an artifact like the bomb which reminds men of their lack of control over their destiny (and their history) is, itself, logically destined to become a religious icon, a symbol of a Godhead as well as a Warhead. Visually and ironically, the worshipped bomb physically resembles an inverted cross; and science is thus alchemically transformed to religion (with a precipitate of associations to the magic of satanism)." Vivian Sobchack, *Screening Space: The American Science Fiction Film* (New York: Ungar, 1987), p. 62.

33. Frederick S. Clarke, review of *Beneath the Planet of the Apes*, *Cinéfantastique* (Fall 1970): 26.

34. This is the way Dehn described the telegram in Winogura's "Dialogues," p. 27. In "Planet of the Apes Revisited," however, the authors quote the telegram as saying "Apes Live! Sequel Required!" p. 47. Although it is awkward, I have used the version appearing in "Dialogues" because it is supposed to be a direct quote.

35. Quoted in Winogura, "Dialogues," p. 22.

36. Penelope Gilliatt, "The Upstanding Chimp," *New Yorker*, June 5, 1971, pp. 102–4.

37. "Onward and Apeward," *Time*, June 5, 1972, p. 62.

38. Frederick S. Clarke, review of *Escape from the Planet of the Apes, Cinéfantastique* (Fall 1971): 28.

Chapter 3

1. Donna Haraway, *Primate Visions: Gender, Race, and Nature in the World of Modern Science*, (New York: Routledge, Chapman and Hall, 1989), p. 145.

2. Ibid., p. 156.

3. Ibid., pp. 152–53.

4. Malcolm X and Alex Haley, *The Autobiography of Malcolm X* (New York: Balentine, 1965), pp. 312, 379.

5. Harvard Sitkoff, *The Struggle for Black Equality 1954–1980* (Toronto: Collins, 1981), pp. 200–2.

6. "Races: The Trigger of Hate," *Time*, August 20, 1965, p. 13.

7. *Time*, August 20, 1965, p. 18. This was not the first time that the simultaneity of violent domestic racial conflict and international war invited metaphoric comparison in the press. Following the Detroit race riots in 1943, a *Life* magazine headline declared, "Race War in Detroit—Americans Maul and Murder Each Other as Hitler Wins a Battle in the Nation's Most Explosive City." *Life*, July 5, 1943, p. 93. The likening of racial conflict at home to the war abroad became increasingly common in the late sixties. This linkage is perhaps typified by the coupling of two stories, "The 'Other War' in Vietnam/To Keep a Village Free" and "The 'Other' Pacification—To Cool U.S. Cities," in the August 25, 1967, issue of *Life* magazine. See Richard Slotkin's analysis of these two stories in *Gunfighter Nation: The Myth of the Frontier in Twentieth Century America* (New York: Atheneum, 1992), pp. 549–54.

8. Cited in *Time*, August 20, 1965, p. 18.

9. Quoted in "Races: The Loneliest Road," *Time*, August 27, 1965, p. 11. My thanks to Richard Slotkin for this reference.

10. Sitkoff, *Struggle for Black Equality*, p. 202.

11. *Conquest* Director J. Lee Thompson, telephone interview with author, January 1991. Unless otherwise indicated, all Thompson quotes are from this interview.

12. Thompson expressed this view to me in our January 1991 interview.

13. Quoted in Dale Winogura, "Dialogues on Apes, Apes, and More Apes," *Cinéfantastique* (Summer 1972): 27.

14. Paul Dehn, *Conquest of the Planet of the Apes*, story outline, undated, pp. 15–16.

15. Ibid., p. 16.

16. Ibid., p. 18.

17. Thompson quoted in Andrew Asch, "Ape Politic," part of "Retrospective/

Monkey Business: The Selling of the Planet of the Apes," *Sci-Fi Universe* 1 (June/July 1994): 38.

18. "From Book—Film—T.V.," *Planet of the Apes Posterbook* (1974): 1.

19. On the image of African-Americans and Native Americans as a rebuke to white society in the "Black Westerns" of the period, see Slotkin, *Gunfighter Nation*, p. 631.

20. The 1973 science fiction film *Westworld* bore some resemblance to *Conquest* because it featured robot servants revolting against their human masters.

21. The tide was starting to turn, however. Whereas in 1971 *Sweetback* was dedicated to those who had had enough of "the man," two years later "the man" had had enough of films like *Sweetback*. In 1973, the year after *Conquest* was released, a white rebuke to "blaxploitation" was embedded in the James Bond film *Live and Let Die*, in which "the man," in the guise of the white James Bond, puts the black "Mr. Big," who had dared to have sexual desires for a white woman, back in his "place."

22. Donald Willis, ed., review of *Conquest of the Planet of the Apes* reprinted in *Variety's Complete Science Fiction Reviews* (New York: Gerald, 1985), p. 279.

23. Quoted in "Onward and Apeward," *Time*, June 5, 1972, p. 62.

24. Vivian Sobchack, *Screening Space: The American Science Fiction Film* (New York: Ungar, 1987), p. 62.

25. Quoted in Winogura, "Dialogues," pp. 23, 25.

26. Indeed, in its depiction of a successful non-white revolt against white power, *Conquest* is very much a reversal of Heston's race-war epics. Even the iconography and graphics of the posters speak to this. The posters and advertisements for *Conquest* have the title written in large block letters that look as if they have been hewn out of stone, thus resembling the graphics on the posters for Heston films like *Ben-Hur: A Tale of the Christ* and *El-Cid*. Consequently, the ad campaign for *Conquest* intimated that, like those films, the fourth *Apes* picture would also be an epic about racial battles and the falling and rising of empires. The poster for this film about a simian Christ figure also bore a striking resemblance to the poster for *King of Kings*, a film about the human Christ figure. See the *King of Kings* poster in Eleanor Clark, Edward Z. Epstein, and Joe Morella, *Those Great Movie Ads* (New Rochelle, NY: Arlington House) 1972, p. 42.

27. From the audience's perspective, *Planet* and *Beneath* take place two thousand years in the audience's future (3978), *Escape* takes place two years in the future (1973), *Conquest* takes place nineteen years in the future (1991), and while *Battle* is unspecific as to time, it seems to take place early in the twenty-first century, approximately forty-five years in the audience's future.

28. Telephone interview with author, January 1991.

29. Telephone interview with author, March 1991.

30. This is similar in strategy, if more subtle in effect, to the use of biblical apocalyptic motifs in *The Confessions of Nat Turner*.

31. In fact, all the *Apes* films written by Dehn have scenes where people are compelled or manipulated into a forced confession of sorts. In *Beneath*, the mutants use mental torture to extract information from Brent, in *Escape* the C.I.A. uses sodium pentothal to induce Zira to reveal her secrets, and in *Conquest* Kolp uses a device called "the authenticator" to force Armando to betray Caesar. Dehn's *Apes* scripts were not unique in this regard. The formerly black-listed Michael Wilson, himself a survivor of state coercion, had Zaius in *Planet* trying to force a confession out of Taylor by threatening to castrate and lobotomize him.

These scenes all seem to speak to a fear of coercion by oppressive authoritarian governments that was probably part of a larger distrust of government provoked by events such as the Vietnam War, the controversy surrounding the sixties assassinations, government harassment of black organizations, government duplicity in the Tonkien Gulf incident, and Watergate that characterized this time period. Kellner and Ryan note that disconfidence in government was manifested in the movie depiction of government as untrustworthy and repressive. Filmic images of authority like the ones in the *Apes* series and other movies of the time were both inspired by and contributed to the questioning of the U.S. government's legitimacy. See Michael Ryan and Douglas Kellner, *Camera Politica: The Politics and Ideology of Contemporary Hollywood Film* (Bloomington: University of Indiana Press, 1990), pp. 49, 76–77. For conspiracy films, see pp. 95–105.

32. I am indebted to Jerry Watts for this point.

33. For a comprehensive history and critical discussion of this and related issues, see Allan Chase, *The Legacy of Malthus: The Social Costs of the New Scientific Racism* (Urbana: University of Illinois Press), 1980.

34. For the latest episode in this sorry public spectacle, see the collection of articles in the November 1994 issue of *Discover* magazine and the symposium by Henry Louis Gates, Jr., et al., in *The New Republic*, October 31, 1994.

35. Paul Dehn, *Conquest of the Planet of the Apes*, final shooting script, January 18, 1972, p. 83.

36. Joel Kovel, *White Racism: A Psychohistory*, (New York: Columbia University Press, 1984), p. xliii. Kovel explains that "The other is assigned some part of the dominant self which is unbearable yet desired; and this alienated part comes to define his or her existence. Therefore the other is not recognized for him/her self, but as the repository of some split-off element of the dominant self. In other words white racism is for whites. Blacks are made to disappear as persons in its course" pp. xliii–xliv.

37. Slotkin, *Gunfighter Nation*, p. 200. See also Slotkin, *Regeneration Through Violence: The Mythology of the American Frontier 1600–1860* (Middletown, Conn.: Wesleyan University Press, 1973).

38. Winthrop Jordan, *The White Man's Burden: Historical Origins of Racism in the United States* (New York: Oxford University Press, 1974), p. 222. The apes in *Planet* and *Beneath* also imputed all that was threatening and negative onto their racial "other." Jordan's last sentence resembles the apes' Sacred Scroll dictate about man: "Shun him, drive him back into his jungle lair, for he is the harbinger of death."

39. Dr. Theodore Lothrop Stoddard, *The Revolt Against Civilization: The Menace of the Underman* (New York: Charles Scribner's Sons, 1922), p. 27. In an interesting reversal of this theory, Kovel argues that the bigot's "worship of the past . . . when everything had its place, and authority was secure" leads to a "frantic rage at disturbances or the slightest changes in the social order. . . . When the object of his prejudice begins to reject his debased role—whenever the fabric of stable authority tears, the bigot rises up, casts off his veneer of conformism, and takes to the streets." Kovel, *White Racism*, p. 56.

40. See Chase, *Legacy of Malthus*, p. 351.

41. See for example Richard Slotkin's discussion of Stoddard's influence on Edgar Rice Burroughs, *Gunfighter Nation*, pp. 198–211. On Stoddard, see also Chase, *The Legacy of Malthus*, pp. 292–95.

42. James Baldwin, *The Devil Finds Work*, in *The Price of the Ticket: Collected Non-Fiction 1948–1985* (New York: St. Martin's/Marek, 1985), p. 606.

43. W. L. Shaefer, letter to the editor, *Time*, September 3, 1965, p. 7.

44. The tragic failure of this "solution" to solve anything has been movingly written about by Winthrop Jordan in *The White Man's Burden*:

> [T]he peace of mind the white man sought by denying his profound inex-orable drives toward creation and destruction (a denial accomplished by affirming virtue in himself and depravity in the Negro) was denied the white man; he sought his own peace at the cost of others and found none. In fearfully hoping to escape the animal within himself the white man debased the Negro surely, but at the same time he debased himself [p. 226].

Compare to Jean Paul Sartre: "Anti-Semitism, in short, is fear of the human condition. The anti–Semite is a man who wishes to be pitiless stone, a furious torrent, a devastating thunderbolt — anything except a man." Jean Paul Sartre, *Anti-Semite and Jew*, trans. George J. Becker (New York: Schocken, 1948), p. 54.

45. David Farber, *Chicago '68* (Chicago: University of Chicago Press, 1988), pp. 145–46.

46. Joel Kovel notes that "Every study of authoritarian prejudice reveals a common truth: the dominative racist is irrationally and profoundly dependent upon the object of his prejudice." Kovel, *White Racism*, pp. 56–57. Sartre similarly pointed out that "the anti–Semite is in the unhappy position of having a virtual need for the very enemy he wishes to destroy," *Anti-Semite and Jew*, p. 28.

47. Baldwin, *The Devil Finds Work*, p. 628.

48. Naming the ape hero "Caesar" could be Dehn's rebuke to Dixon's *The Clansman*, the literary source for the film *Birth of a Nation*, which featured an African-American character named August Caesar who, true to stereotype, rapes a white woman and thus "justifies" attacks by the Ku Klux Klan. Calling the leader of the ape revolution "Caesar" may also recall Ignatius Donnelly's dystopian *Caesar's Column: A Story of the Twentieth Century* in which proletarian leader Cesare Lombro leads a working class war of extermination. See Slotkin, *Gunfighter Nation*, p. 696, n. 79. On the more positive side, the name may have sparked associations with Cesar Chavez, the union organizer whose heroic struggles on behalf of Latino farm workers were contemporary with the release of *Conquest*.

49. Paul Dehn, *Conquest of the Planet of the Apes*, revised screenplay, January 24, 1972, p. 14.

50. Paul Dehn, *Escape from the Planet of the Apes*, revised screenplay, October 22, 1970, p. 19.

51. This is a significant change from Dehn's early *Conquest* outline, in which Dehn wrote: "Gorillas are the best and costliest slaves because they are the mildest-natured. But orangutans and chimps are available at cheaper prices to poorer whites and blacks," thus suggesting African-Americans are still less-advantaged than non-poor whites (Dehn *Conquest* outline, p. 16). In addition to less economic power, the absence of MacDonald in the original proposal suggests less political power for African-Americans than in the final script.

52. African-Americans were not intended to be the only racial minorities to have taken on the role of oppressor in *Conquest*. Dehn's final screenplay notes a Chinese proprietor who uses slave labor at his restaurant.

53. Telephone interview with author, January 1991.

54. In the *Planet* novel, the apes similarly conditioned humans with shocks administered following the ringing of a bell. Pierre Boulle, *Planet of the Apes*, trans. Xan Fielding (New York: Vanguard, 1963), pp. 70–71.

55. Paul Dehn, *Conquest of the Planet of the Apes* script, January 18, 1972, pp. 84–85.

56. Telephone interview with author, January 1991.

57. This is partly due to editorial changes, discussed below, made prior to the film's release.

58. Information regarding Fox's reaction to the initial cut and about the editing of *Conquest* comes from a telephone conversation with Thompson, January 1991.

59. For examples of the use of this convention, see Slotkin, *Gunfighter Nation*, pp. 299–300, 357–58, 388–89, 391, 395, 402.

60. Dehn, *Conquest* script, January 18, 1972, p. 86.

61. Images of the fearsome "other" seem depressingly consistent. Compare, for instance, the description of the above scene with Mary Rowlandson's three-and-a-half-centuries-old description of Native Americans following a killing spree: "oh the roaring, and singing and dancing, and yelling of those black creatures in the night, which made the place a lively resemblance of hell." Cited in Richard Slotkin, *Regeneration Through Violence* (Middletown: Wesleyan University Press, 1973), p. 109.

62. Consider that the elections of Ronald Reagan as California governor and Richard Nixon as president followed the Watts riots and the violence at the 1968 Democratic national convention.

63. Baldwin, *The Devil Finds Work*, p. 609.

64. James Baldwin, *The Fire Next Time*, in *The Price of the Ticket*, p. 368.

Chapter 4

1. "Onward and Apeward," *Time*, June 5, 1972, p. 62.

2. Paul Dehn, *The Battle for the Planet of the Apes*, first draft story outline, July 5, 1972, p. 66.

3. Ibid., p. 68.

4. Telephone interview with author, January 1991.

5. The need to make sense of the painful events of the preceding ten years and the desire for reconciliation following them were taken up in a number of other films released in the early and mid-seventies. In 1975, Clint Eastwood's *The Outlaw Josey Wales* (written by Eastwood and Phillip Kaufman, directed by Eastwood), set during and just after the Civil War, depicted the symbolic reconciliation of Native and European-Americans, women and men, and North and South in terms that spoke to the need for national forgiveness of the hurts and wrongs of the past decade. The 1976 *Robin and Marian* (written by James Goldman, directed by Richard Lester) evoked post–Vietnam soul-searching as a middle-aged Robin Hood returns to England after twenty years of fighting in the Crusades. Robin (Sean

Connery) seeks reconciliation with Marian (Audrey Hepburn) whom he abandoned and who struggles to understand why he fought in a brutal war in which he did not believe. On *Wales*, see Richard Slotkin, *Gunfighter Nation: The Myth of the Frontier in Twentieth Century America* (New York: Atheneum, 1992), pp. 632–33.

6. Donna Haraway, *Primate Visions: Gender, Race, and Nature in the World of Modern Science* (New York: Routledge, Chapman and Hall, 1989), p. 9.

7. All quotes from Joyce Hooper Corrington are from a telephone interview with the author, March 1991.

8. Richard Slotkin, *Regeneration Through Violence: The Mythology of the American Frontier 1600–1860* (Middletown, Conn.: Wesleyan University Press, 1973), p. 6.

9. This term is all too often used but all too seldom defined. I use it with reservation, remembering a talk in which Toni Cade Bambarra rhetorically asked, "Why is it that when Black people expect what White people expect they are called 'militant' when they should be called 'expectant'?"

10. Quoted in Harvard Sitkoff, *The Struggle for Black Equality, 1954–1980* (Toronto: Collins, 1981), p. 216.

11. On this debate, see, for example, Dr. Martin Luther King, Jr., *Where Do We Go from Here: Chaos or Community*. For an analysis of the effect of the "Black Power" slogan on Dr. King, see Robert L. Scott, "Black Power Bends Martin Luther King," in Wayne Brockriede and Robert L. Scott, *The Rhetoric of Black Power* (New York: Harper and Row, 1969), pp. 166–77.

12. Roy Wilkins from *The Crisis* magazine (Aug.-Sept. 1966), quoted in Charles E. Fager, *White Reflections on Black Power* (Grand Rapids: William B. Eerdmons, 1967), p. 42.

13. On the rhetorical strategy of Carmichael, see Wayne Brockriede and Robert L. Scott, "Stokely Carmichael: 2 Speeches on Black Power," in Brockriede and Scott, *The Rhetoric of Black Power* (New York: Harper and Row, 1969).

14. Quoted in "Newark: Post-Riot Summit for Black Power," in *Life*, August 4, 1967, p. 28.

15. Compare with Slotkin's point that "The torments . . . we have inflicted make the image of what the enemy may do to *us* all the more vivid. . . . The mechanisms of projection continue to work, and the perpetrator of an atrocity now attributes to the Filipino, Indian or 'nigger' the desire to do to the White man exactly what has been done to him (or his likeness) in the way of torment, emasculation and unjust slaying." Slotkin, *Gunfighter Nation*, p. 116.

16. John William Corrington and Joyce Hooper Corrington, *Battle for the Planet of the Apes* screenplay, December 20, 1972, p. 15.

17. White backlash could also be seen in films dealing with Native Americans during this period. Slotkin notes that between 1965 and 1970 sympathetic film portrayals of Native Americans "gave way" to traditional film portrayals of them as "savages." Slotkin, *Gunfighter Nation*, p. 561.

18. David Gerrold, *Battle for the Planet of the Apes* (New York: Award Books, 1973), p. 9.

19. Gerrold, *Battle for the Planet of the Apes*, p. 155.

20. Quoted in Sitkoff, *Struggle for Black Equality*, p. 172.

21. Paul Dehn, John William Corrington and Joyce Hooper Corrington, *Battle* revised screenplay, December 20, 1972, p. 84.

22. Paul Dehn, John William Corrington and Joyce Hooper Corrington, *Battle* revised screenplay, December 20, 1972, p. 98. Although Aldo's attack on the school made the film's final cut, his ascension to the top of the bus was edited out. But the complete bus scene occasionally appears in television broadcasts.

23. John William Corrington and Joyce Hooper Corrington, *Battle for the Planet of the Apes*, first draft, October 30, 1972, p. 91.

24. Of course this can allow some viewers to have their vengeance cake and eat it too by both lauding Caesar's mercy and enjoying Aldo's slaughter of the humans.

25. Haraway discusses the Western fascination with the language barrier between apes and humans and with crossing that barrier as a means of reconnecting with nature. See *Primate Visions*, p. 132.

26. Winthrop D. Jordan, *The White Man's Burden* (New York: Oxford University Press, 1974), p. 226.

27. James Baldwin, *The Devil Finds Work*, in *The Price of the Ticket: Collected Non-Fiction 1948–1985* (New York: St. Martin's/Marek, 1985), p. 610.

28. A less generous interpretation of the gorillas' repudiation of Aldo could be that they simply abandoned Aldo once it was clear that he could not win.

29. Baldwin, *The Devil Finds Work*, pp. 606–7.

30. See Joel Kovel, *White Racism: A Psychohistory* (New York: Columbia University Press, 1984), pp. xlii, xlv, xlvii–lii. For a discussion of the nature-nurture debate in the changing constructions of race after World War II, see Haraway, *Primate Visions*, Chapter 6, especially pp. 126–29 and Chapter 8, especially pp. 197–203. See also Linden, "A Curious Kinship: Apes and Humans," *National Geographic* (March 1992): 2–45.

31. Haraway, *Primate Visions*, pp. 368–69, discussing Smuts et al, *Primate Studies* (Chicago: University of Chicago Press, 1987).

32. Slotkin, for instance, notes the ideological contradictions in *Broken Arrow* regarding racial coexistence and points out that in the film, whites "can trust the Indians and make peace with them because they are 'just like us'; but to demonstrate that 'truth' we have to transform them into Whites and expel or suppress the ethnic Indian from the picture." Slotkin, *Gunfighter Nation*, p. 376. On the U.S. culture's uneasy relationship to ethnic difference, see also Alan Spiegel, "The Vanishing Act: A Typology of the Jew in Contemporary American Film," in Sarah Blacher Cohen, *From Hester Street to Hollywood: The Jewish American Stage and Screen* (Bloomington: Indiana University Press, 1983), pp. 257–75.

33. Unlike the final cut, the *Battle* screenplay did *not* completely fall into the trap of making the denial of difference the price of acceptance. After MacDonald demands to be freed completely, the screenplay has the young white woman named "Doctor," with whom he is in love, come close to MacDonald, hold his hand, and explain "We want to live our own way, Caesar, a human way, with you, with the apes. But our way." Her plea for interracial understanding and love on a societal level is reinforced by the image of interracial love on an individual level. As with the friendship between Caesar, Virgil, and MacDonald, the personal is offered as a model for the collective. As written, Caesar's eventual determination to right the racial wrongs of the village indicates his acceptance of the differences between ape and human and his recognition that the humans can live "with the apes. But [their] way." Paul Dehn, John William Corrington and Joyce Hooper Corrington, *Battle*, revised screenplay, December 20, 1972, p. 111.

34. This point was made somewhat more directly in the Corringtons' first draft screenplay, in which Caesar, having been exposed to radiation in the Forbidden City, is losing his hair. Caesar thus outwardly looks more like a human at the same time that he realizes the growing internal resemblances between ape and human. His exposure to the postbomb radiation links him not only with humans in general but also, specifically, with the mutants in the Forbidden City: both he and they have gone through a human-created traumatic experience—like racism and war—that malforms them.

35. Kovel, *White Racism*, p. xxxvii.

36. Judith Shatnoff, "A Gorilla to Remember," *Film Quarterly* (Fall 1968): 56. It is also possible to interpret *Battle* as not rebuking *Planet*'s theory of racial conflict but *adding* to it, that is, saying that racial warfare is both cultural *and* genetic. In this case the film is quite consistent with Dehn's picture of an inescapable cycle of hatred, brutality, and retaliation.

37. Paul Dehn, John William Corrington, and Joyce Hooper Corrington, *Battle for the Planet of the Apes*, revised screenplay, December 20, 1972, p. 100.

38. Kevin Thomas, "Battle Completes Ape Cycle," *Los Angeles Times*, June 12, 1973, p. 13.

39. An earlier, somewhat less ambiguous, ending had the Lawgiver and the children anticipating in messianic expectation the future day when Taylor would arrive and hoping that "if when he comes, finds not a planet of lords and slaves, ape or human [Taylor] will bless us and live among us and make all things new once more." (John William Corrington and Joyce Hooper Corrington, *Battle for the Planet of the Apes*, first draft screenplay, p. 99.) What Taylor finds will be the measure of the apes' and humans' success in avoiding the dire future depicted in *Planet* and *Beneath*. The screenplay ends with a human child and an ape child of unspecified races fighting and the Lawgiver predicting that until that hoped for golden age when Taylor arrives, they "must wait a very long time yet. . . . A very long time." The last image in the screenplay is the ape child's hand holding a stick and smashing it down, an image reminiscent of Stanley Kubrick's image of the first use of weapons in *2001: A Space Oddessy*. This homage to *2001*'s "Dawn of Man" segment would have again suggested that the past—even if only the movie past—is the future. (John William Corrington and Joyce Hooper Corrington, *Battle for the Planet of the Apes*, p. 100.)

40. The Corringtons did not come up with the idea of the crying Caesar statue. It was taken from one of Dehn's early *Conquest* screenplays and added in a later rewrite by an uncredited author.

Chapter 5

1. Richard Slotkin, *Regeneration Through Violence: The Mythology of the American Frontier 1600–1860* (Middletown, Conn: Wesleyan University Press, 1973), p. 7.

2. Quoted in Mark Olshaker, "Requiem for a Heavyweight: Final Tribute" in *New Times*, July 25, 1975, p. 68.

3. Rod Serling quoted in Andrew Sarris, "Rod Serling Viewed from Beyond the Twilight Zone," *Television Quarterly* 21, no. 2 (Summer 1984): 37.

4. A notable exception is Lisa's decisive intervention at the climax of *Conquest*. Up until that point, however, Lisa is fairly passive.

5. See Richard Slotkin, *Gunfighter Nation: The Myth of the Frontier in Twentieth Century America* (New York: Atheneum, 1992), p. 654–60.

6. The show does not indicate that this Zaius is an ancestor of the Zaius from *Planet* and *Beneath*, nor that Galen is related to Zira's colleague Dr. Galen from *Planet*, though it is possible that these characters are the ancestors of their namesakes from the films.

7. The format of the *Apes* television series—a group of fugitives or wanderers moving from place to place, often after some kind of cataclysm, encountering and aiding various cultures and subcultures—was a staple of science fiction television series during the seventies. "Starlost," "Genesis II," "Ark II," "Space: 1999," "Logan's Run," "Fantastic Journey" (with *Apes* star Roddy McDowall) and "Battlestar Galactica," all shared this concept with the "Planet of the Apes" television show. In most of these shows, the characters are in a situation not of their own choosing (i.e., roaming a postapocalyptic landscape) and are running or wandering with little or no direction. The frequency of these shows appears to express a feeling of lack of control over one's life—probably a cultural response to the feeling of disorientation inspired by the political conflicts of the era. Ironically, each of these shows, except for "Space: 1999," was canceled after or within its first year, and it remains puzzling why so many producers used a format which was consistently ill-received by audiences.

8. The ideological basis underlying the show bears significant resemblance to attitudes towards the Vietnamese in U.S. tactical and strategic doctrine. See Slotkin, *Gunfighter Nation*, p. 494.

9. The inferiority of religious tradition was not a message that all audiences accepted. In Indonesia, viewers sent letters to the television station complaining that the show "was not making any sense." They protested that "it is inconceivable that the government television station [has] run such a series, forgetting that Man was God's most perfect creature. It is unbelievable that Man could fall under apes' orders." ("*Planet of the Apes* T.V. Series Draws Criticism in Indonesia," *Los Angeles Times*, July 25, 1980.)

10. "Planet of the Apes" was replaced by CBS in its Friday night 8 P.M. time slot by "Khan" a series about a Chinese-American detective in San Francisco's Chinatown. Meanwhile, in the same time slot, ABC featured "Kodiak," a program about a white man among Eskimos, and NBC had "Sanford and Son," about an African-American father and son, followed by Latino comic Freddie Prinze in "Chico and the Man." It was as if each network had designated Friday at 8 P.M., generally considered a poor time slot, its "racial 'other' hour."

11. The "Apes" animated series makes no reference to events from the movies or live-action TV show and the producers did not try to tie the show into the continuity previously established. Thus, for example, the show is set one year after the first film but features a much more technically advanced ape population and mixes characters and elements of *Planet* and *Beneath* along with the name "Urko" from the live-action television series.

12. This simultaneous absorption and deflection of the social demands of the time also resembles "Star Trek," which, in the midst of sixties racial strife, featured a multiracial, multinational, bigendered crew happily united under the command of a white American male captain.

13. All quotes from Wildey are from a telephone interview with the author, December 1992.

14. Wildey told me that no deliberate parallel between Urko and Nixon was intended, and there is no reason to doubt his word. Nonetheless, the similarities of Urko's temperament and appearance to Nixon's are conspicuous to say the least, especially in the context of the Vietnam and Watergate-influenced storylines.

15. See Slotkin, *Gunfighter Nation*, pp. 3, 492–96.

16. My thanks to Richard Slotkin for this point.

17. See Slotkin on the multi-ethnic platoon in *Bataan, Gunfighter Nation*, pp. 322–26.

18. A standoff was the most definitive resolution Wildey could imagine for the show. In an unproduced episode, Wildey planned to have the humans destroy the apes' munitions depot and so force the apes into a truce.

19. *Planet of the Apes* 6 (March 1975): 40.

20. Pournelle, who wrote the novelization of *Escape*, later wrote, with Larry Niven, the books *Lucifer's Hammer* and *The Mote in God's Eye*. Jakes, the author of the *Conquest* novel, is a former president of Science Fiction Writers of America and later authored the popular *Kent Family Chronicles* and the *North and South* novels, both very successful historical fiction series. David Gerrold, the writer of the *Battle* novelization, had written "The Trouble with Tribbles," one of the most beloved episodes of "Star Trek."

21. McDonald quoted in Karen Schoemer, "Tuning in on College Radio Bands at Clubs Around Town," *New York Times*, October 26, 1990, p. C24.

22. Robert McDonald, "'Meal in Three Courses' Is Not a Very Tasty Dish," *Los Angeles Times*, May 30, 1986, Calendar, Part 6, p. 15.

23. Amei Wallach, "Art with an Attitude," *Newsday*, March 5, 1993, Part II/Weekend, p. 52.

24. Quoted in Lynn Voedisch, "Nimoy in Comic Land; Enterprising Actor Fuels New Project," *Chicago Sun-Times*, November 14, 1994, Sec. 2, p. 35.

25. Jeff Krueger, letter to the editor, *Planet of the Apes* 14 (July 1991): 28. Although the comic is dated July 1991, the letter was written months before, when the Persian Gulf War was still "on the horizon."

26. Telephone interview with Tom Mason, creative director, Adventure Comics, December 1991.

27. Gary Chaloner, *Planet of the Apes: Urchak's Folly* 2 (February 1991): 15.

28. Chaloner, *Urchak's Folly*, p. 11. "Mud people" is also a term used among white supremacists to refer to those they see as racially impure.

29. Roland Mann, *Planet of the Apes: Blood of the Apes* 3 (January 1992): 21.

30. Roland Mann, *Planet of the Apes: Blood of the Apes* 4 (February 1992): 15.

31. Ibid., p. 24. This ending is similar to that of "The Deception," an episode of the live-action television show in which a blind ape named Fauna, thinking human Pete Burke is an ape, falls in love with him.

32. Lowell Cunningham, *Planet of the Apes: The Forbidden Zone* 4 (March 1993): 10.

33. For instance, a human named Simon tries to kill Alexander, the leader of the ape city in *Planet of the Apes* and later joins up with the renegade General Ollo and the villainous invader Danada from the planet Tenchton in *Ape Nation*. And, borrowing from *The Dirty Dozen*, in *Ape City*, a heavily armed, biracial, bigendered, Green Berets–style team of human criminals, in return for pardons, is sent into the future to kill enough apes to give the humans of the time a fighting chance against

the simians. The team includes Jo Taylor, daughter of Taylor from *Planet* and *Beneath*, who is seeking to avenge her father.

34. Cunningham, *The Forbidden Zone* 4 (March 1993): 9.

35. Personal correspondence with author, July 14, 1993.

36. Telephone interview with author, July 1992.

37. See Ed Whitelaw, "Guessing at the 'hood: An Urban Future," in *Oregon Business* 17, no. 1 (January 1994): sec. 1, p. 20; Sam Walker, "U.S. Activists Seek a Wider Audience for Sarajevo's Paper," *Christian Science Monitor*, February 28, 1994, p. 4.; Andrew Armstrong, "Parroting Perot on NAFTA," *Washington Times*, September 26, 1993, p. B5; and Peter Kerr, "Vote on Guns Pits Lobbyists Against Florio," *New York Times*, May 17, 1990, p. B1.

38. See Slotkin, *Gunfighter Nation*, p. 350.

39. Adam Rifkin, from a story by Cassian Elwes and Adam Rifkin, *Return to the Planet of the Apes*, first revision, December 21, 1988, p. 1.

40. Ibid., p. 10.

41. Ibid., p. 69.

42. Ibid., p. 97.

43. Ibid., p. 98.

44. *Time*, November 8, 1993, p. 88.

45. David Williams, "Oliver's Apes," *Sci Fi Universe* 1, no. 1 (July 1994): 44.

46. Ted Post cited in Dale Winogura, "Dialogues on Apes, Apes, and More Apes," *Cinéfantastique* (Summer 1972): 22.

Afterword

1. Sam Roberts, "50 Years of Crime, and Stereotypes," *New York Times*, March 2, 1992, p. B12.

2. See Juan Williams, "Violence, Genes, and Prejudice" in *Discover*, November 1994, p. 97.

3. Jefferson cited in Winthrop D. Jordan, *The White Man's Burden* (New York: Oxford University Press, 1974), p. 170.

Filmography

Planet of the Apes (1968). 112 minutes. Produced by Arthur P. Jacobs. Associate Producer Mort Abrahams. Based on the book *Monkey Planet* by Pierre Boulle. Screenplay by Rod Serling and Michael Wilson, uncredited rewrite by John T. Kelly. Directed by Franklin Schaffner.

Cast
George Taylor: Charlton Heston; Cornelius: Roddy McDowall; Zira: Kim Hunter; Dr. Zaius: Maurice Evans; President of the Assembly: James Whitmore; Honorius: James Daly; Nova: Linda Harrison; Landon: Robert Gunner; Lucius: Lou Wagner; Maximus: Woodrow Parfrey; Dodge: Jeff Burton; Julius: Buck Kartalian; Hunt Leader: Norman Burton; Dr. Galen: Wright King; Minister: Paul Lambert.

Minor parts
First Human: Priscilla Boyd; Female Human: Jane Ross; Child Gorilla: Felix Silla; Astronaut Stewart: Dianne Stanley; Ape Photographer: Robert Lombardo; Child Apes: Billy Curtis, Harry Monty, Frank Delfino, Jerry Maren, Emory Souza, Buddy Douglas; Chimpanzees: Cass Martin, Smokey Roberds, George Sasaki, David Chow, Norma Jean Kron; Gorillas: Chuck Fisher, John Quijada, Eldon Burke, Bill Graeff, Joseph Anthony Tornatore, Bob Lombardo, Dave Rodgers, Army Archerd; Chimpanzee Woman: Erlynn Botelho.

Crew
Music: Jerry Goldsmith; Creative Makeup Design: John Chambers; Director of Photography: Leon Shamroy, A.S.C.; Art Direction: Jack Martin Smith and William Creber; Set Decorations: Walter M. Scott and Norman Rockett; Special Photographic Effects: L. B. Abbott, A.S.C., Art Cruickshank and Emil Kosa, Jr.; Film Editor: Hugh S. Fowler, A.C.E.; Unit Production Manager: William Eckhardt; Assistant Director: William Kissel; Sound: Herman Lewis and David Dockendorf; Costume Design: Morton Haack; Makeup: Ben Nye and Dan Striepeke, S.M.A.; Hairstyling: Edith Lindon; Orchestration: Arthur Morton; Filmed in Panavision. Color by DeLuxe.

Academy of Motion Pictures Arts and Sciences Recognition. Academy Award Nominations: Music — Jerry Goldsmith; Costumes — Morton Haack. Special Academy Award given to John Chambers.

Beneath the Planet of the Apes (1970). 95 Minutes. Produced by Arthur P. Jacobs. Associate Producer Mort Abrahams. Story by Paul Dehn and Mort Abrahams. Screenplay by Paul Dehn. Directed by Ted Post.

Cast

Brent: James Franciscus; Zira: Kim Hunter; Zaius: Maurice Evans; Nova: Linda Harrison; Mendez: Paul Richards; Fat Man: Victor Buono; Ursus: James Gregory; Caspay: Jeff Corey; Albina: Natalie Trundy; Minister: Thomas Gomez; Cornelius: David Watson; Negro: Don Pedro Colley; Skipper: Tod Andrews; Verger: Gregory Sierra; Gorilla Sgt.: Eldon Burke; Lucius: Lou Wagner; Astronaut Taylor: Charlton Heston.

Minor parts

Soldier #2: Eldon Burke; Gorilla: Bruce Fleischer; Stock Ape: Phillip Wilson; Stunt: Loren Janes; Stunt: Chuck Roberson; Gorilla: Army Archerd; Chimp Protestor: Edward J. Aubry; Picket (dubbing): Edward Bach; Gorilla (Publicity): James Bacon; Stunt Gorilla: Stan Barrett; Chimp Protestor: Angelina Bauer; Stock Ape: Calvert Botelho; Ad Lib: Erlynn Botelho; Chimp Protestor: Maxine Botelho; Stunt Gorilla: Dick Bullock; Picket (dubbing): Tim Burns; Stunt Masked Gorilla: Bill Burton; Stunt Wagon Driver: Hank Calia; Stunt Double: Tap Canutt; Dubbing Soldier: Richard Carlyle; Stunt: Eddie Donno; Stunt Masked Gorilla: Gary Epper; Stunt Double: Tony Epper; Chimp Protestor: Frisco Estes; Chimp Protestor: Paul A. Fabian; Stunt Ape: Alan Gibbs; Stunt Gorilla: Mickey Gilbert; Stock Ape Ad-Lib: William Graeff; Chimp Protestor: Lenmana Guerin; Stunt Masked Gorilla: Orwin Harvey; Soldier (dubbing): Tom Hatten; Stunt Ape: Kent Hayes; Stunt Gorilla: Eddie Hice; Stunt Gorilla: Clyde "Ace" Hudkins; Stunt Ape: Dick Hudkins; Stunt Masked Gorilla: Whitey Hughes; Picket (dubbing): Judd Laurance; Stunt Double: Terry Leonard; Soldier (dubbing): John Logan; Stunt Ape: Gary McLarty; Stock Ape Ad-Lib: George R. Miller; Stock Ape Ad-Lib: Mel Pittenger; Stunt: Carl Rizzo; Stock Ape Ad-Lib: Dave Rogers; Stunt Masked Gorilla: George Sawaya; Stunt Masked Gorilla: Walter Scott; Ad-Lib: Eddie Smith; Picket (dubbing): Michael Sterling; Picket (dubbing): Wayne Storm; Stunt Double: Pat Thompson; Picket (dubbing): David Westberg; Stunt: Jack Williams; Soldier (dubbing): Richard Wilson.

Crew

Music: Leonard Rosenman; Creative Makeup Design: John Chambers; Costume Design: Morton Haack; Director of Photography: Milton Krasner, A.S.C.; Art Direction: Jack Martin Smith, William Creber; Set Decoration: Walter M. Scott, Sven Wickman; Makeup Supervision: Dan Striepeke; Hairstyling: Edith Lindon; Orchestration: Ralph Ferraro; Film Editor: Marion Rothman; Sound: Stephen Bass, David Dockendorf; Special Photographic Effects: L. B. Abbott, A.S.C., Art Cruickshank; Second Unit Director: Chuck Roberson; Unit Production Manager: Joseph C. Behm; Assistant Director: Fred Simpson; Costumes: Head Wardrobe Man: Wally Harton; Wardrobe Man: Norman Salling; Wardrobe Women: Phyllis Garr, Adelle

Balkan; Camera Operator: Moe Rosenberg; First Assistant Cameraman: Arthur Gerstle; Second Assistant Cameraman: Mervin Becker; Still Photographer: George Hurrell; Art Illustrator: Fred Harpman: Property Man: Pat O'Connor; Property Master: Bob McLaughlin; Special Effects Man: Jerry Endler; Makeup Artists: Norman Pringle, Jack Barron; Hair Stylists: Madine Reed, Sharleen Walsh; Supervising Music Film Editor: Leonard Engle; Music Film Editor: Kenneth Wannberg; Supervising Sound Effects Editor: Don Hall; Sound Effects Editors: Jack Cornell, John Jolliffe; Sound Mixer: Stephen Bass; Sound Recorder: David Dockendorf; Chief Set Electrician (Gaffer): Fred Hall; First Company Grip: Fred Richter; Script Supervisor: Joan Eremin; First Aid Woman: Helen Jackson; Unit Publicist: Jack Hirschberg; Filmed in Panavision. Color by De Luxe. Motion Picture Association of America Rated G.

Escape from the Planet of the Apes (1971). 97 Minutes, 23 Seconds. Produced by Arthur P. Jacobs. Associate Producer Frank Capra, Jr. Screenplay by Paul Dehn. Directed by Don Taylor.

Cast
Cornelius: Roddy McDowall; Zira: Kim Hunter; Dr. Lewis Dixon: Bradford Dillman; Dr. Stephanie Branton: Natalie Trundy; Dr. Otto Hasslein: Eric Braeden; The President: William Windom; Milo: Sal Mineo; Armando: Ricardo Montalban; E-1: Albert Salmi; E-2: Jason Evers; Chairman: John Randolph; General Brody: Steve Roberts; General Winthrop: Harry Lauter; Aide: M. Emmet Walsh; Lawyer: Roy E. Glenn, Sr.; Cardinal: Peter Forster; Army Officer: Norman Burton; Naval Officer: William Woodson; Orderly: Tom Lowell; Marine Captain: Gene Whittington; Curator: Donald Elson; TV Newscaster: Bill Bonds; Referee: Army Archerd; Hercules: Ed Holliday; Brunhilde: Raylene Holliday; General Faulkner: James Bacon.

Crew
Music: Jerry Goldsmith; Director of Photography: Joseph Biroc, A.S.C.; Film Editor: Marion Rothman; Creative Makeup Design: John Chambers; Unit Production Manager: Francisco Day; Assistant Director: Pepi Lenzi; Art Illustrator: Billy Sully; Sound: Dean Vernon, Theodore Soderberg; Special Photographic Effects: Howard A. Anderson Co.; Art Directors: Jack Martin Smith, William Creber; Set Decorators: Walter M. Scott, Stuart A. Reiss; Makeup Supervision: Dan Streipeke; Makeup Artist: Jack Barron; Hair Stylist: Mary Babcock; Orchestration: Arthur Morton; Unit Publicist: Jack Hirschberg; Animals Furnished by: Roy Kabat. Filmed in Panavision. Color by De Luxe. MPAA Rated G.

Conquest of the Planet of the Apes (1972). 88 Minutes. Produced by Arthur P. Jacobs. Associate Producer Frank Capra, Jr. Screenplay by Paul Dehn. Directed by J. Lee Thompson.

Cast
Caesar: Roddy McDowall; Breck: Don Murray; Armando: Ricardo Montalban; Lisa: Natalie Trundy; MacDonald: Hari Rhodes; Kolp: Severn Darden; Busboy: Lou Wagner; Commission Chairman: John Randolph; Mrs. Riley: Asa Maynor; Hoskyns:

H. M. Wynant; Aldo: David Chow; Frank: Buck Kartalian; Policeman: John Dennis; Auctioneer: Gordon Jump; Announcer: Dick Spangler; Zelda: Joyce Harber; Ape with Chain: Hector Soucey; 2nd Policeman: Paul Comi; Stunt Coordinator: Paul Stader; Stuntmen included: Alan Gibbs, Dave Sharpe, George Robotham, Allen Pinson, George Wilbur, Larry Holt, Hubie Kerns, Victor Paul, Chuck and Bill Couch, Alex Sharp, Loren Janes, Chuck Waters, Ernie Robinson and Henry Kingi.

Crew
Music: Tom Scott; Director of Photography: Bruce Surtes; Film Editors: Marjorie Fowler, A.C.E., Alan Jaggs, A.C.E.; Creative Makeup Design: John Chambers; Unit Production Manager: William G. Eckhardt; Assistant Director: David "Buck" Hall; Sound: Herman Lewis, Don Bassman; Unit Publicist: Jack Hirshberg; Titles: Don Record; Art Director: Phillip Jefferies; Set Decorator: Norman Rockett; Makeup Supervision: Dan Striepeke; Makeup Artists: Joe DiBella, Jack Barron; Hair Stylist: Carol Pershing. Filmed in TODD-AO 35. Color by DeLuxe. MPAA Rated G.

Battle for the Planet of the Apes (1973). 86 Minutes, 21½ seconds. Produced by Arthur P. Jacobs. Associate Producer Frank Capra, Jr. Story by Paul Dehn. Screenplay by John William Corrington and Joyce Hooper Corrington. Directed by J. Lee Thompson.

Cast
Caesar: Roddy McDowall; Aldo: Claude Akins; Lisa: Natalie Trundy; Kolp: Severn Darden; Mandemus: Lew Ayres; Virgil: Paul Williams; The Lawgiver: John Huston; MacDonald: Austin Stoker; Teacher: Noah Keen; Mutant Captain: Richard Eastham; Alma: France Nuyen; Mendez: Paul Stevens; Doctor: Heather Lowe; Cornelius: Bobby Porter; Jake: Michael Sterns; Soldier: Cal Wilson; Young Chimp: Pat Cardi; Jake's Friend: John Landis; Mutant on Motorcycle: Andy Knight.

Crew
Music: Leonard Rosenman; Director of Photography: Richard H. Kline, A.S.C.; Film Editors: Alan L. Jaggs, A.C.E., John C. Horger; Art Director: Dale Hennesy; Set Decorator: Robert de Vestel; Special Mechanical Effects: Gerald Endler; Creative Makeup Design: John Chambers; Makeup Supervision: Jo DiBella; Makeup Artists: Jack Barron, Werner Keppler; Hair Stylist: Carol Pershing; Unit Production Manager: Michael S. Glick; Assistant Director: Ric Rondell; Second Assistant Director: Barry Stern; Sound: Herman Lewis, Don Bassman; Casting: Ross Brown; Title Design: Don Record. Filmed in Panavision. Color by DeLuxe. MPAA Rated G.

LIVE-ACTION TELEVISION SERIES *PLANET OF THE APES*

Broadcast on CBS Fridays at 8:00 P.M. from September 13, 1974, through December 20, 1974. Executive Producer: Herbert Hirschman. Producer: Stan Hough. Developed by Anthony Wilson.

Cast
Galen: Roddy McDowall; Alan Virdon: Ron Harper; Peter Burke: James Naughton; Urko: Mark Lenard; Dr. Zaius: Booth Colman.

Crew
Executive Story Consultant: Howard Dimsdale; Story Consultants: Ken Spears, Joe Ruby; Production Supervisor: Mark Evans; Unit Production Manager: Richard Glassman; Director of Photography: Gerald Perry Finnerman, A.S.C.; Art Director: Arch Bacon; Makeup Artist: Dan Striepeke; Set Decorator: Stuart A. Reiss; Casting: Marvin Paige; Theme Music: Lalo Schifrin; Music Supervision: Lionel Newman; Post Production Supervisor: Joseph Silver, A.C.E. Color by DeLuxe. Titles designed by: Jack Cole Film Group.

Episode Guide

"Escape from Tomorrow" (Broadcast on September 13, 1974). Teleplay by Art Wallace. Directed by Don Weis. Assistant Director: Bill Derwin. Film Editor: J. Frank O'Neill. Music: Lalo Schiffrin.

Guest cast
Farrow: Royal Dano; Turvo: Ron Stein; Verska: Woodrow Parfrey; Ullman: Biff Elliott; Proto: Jerome Thor; Grundig: William Beckley; Gorilla Guard: Eldon Burke; Man: Alvin Hammer; Arno: Bobby Porter; Gorilla Lt.: Shelly Snell.

"The Gladiators" (September 20, 1974). Teleplay by Art Wallace. Directed by Don McDougall. Assistant Director: Gil Mandelik. Film Editor: Axel Hubert, A.C.E. Music: Lalo Schiffrin.

Guest cast
Jason: Pat Renella; Tolar: William Smith; Dalton: Marc Singer; Barlow: John Hoyt; Gorilla Sergeant: Eddie Fontaine; Man: Andy Albin; Gorilla: Nick Dimitri; First Gorilla: Ron Stein; Second Gorilla: Jim Stader; Stunt Doubles: Nick Dimitri; Craig Buxley, Erik Cord, Jack Tyree.

"The Trap" (September 27, 1974). Teleplay by Edward J. Lakso. Directed by Arnold Lavin. Assistant Director: Bill Derwin. Editor: Alex Hubert, A.C.E. Music: Richard Lasalle.

Guest cast
Zako: Norm Alden; Mema: Ron Stein; Olam: Eldon Burke; Miller: John Milford; Jick Miller: Mickey Leclair; Mary Miller: Wallace Earl; Lisa Miller: Cindy Eilbacher; Old Woman: Gail Bonney; Tower Gorilla: Ted White; Farmer: Robert Munk.

"The Good Seeds" (October 4, 1974). Teleplay by Robert W. Lenski. Directed by Don Weis. Assistant Director: Bill Derwin. Editor: Clay Bartels. Music: Lalo Schiffrin.

Guest cast
Anto: Geoffrey Deuel; Polar: Lonny Chapman; Zantes: Jacqueline Scott; Remus: Bobby Porter; Jillia: Eileen Ditz; Police Gorilla: John Garwood; Gorilla Officer: Dennis Cross; Patrol Gorilla: Michael Carr; Police Gorilla: Fred Lerner.

"The Legacy" (October 11, 1974). Teleplay by Robert Hamner. Directed by Bernard

McEveety. Assistant Director: Gil Mandelik. Editor: Clay Bartels. Music: Earle Hagen.

Guest cast
Scientist: Jon Lormer; Gorilla Captain: Robert Phillips; Gorilla Sergeant: Wayne Foster; Kraik: Jackie Earle Haley; Arn: Zina Bethune; Gorilla Guard #1: Dave Rodgers; Gorilla Guard #2: Ron Stein; Gorilla Guard #3: Shelly Snell; Human: Victor Kilian.

"Tomorrow's Tide" (October 18, 1974). Teleplay by Robert W. Lenski. Directed by Robert W. Lenski. Assistant Director: Gil Mandelik. Editor: Axel Hubert, A.C.E. Music: Earle Hagen.

Guest cast
Hurton: Roscoe Lee Browne; Romar: Jim Storm; Soma: Kathleen Bracken; Gahto: John McLiam; Bandor: Jay Robinson; Armed Guard: Ron Stein; Armed Aide: Eldon Burke; Mounted Patrol: Tom McDonough; Drayman #1: Alex Brown; Drayman #2: Larry Ellis; Young Human: Frank Orsatti.

"The Surgeon" (October 25, 1974). Teleplay by Barry Oringer. Directed by Arnold Lavin. Assistant Director: Bill Derwin. Film Editor: J. Frank O'Neill.

Guest cast
Kira: Jacqueline Scott; Leander: Martin Brooks; Hamen: Ron Stein; Travin: Michael Strong; Girl: Jamie Smith Jackson; Jordo: Phil Montgomery; Lafer: Ron Stein; Cleon: Peter Ireland; Chester: Eldon Burke; Dr. Stole: David Naughton; Brigid: Diana Hale; Human: Raymond Mayo.

"The Deception" (November 1, 1974). Story by Anthony Lawrence. Teleplay by Anthony Lawrence and Ken Spears and Joe Ruby. Directed by Don McDougall. Assistant Director: Gil Mandelik. Film Editor: Bill Martin.

Guest cast
Sestus: John Milford; Fauna: Jane Actman; Perdix: Baynes Barron; Zon: Pat Renella; Chilot: Eldon Burke; Macor: Tom McDonough; Krona: Ron Stein; Jasko: Hal Baylor; Gorilla: Ron Stein.

"The Horse Race" (November 8, 1974). Teleplay by David P. Lewis and Booker Bradshaw. Directed by Jack Starrett. Assistant Director: Bill Derwin. Editor: Axel Hubert, A.C.E.

Guest cast
Barlow: John Hoyt; Prefect: Henry Levin; Kagan: Wesley Fuller; Zandar: Reichard Devon; Martin: Morgan Woodward; Greger: Meegan King; Zilo: Joseph Anthony Tornatore; Nurse: Adriana Shaw; Damon: Russ Marin; Handler: Stephan Whittaker; Moro: Peter Ireland; Official: Tom McDonough; Chimp Jockey: Eldon Burke; Tumbler: Bill (Hooker) Harrison.

"The Interrogation" (November 15, 1974). Teleplay by Richard Collins. Directed by Alf Kjellian. Assistant Director: Gil Mandelik. Editor: Bill Martin.

Guest cast
Wanda: Beverly Garland; Peasant Gorilla: Eldon Burke; Lt. Gorilla: Wayne Foster; Gorilla Aide: Peter Ireland; Tall Police: Tom McDonough; Ann: Anne Seymour; Yalu: Norman Burton; Officer Gorilla: Lee Delano; Gorilla Leader: Ron Stein; Inside Jailer: Ron Stein; Nora: Lynn Benesch; Dr. Malthus: Harry Townes; Chimpenzee: Bill Blake.

"The Tyrant" (November 22, 1974). Teleplay by Walter Black; Directed by Ralph Senesky; Assistant Director: Bill Derwin; Editor: Clay Bartels.

Guest cast
Aboro: Percy Rodrigues; Daku: Joseph Ruskin; Augustus: Tom Troupe; Janor: Michael Conrad; Mikal: James Daughton; Gorilla: Gary Combs; Gorilla Guard: Ron Stein; Gola: Arlen Stuart; Gorilla Trooper: Tom McDonough; Gorilla Sgt.: Ron Troncotty; Road Guard: Eldon Burke.

"The Cure" (November 29, 1974). Teleplay by Edward J. Lakso. Directed by Alf Kjellian. Assistant Director: Gil Mandelik. Editor: J. Frank O'Neill.

Guest cast
Zoran: David Sheiner; Amy: Sondra Locke; Talbert: George Wallace; Orangutan: Biff Elliot; Mason: Albert Cole; Inta: Eldon Burke; Neesa: Ron Stein; Kava: Ron Soble; Dying Man: Charles Leland; Gorilla Guard: Ron Stein; Elderly Man: Eugene O. Roth; Elderly Woman: Georgia Schmidt.

"The Liberator" (December 6, 1974). Teleplay by Howard Dimsdale. Directed by Arnold Lavin. Assistant Director: Bill Derwin. Editor: Clay Bartels.

Guest cast
Brun: John Ireland; Miro: Ben Andrews; Clim: Peter G. Skinner; Talia: Jennifer Ashley; Villager: Mark Bailey; 1st Gorilla Guard: Ron Stein; 2nd Gorilla Guard: Tom McDonough.

"Up Above the World So High" (December 20, 1974). Story by S. Bar-David. Teleplay by S. Bar-David and Arthur Browne, Jr. Directed by John Meredyth Lucas. Assistant Director: Gil Mandelik. Music: Earle Hagen.

Guest cast
Leuric: Frank Aletter; Konag: Martin Brooks; Carsia: Joanna Barnes; Gorilla Guard: Ron Stein; 2nd Trooper: Eldon Burke; Council Orangutan: William Beckley; Human Driver: Glenn Wilder.

ANIMATED TELEVISION SERIES
RETURN TO THE PLANET OF THE APES

Broadcast on NBC Saturday mornings September 6, 1975–September 4, 1976. Developed for Television and Produced by: David H. Depatie and Friz Freleng. Supervising Director and Associate Producer: Doug Wildey.

Cast

Jeff Allen: Austin Stoker; Bill Hudson: Tom Williams; Judy: Claudette Nevins; Urko: Henry Cordin; Dr. Cornelius: Edwin Mills; Zira: Phillipa Harris; Zaius: Richard Blackburn.

Crew

Animation Director: Cullen Houghtaling; Storyboard Directors: Morris Gollub, Doug Wildey, Jan Green; Graphic Design: Moe Gollub, Leo Swenson, Tony Sgroi, George Wheeler, Zygamond Jablecki, Hak Ficq, Norley Paat, Earl Martin, John Dorman, John Messina; Animation: Reuben Timmins, Ed Aardal, Lee Halpern, Bob Kirk, Jim Brummett, Joe Roman, Jr., Jack Foster, Janice Stocks; Backgrounds Supervised by: Richard H. Thomas; Backgrounds: Mary O'Laughlin, Don Watson; Ink and Paint Supervision: Gertrude Timmins; Xerography: Greg Marshall; Editing Supervised by: Bob Gillis; Film Editors: Allan Potter, Rick Steward; Music Editor: Joe Siralusa; Anthropological Dialogue Researched by: MacDonald Stearns PhD, U.C.L.A., Department of Germanic Languages; Music by: Dean Elliott, Conducted by Eric Rogers; In Charge of Production: Lee Gunther; Camera by: Ray Lee, Larry Hogan, John Burton, Jr.; Production Mixer: Steve Orr; Music Mixer: Eric Tomlinson; Sound by: Producers Sound Service, Inc.

Episode Guide

"Flames of Doom." Teleplay by Larry Spiegel.

"Escape from Ape City." Teleplay by Larry Spiegel.

"The Unearthly Prophecy." Teleplay by Jack Kaplan and John Barrett.

"Tunnel of Fear." Teleplay by Larry Spiegel.

"Lagoon of Peril." Teleplay by J. C. Strong.

"Terror on Ice Mountain." Teleplay by Bruce Shelley.

"River of Flames." Teleplay by Jack Kaplan and John Barrett.

"Screaming Wings." Teleplay by Jack Kaplan and John Barrett.

"Trail to the Unknown." Teleplay by Larry Spiegel.

"Attack from the Clouds." Teleplay by Larry Spiegel.

"Mission of Mercy." Teleplay by Larry Spiegel.

"Invasion of the Underdwellers." Teleplay by J. C. Strong.

"Battle of the Titans." Teleplay by Bruce Shelly.

Bibliography

BOOKS

Baldwin, James. "The Devil Finds Work." In *The Price of the Ticket: Collected Non-Fiction 1948–1985*. New York: St. Martin's/Marek, 1985.

————. "The Fire Next Time." In *The Price of the Ticket: Collected Non-Fiction 1948–1985*. New York: St. Martin's/Marek, 1985.

Bell, Derrick A. *Race, Racism, and American Law*. Boston: Little, Brown, 1973.

Bennett, Tony, and Janet Wollacott. *Bond and Beyond: The Political Career of a Popular Hero*. New York: Methuen, 1987.

Boulle, Pierre. *Planet of the Apes*. Translated by Xan Fielding. New York: Vanguard, 1963.

Brockriede, Wayne, and Robert L. Scott. *The Rhetoric of Black Power* (New York: Harper and Row, 1969).

Carson, Clayborne, ed. *A Readers Guide, Eyes on the Prize: America's Civil Rights Years*. New York: Penguin Books, 1987.

Chaloner, Gary. *Planet of the Apes: Urchak's Folly* 2 (February 1991).

Chase, Allan. *The Legacy of Malthus: The Social Costs of the New Scientific Racism*. Urbana: University of Illinois Press, 1980.

Christensen, Terry. *Reel Politics*. New York: Basil Blackwell, 1987.

Clark, Eleanor, Joe Morella, and Edward Z. Epstein. *Those Great Movie Ads*. New Rochelle, N.Y.: Arlington House, 1972.

Cunningham, Lowell. *Planet of the Apes: The Forbidden Zone* 4 (March 1993).

Denning, Michael. *Mechanic Accents: Dime Novels and Working Class Culture in America*. New York: Verso, 1987.

Fager, Charles E. *White Reflections on Black Power*. Grand Rapids: William B. Eerdmans, 1967.

Farber, David. *Chicago '68*. Chicago: University of Chicago Press, 1988.

Geertz, Clifford. *The Interpretation of Cultures*. New York: Basic Books, 1973.

Gerrold, David. *Battle for the Planet of the Apes*. New York: Award Books, 1973.

Gilman, Sander. *The Jew's Body*. New York: Routledge, 1991.

Gould, Stephan Jay. *The Mismeasure of Man*. New York: Norton, 1981.

Haraway, Donna. *Primate Visions: Gender, Race, and Nature in the World of Modern Science*. New York: Routledge, Chapman and Hall, 1989.

Holdstock, Robert, consulting editor. *Encyclopedia of Science Fiction*. London: Octopus Books, 1978.

Jordon, Winthrop D. *The White Man's Burden*. New York: Oxford University Press, 1974.

Kim, Erwin. *Franklin J. Schaffner*. Metuchen, N.J. and London: Scarecrow, 1985.

King, Dr. Martin Luther, Jr. *Where Do We Go from Here: Chaos or Community*. Boston: Beacon, 1967.

Kovel, Joel. *White Racism: A Psychohistory*. New York: Columbia University Press, 1984.

Mann, Roland. *Planet of the Apes: Blood of the Apes* 3 (January 1992).

_____. *Planet of the Apes: Blood of the Apes* 4 (February 1992).

Maynard, Richard A. *The Black Man on Film: Racial Stereotyping*. Rochelle Park, N.J.: Hayden, 1974.

Planet of the Apes 6 (March 1975).

Preston, Ruth, and L. L. Thurstone. *Motion Pictures and the Social Attitudes of Children*. New York: Macmillan, 1933.

Reed, Joseph W. *American Scenarios: The Uses of Film Genre*. Middletown, Conn.: Wesleyan University Press, 1989.

Ryan, Michael and Douglas Kellner. *Camera Politica: The Politics and Ideology of Contemporary Hollywood Film*. Bloomington: Indiana University Press, 1990.

Sartre, Jean Paul. *Anti-Semite and Jew*. Translated by George J. Becker. New York: Schocken, Inc., 1948.

Sitkoff, Harvard. *The Struggle for Black Equality 1954–1980*. Toronto: Collins, 1981.

Slotkin, Richard. *The Fatal Environment: The Myth of the Frontier in the Age of Industrialization 1800–1890*. Middletown, Conn.: Wesleyan University Press, 1986.

_____. *Gunfighter Nation: The Myth of the Frontier in Twentieth Century America*. New York: Atheneum, 1992.

_____. *Regeneration Through Violence: The Mythology of the American Frontier 1600–1860*. Middletown, Conn.: Wesleyan University Press, 1973.

Sobchack, Vivian. *Screening Space: The American Science Fiction Film*. New York: Ungar, 1987.

Stoddard, Lothrop. *The Revolt Against Civilization: The Menace of the Underman*. New York: Charles Scribner's Sons, 1922.

Turner, Victor. *Dramas, Fields, and Metaphors*. Ithaca: Cornell University Press, 1974.

Washington, James M., ed. *A Testament of Hope: The Essential Writings and Speeches of Martin Luther King, Jr.* San Francisco: HarperCollins, 1991.

X, Malcolm, and Alex Haley. *The Autobiography of Malcolm X*. New York: Ballantine, 1964.

ARTICLES AND ESSAYS

Armstrong, Andrew. "Parroting Perot on NAFTA." *Washington Times*, September 26, 1993, p. B5.

Asch, Andrew. "Ape Politic," part of "Retrospective/Monkey Business: The Selling of the Planet of the Apes." *Sci-Fi Universe* (June/July 1994).

Barber, Rowland. "How Much Milk Can You Get from an Ape?" *TV Guide*, December 7, 1974, pp. 6–10.

Clarke, Frederick S. Article in *Cinéfantastique* (Fall 1970).

_____. Review of *Beneath the Planet of the Apes*. *Cinéfantastique* (Fall 1971).

Conquest of the Planet of the Apes review, June 14, 1972. Reprinted in *Variety's Complete Science Fiction Reviews*, edited by Donald Willis. New York: Garland, 1985.

Desser, David. "The Cinematic Melting Pot: Ethnicity, Jews, and Psychoanalysis." In *Unspeakable Images: Ethnicity and the American Cinema*, edited by Lester D. Friedman, Urbana: University of Illinois Press, 1991.

Elmore, Patt. Letter to the editor. *Planet of the Apes* 8 (May 1975): 5.

Fox, David J. and Larry B. Stammer. "Mahony Urges 'Human Values' in Films, TV." *Los Angeles Times*, October 1, 1992, pp. 1, 22.

"From Book — Film — T.V." In *Planet of the Apes Posterbook*. London: Top Sellers, 1974.

"Furthermore." *Time* Magazine, November 8, 1993, p. 88.

Gates, Henry Louis, Jr., et al. Symposium in *The New Republic*, October 31, 1994.

Gerani, Gary. "Knowing Your Place on the Planet of the Apes." In *Planet of the Apes* 8 (May 1975).

Gilliatt, Penelope. "The Upstanding Chimp." *New Yorker*, June 5, 1971, pp. 102–4.

Hall, Stuart. "The Whites of Their Eyes: Racist Ideologies and the Media." In *Silver Linings: Some Strategies for the Eighties*, edited by George Bridges and Rosalind Brunt. London: Lawrence and Wishart, 1981.

Howard, Alan R. *Battle for the Planet of the Apes* review. *Hollywood Reporter*, May 18, 1973.

Johnson, David. "Michael Wilson: The Other 'APES' Writer." *Planet of the Apes* 2 (October 1974): 48–52.

Kael, Pauline. "Apes Must Be Remembered, Charlie." *New Yorker*, February 17, 1968, pp. 108–9.

_____. Commencement Address. Smith College, May 27, 1973.

Kerr, Peter. "Vote on Guns Pits Lobbyists Against Florio." *New York Times*, May 17, 1990, p. B1.

Krueger, Jeff. Letter to the editor. *Planet of the Apes* 14 (July 1991).

Linden, Eugene. "A Curious Kinship: Apes and Humans." *National Geographic* (March 1992): 2–45.

May, Ellen Cameron. "Serling in Creative Mainstream." *Los Angeles Times*, June 25, 1967.

Morgerstern, Joseph. "Monkey Lands." *Newsweek*, February 26, 1968, p. 84.

Morrow, Lance. "Folklore in a Box." *Time* September 21, 1992, p. 50.

"Newark: Post-Riot Summit for Black Power." *Life*, August 4, 1967.

Olshaker, Mark. "Requiem for a Heavyweight: Final Tribute." *New Times*, July 25, 1975, p. 68.

"Onward and Apeward." *Time*, June 5, 1972, p. 62.

Ornstein, Bill. "Jacobs Plans Enter Television" *(sic)*. *Hollywood Reporter*, May 6, 1971, pp. 1, 4.

"The 'Other' Pacification — To Cool U.S. Cities." *Life*, August 25, 1967.

"The 'Other War' in Vietnam/To Keep a Village Free." *Life*, August 25, 1967.

Phillips, Mark. Letter to the editor. *Planet of the Apes* (April 1991).

Planet of the Apes review. *Daily Variety*, February 7, 1968.

"*Planet of the Apes* T.V. Series Draws Criticism in Indonesia." *Los Angeles Times*, July 25, 1980.

"Race War in Detroit — Americans Maul and Murder Each Other as Hitler Wins a Battle in the Nation's Most Explosive City." *Life*, July 5, 1943, p. 93.

"Races: The Loneliest Road." *Time*, August 27, 1965, p. 11.

"Races: The Trigger of Hate." *Time*, August 20, 1965, p. 13.

Rice, Susan. "Teaching Apes: A Review of *Planet of the Apes*." *Media and Methods Magazine*, October 1973, pp. 32–50.

Roberts, Sam. "50 Years of Crime, and Stereotypes." *New York Times*, March 2, 1992, sec. B1, p. 12.

"Rod Serling Clarifies Comments on His Attitude Toward Contemporary TV." *Daily Variety*, January 19, 1968.

Rod Serling interview. *Show Business Illustrated*, November 28, 1961.

Russo, Joe, and Larry Landsman, with Edward Gross. "Planet of the Apes Revisited." *Starlog* (April 1986): 42–47.

Sarris, Andrew. "Rod Serling Viewed from Beyond the Twilight Zone." *Television Quarterly* 21, no. 2 (Summer 1984): 37.

Schickel, Richard. "Second Thoughts on Ape-Men." *Life*, May 10, 1968.

Scott, Robert L. "Black Power Bends Martin Luther King." In Brockriede and Scott, *The Rhetoric of Black Power*.

——— and Wayne Brockriede. "Stokely Carmichael: 2 Speeches on Black Power." In Brockriede and Scott, *The Rhetoric of Black Power*.

Serling, Rod. "Bitter Sadness, Special Irony Seen in the Passing of Dr. King." Letter to the editor. *Los Angeles Times*, April 8, 1968.

Shaefer, W. L. Letter to the editor. *Time*, September 3, 1965.

Shatnoff, Judith. "A Gorilla to Remember." *Film Quarterly* (Fall 1968): 56.

Shreeve, James, et al. *Discover*, special issue, *The Science of Race* 15, no. 11 (November 1994).

Slotkin, Richard. "The Continuity of Forms: Myth and Genre in Warner Brothers' *The Charge of the Light Brigade*." *Representations* 29 (Winter 1990).

———. "Nostalgia and Progress: Theodore Roosevelt's Myth of the Frontier." *American Quarterly* 33: 5 (1981), pp. 608–38.

Spiegel, Alan. "The Vanishing Act: A Typology of the Jew in the Contemporary American Film." *From Hester Street to Hollywood: The Jewish American Stage and Screen*, edited by Sarah Blacher Cohen, pp. 257–75. Bloomington: Indiana University Press, 1983.

Sterba, Richard. "Some Psychological Factors in Negro Race Hatred and Anti-Negro Riots." *Psychoanalysis and the Social Sciences* 1 (Vol. 1, New York: Int. Univ. Press, 1947).

Thomas, Kevin. "Balancing Act Pays Off for Patton Director." *Los Angeles Times*, May 7, 1970, part IV, p. 24.

———. "Battle Completes Ape Cycle." *Los Angeles Times*, June 12, 1973, p. 13.

Voedisch, Lynn. "Nimoy in Comic Land: Entertaining Actor Fuels New Project" *Chicago Sun Times*, November 14, 1994, Sec. 2, Features, p. 35.

"Vote No Censure by SWG on Michael Wilson, But Leak Is Embarrassing." *Daily Variety*, September 16, 1953.

Walker, Sam. "U.S. Activists Seek a Wider Audience for Sarajevo's Paper." *Christian Science Monitor*, February 28, 1994, p. 4.

"The Weary Young Man." *Newsweek*, September 28, 1959.

Wallach, Amei. "Art with an Attitude." *Newsday* city edition, March 5, 1993, Part II/Weekend, p. 52.

Whitelaw, Ed. "Guessing at the 'hood: An Urban Future." *Oregon Business* 17, no. 1 (January 1994): sect. 1, p. 20.

Wines, Michael. "Views on Single Motherhood Are Multiple at White House." *New York Times*, May 21, 1992, p. B16.

Winogura, Dale. "Dialogues on Apes, Apes, and More Apes." *Cinéfantastique* (Summer 1972): 16–37.

Zoglin, Richard. "Sitcom Politics." *Time*, September 21, 1992, p. 44.

Screenplays and Screenplay Proposals

Boulle, Pierre. *Planet of the Men.* July 1968.

Corrington, John William, and Joyce Hooper Corrington. *Battle for the Planet of the Apes.* First draft screenplay. October 30, 1972.

The Dark Side of the Earth. Unsigned and undated.

Dehn, Paul. *The Battle for the Planet of the Apes.* First draft story outline. July 5, 1972.

_____. *Beneath the Planet of the Apes.* April 10, 1969.

_____. *Conquest of the Planet of the Apes.* Story outline, undated.

_____. *Conquest of the Planet of the Apes.* Final shooting script. January 18, 1972.

_____. *Planet of the Apes Revisited.* Story outline. September 13, 1968.

_____, John William Corrington and Joyce Hooper Corrington. *Battle for the Planet of the Apes.* Revised screenplay. December 20, 1972.

Rifkin, Adam. *Return to the Planet of the Apes.* First revision, from a story by Cassian Elwes and Adam Rifkin. December 21, 1988.

_____. *Return to the Planet of the Apes,* July 6, 1989.

Serling, Rod. *Planet of the Apes.* Second draft. December 23, 1964.

_____. *Planet of the Apes.* March 1, 1965.

Wilson, Michael. *Planet of the Apes,* January 13, 1967.

_____. *Planet of the Apes,* January 17, 1967.

Correspondence

Boulle, Pierre. Letter to Arthur Jacobs, April 29, 1965.

Hoknes, Terry. Letter to Eric Greene, July 14, 1993.

Serling, Rod. Letter to Mort Abrahams, April 8, 1968.

Index

Numbers in **boldface** refer to pages with photographs. Bullets (•) indicate names of *Planet of the Apes* characters.

227